THE UNLIKELY CHOSEN

Dear Dirk and Linda,

Blessings and peace to you.

You are always in my prayers.

Earnest Graham III

THE UNLIKELY CHOSEN

A Graphic Novel Translation of
the Biblical Books of **Jonah, Esther,** and **Amos**

Word translation by **Shirley Smith Graham**
Graphic translation by **Earnest N. Graham III**

Seabury Books

Word translation by Shirley Smith Graham
Graphic translation by Earnest N. Graham III

Lettering and production by Dave Sharpe

A catalog record of this book is available from the Library of Congress.

ISBN: 978-1-59627-078-7

Seabury Books
445 Fifth Avenue
New York, New York 10016

www.seaburybooks.com

An imprint of Church Publishing Incorporated

5 4 3 2 1

DEDICATION

To Nana
your generous spirit continues to inspire and amaze us.

To EMG
that you may be like a green olive tree in the house of God,
trusting in the steadfast love of God forever and ever.

Acknowledgments
(Gratitudes)

The production of this book depended on many persons, all of whom have
showed us the wonders of God's grace. We would especially like to acknowledge:

The Rev. John Schively, who did not laugh when Shirley first expressed
an interest in translating the Bible.

Professor Ellen F. Davis, from whose teaching in the Hebrew Bible we both benefited
and who was Shirley's first teacher of Hebrew. The best aspects of this work reflect her
fine teaching; the worst are our own mistakes.

The members of Temple Beth El in Alexandria, Virginia, who helped
Shirley broaden her perspective.

Dr. Cynthia L. Shattuck for inviting us to expand the scope of the work.

The various members of the youth groups, Sunday school classes, Bible studies and
art groups and colleagues at Christ Church, St. Francis, and St. Martin's who provided
listening ears and encouraging voices along the way.

INTRODUCTION

Can you imagine receiving a Christmas present but not opening it? Perhaps the present is from Aunt Millie, who always ties the ribbon in such intricate knots that it's impossible to untie and get to the wrapping paper. Perhaps the present is from Grandpa Joe, who must have shares in Scotch tape the way he covers every inch of paper with it. But no matter how difficult it is to open the present, you know that there's treasure inside, treasure that has been prepared just for you. You just can't figure out how to open the package.

Our experience as parish priests is that people often feel this way about the Bible. Perhaps a couple of times in their lives, they've resolved to read the Bible because they know in their guts that mysteries of life with God are within. So, they start with Genesis and, proceeding sequentially, they are lucky to get past Leviticus. Or, folks start reading the Gospels in the New Testament but find themselves bewildered by the historical references or the things that simply are not explained in the biblical text.

When we went to seminary, we had the extraordinary experience of being taught the biblical languages of Hebrew and Greek. As a result, we were able to dive deeply into the text and work on the slow art of interpretation. We realize this learning is a luxury. How many people, even if they're interested, have the opportunity to learn a biblical language? And, once the language is learned, how many people have the chance to practice it enough to develop some proficiency?

So we want as many people as possible--young people and adults alike--to have the powerful experience of reading the Bible in the original language without having to learn it. The Bible speaks to teens powerfully and viscerally because they share many of the same concerns as the prophets, Jesus, and the earliest Christians: What does it mean to live in relationship with God? What does it mean to live a moral life? What about a good life? Does God get angry? Is there punishment? Why? How can people say one thing and do another? How can people find love, and what does love look like? We hear teens asking these questions, and if we "listen" carefully to the biblical text, we hear the answers as well.

We chose the stories of Jonah, Esther, and Amos because they provide three fascinating examples of the unlikely people whom God chooses. Jonah is a prophet who runs away from God's will. He is chosen by God to bring a message of repentance to Nineveh, the capital of the Assyrian Empire and a fierce and often merciless enemy to the Hebrew people. In the story, Jonah is faced with the unwelcome possibility that the nation may repent and a merciful God will forgive Israel's sworn enemy.

Esther is an orphan and an exiled Jew who is called to be the queen of Persia. She lives in the household of her cousin Mordechai in Shushan, part of the fourth-century-BCE Persian Empire. Her Hebrew name is Hadassah, but she is known by her Persian name, Esther. Chosen to be queen of Persia, she is faced with a decision that will mean life or death for her people, the Jews living throughout the Persian Empire.

Amos, by his own admission, is a shepherd and a tree trimmer, a rugged rancher figure who was far from qualified to prophesy to the sophisticated elite of historic Israel. In the eighth century BCE there were two Hebrew kingdoms in the promised land, the southern kingdom of Judah and the northern kingdom of Israel. The ruling elite of both kingdoms enjoyed great wealth, peace, and security while grinding the faces of the poor into the dust. In this time, God chooses Amos to proclaim a prophetic message of repentance to the people of Israel in the north.

These people of faith challenge the notion that God chooses one kind of person. All of them are flawed in some way, and none of them are heroic in the absolute sense. However, they show us that chosen people are not favored above others but rather are chosen for the purpose of carrying out the special responsibilities to God and God's world. While the stories offer three distinct people responding to God, it is the character of God that stands out in these stories. God is outrageously and unpredictably gracious, concerned with justice, and active in the affairs of the nations.

The combination of art and text in the graphic novel format is uniquely able to portray the social and historical context of the Bible in a way that speaks to a highly visual culture such as our own. In *The Unlikely Chosen* the text and art work together to represent the full text of the books of Jonah, Esther, and Amos. The relatively short length of these stories allows us to present verse-by-verse translations from the original Hebrew of the Masoretic text. The words of Hebrew, as other languages, offer a range of meaning and therefore present the translator with choices. The style used here is to choose English words that closely mirror the Hebrew meaning, as best as it can be discerned, while retaining images, feeling, or sense contained in the original Hebrew. As a result, this translation at times may read awkwardly in English--always a clue that something interesting is in the Hebrew text. The resulting English translation forms the basis of the graphic interpretation, as well as providing the dialog and narrative used in the stories.

We hope that this new, visual translation will help people unwrap the package and discover the gift of God's word in a refreshing way. The true gift is the message itself--the story of God and God's people--which transcends space and time, and speaks to our lives today.

Shirley Smith Graham
Earnest N. Graham III

JONAH

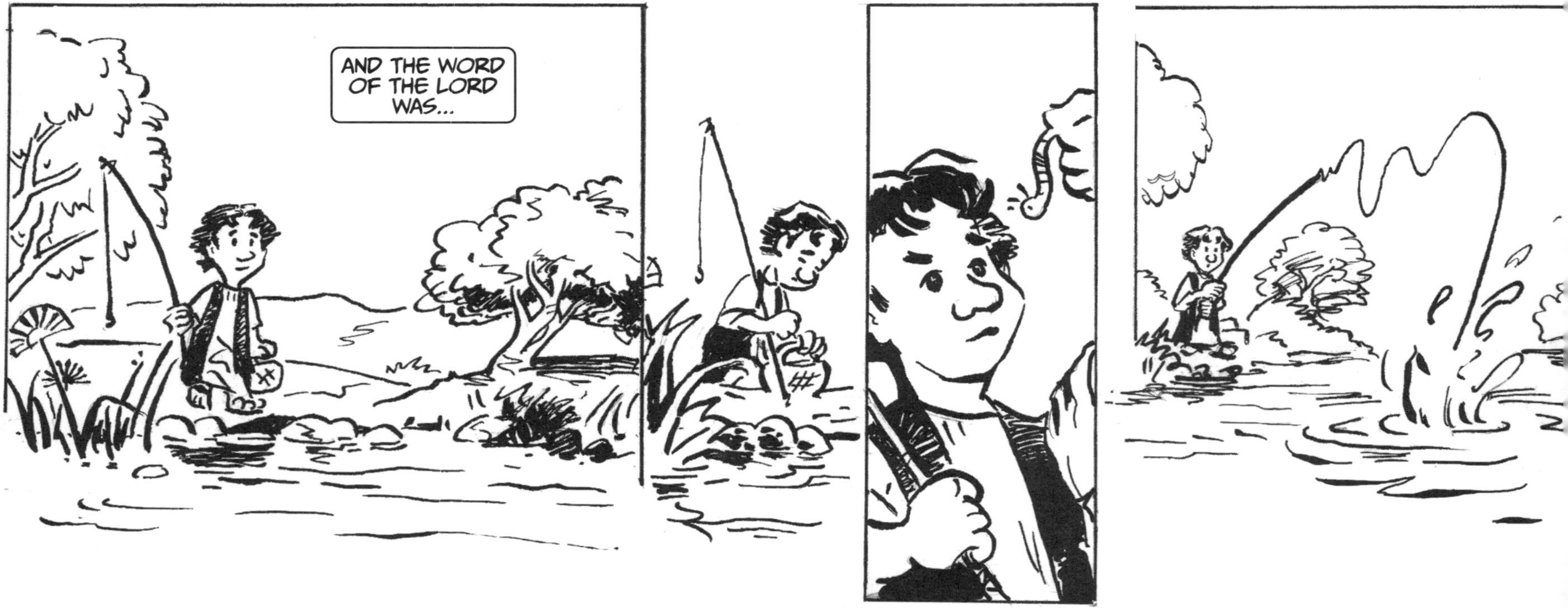
AND THE WORD OF THE LORD WAS...

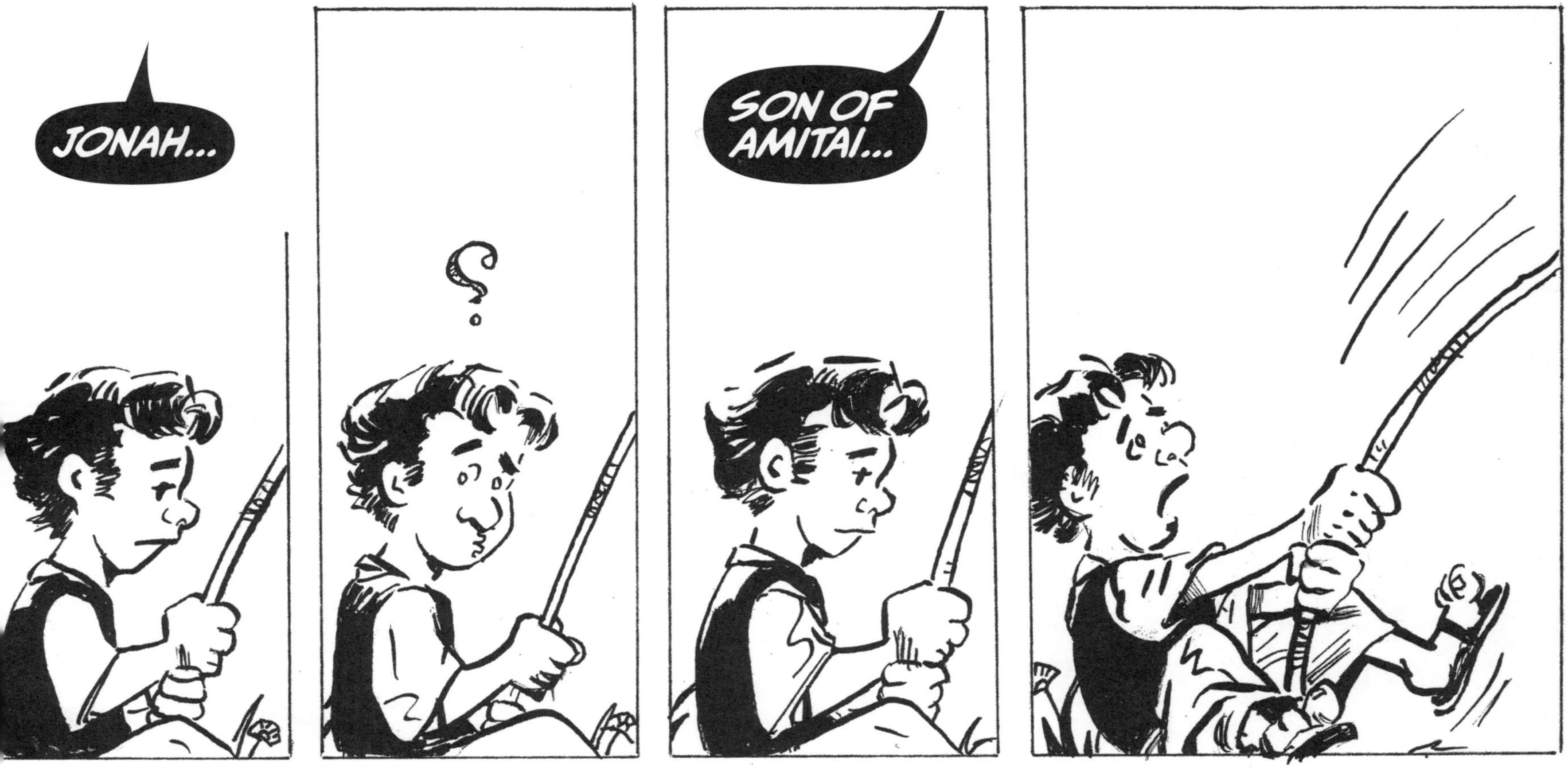
JONAH...
SON OF AMITAI...

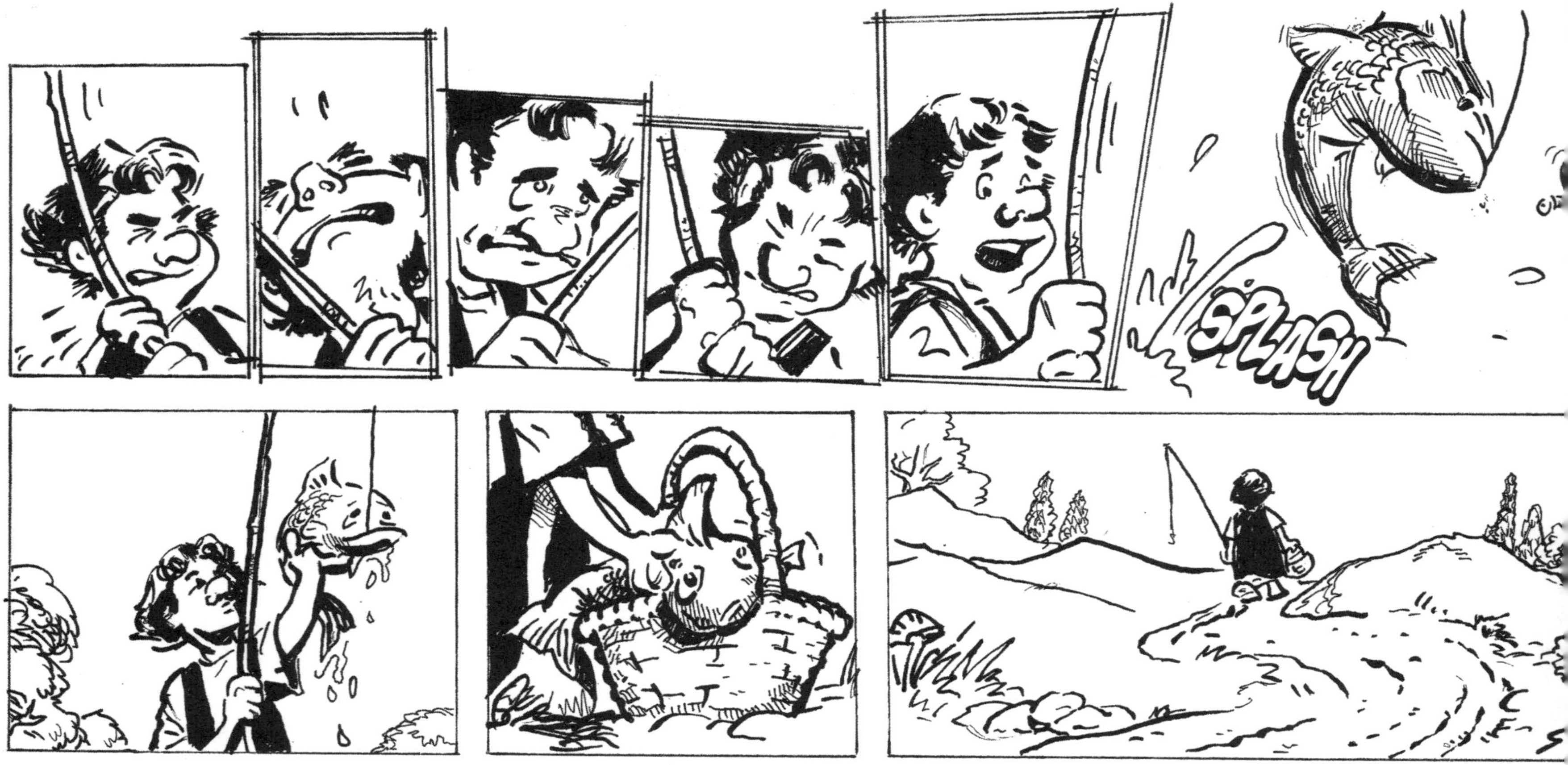
SPLASH

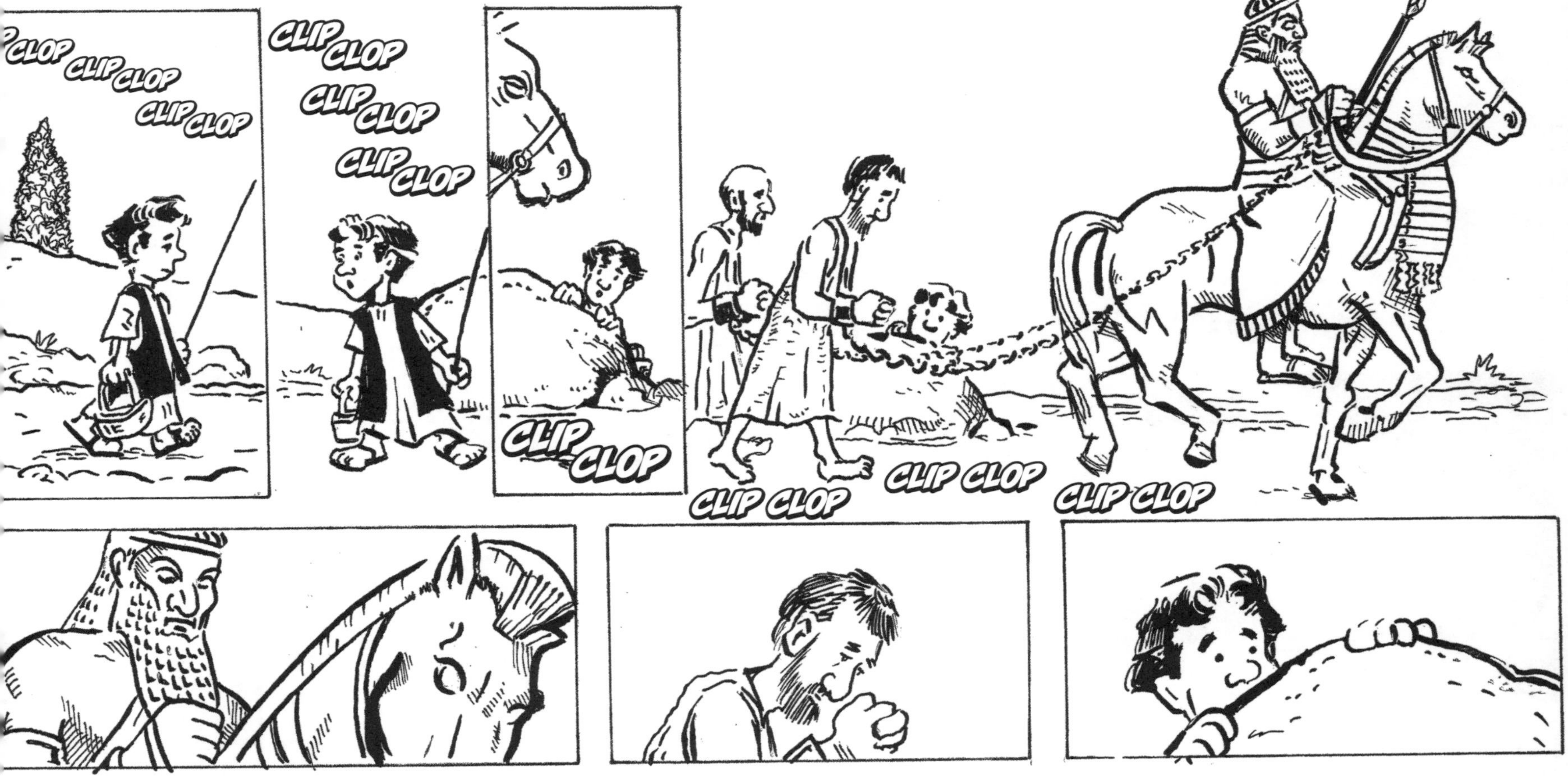
P CLOP CLIP CLOP
CLIP CLOP
CLIP CLOP
CLIP CLOP
CLIP CLOP
CLIP CLOP
CLIP CLOP
CLIP CLOP
CLIP CLOP
CLIP CLOP

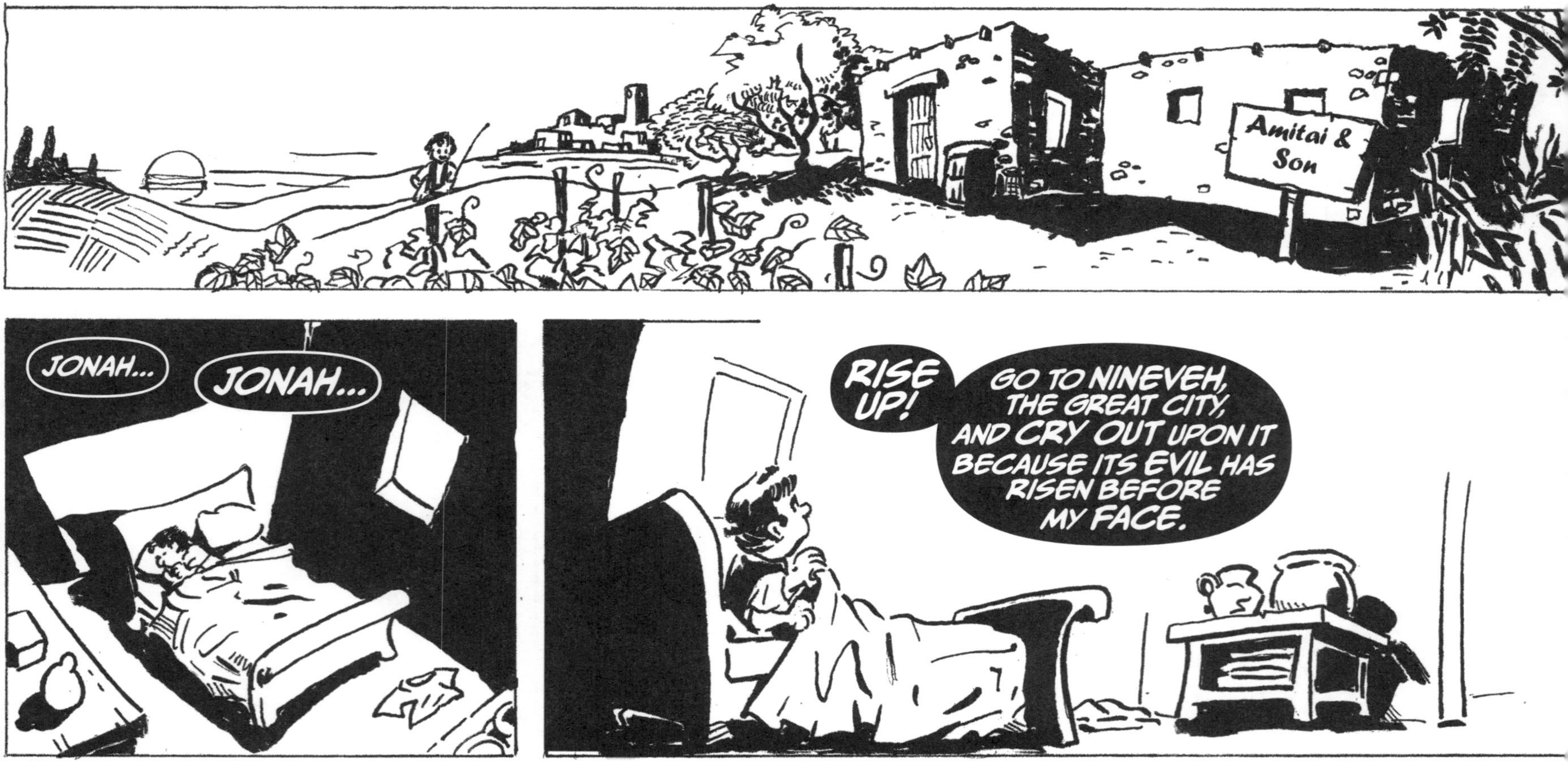
Amitai & Son
JONAH...
JONAH...
RISE UP!
GO TO NINEVEH, THE GREAT CITY, AND CRY OUT UPON IT BECAUSE ITS EVIL HAS RISEN BEFORE MY FACE.

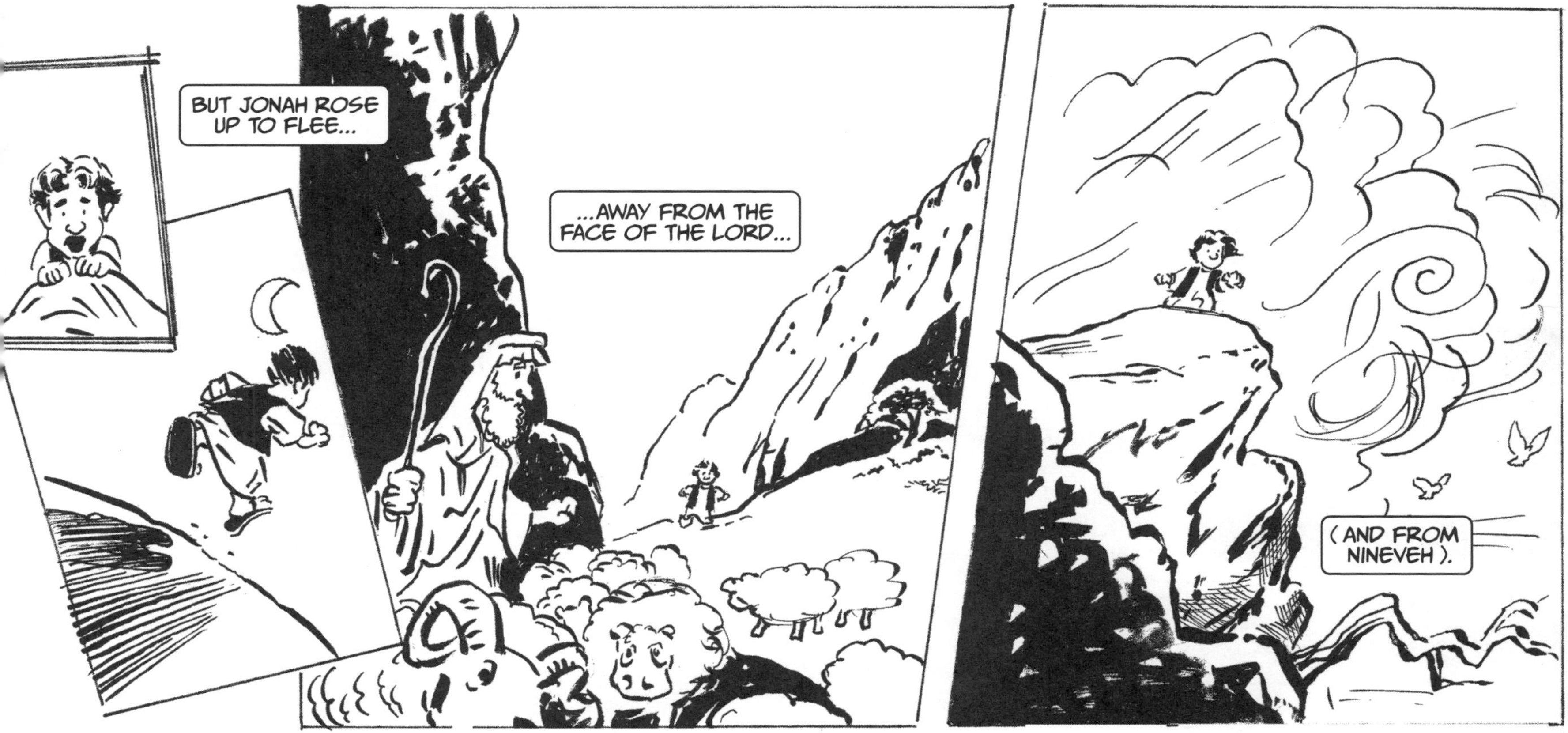
BUT JONAH ROSE UP TO FLEE...
...AWAY FROM THE FACE OF THE LORD...
(AND FROM NINEVEH).

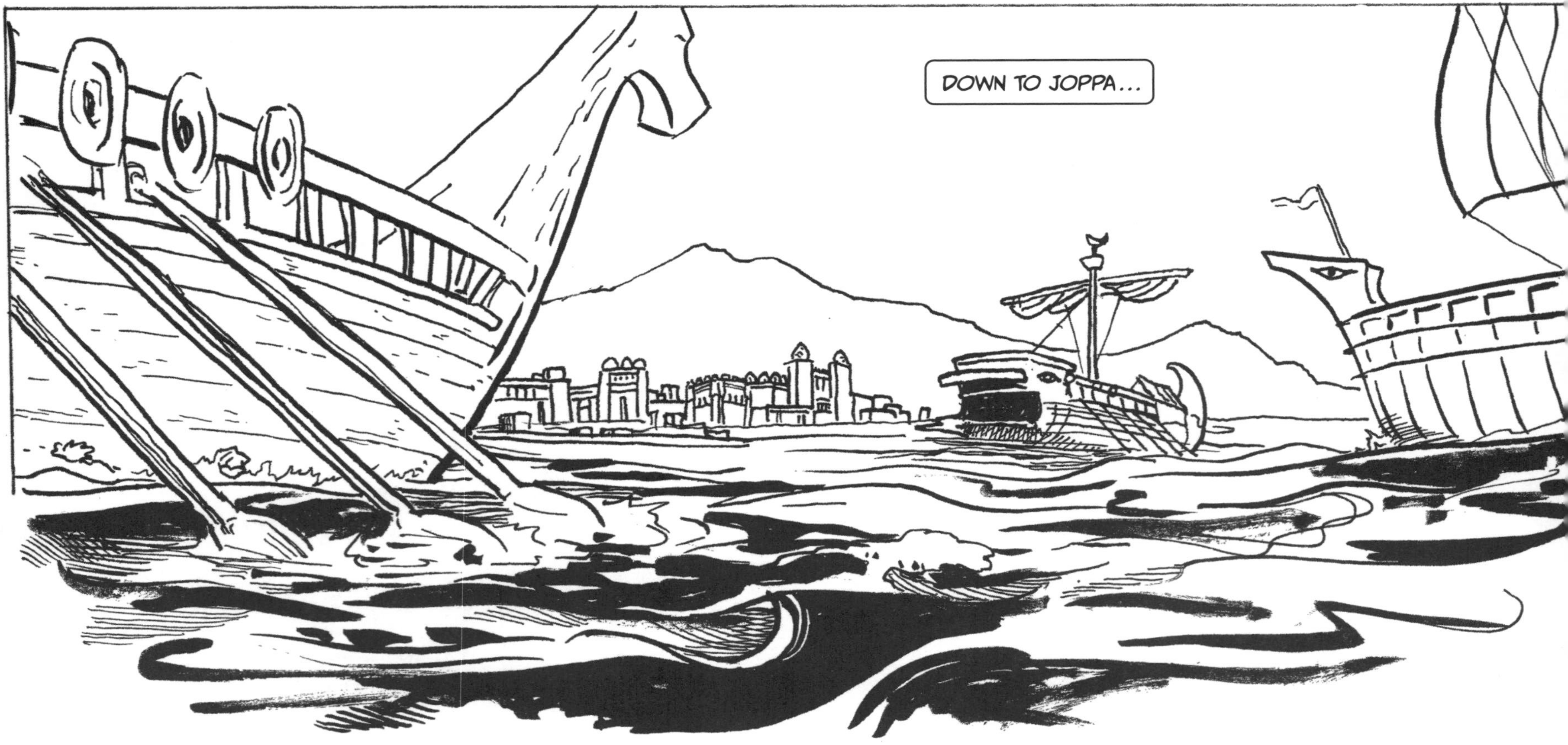
DOWN TO JOPPA...

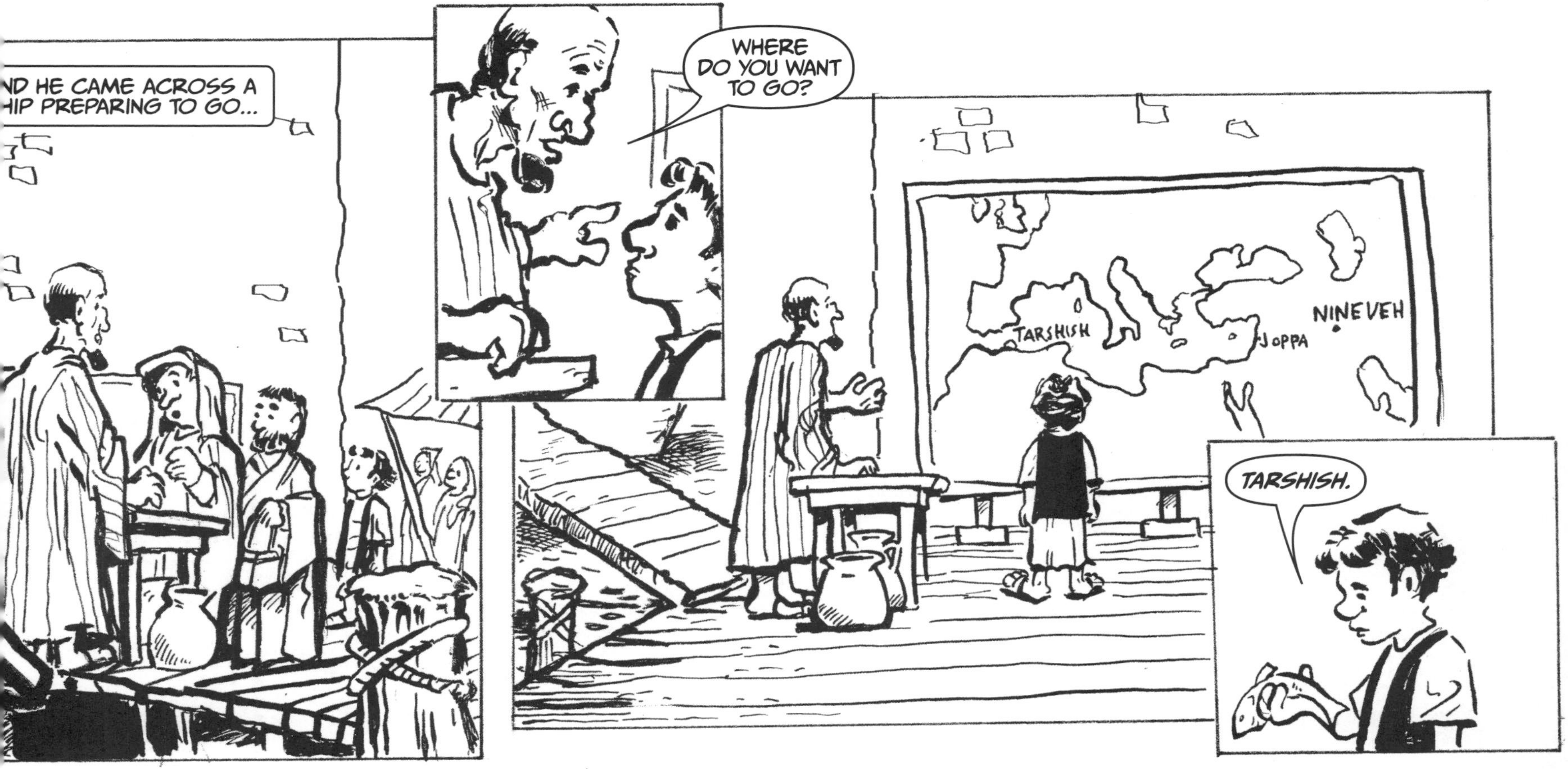
ND HE CAME ACROSS A
HIP PREPARING TO GO...
WHERE
DO YOU WANT
TO GO?
TARSHISH
JOPPA
NINEVEH
TARSHISH.

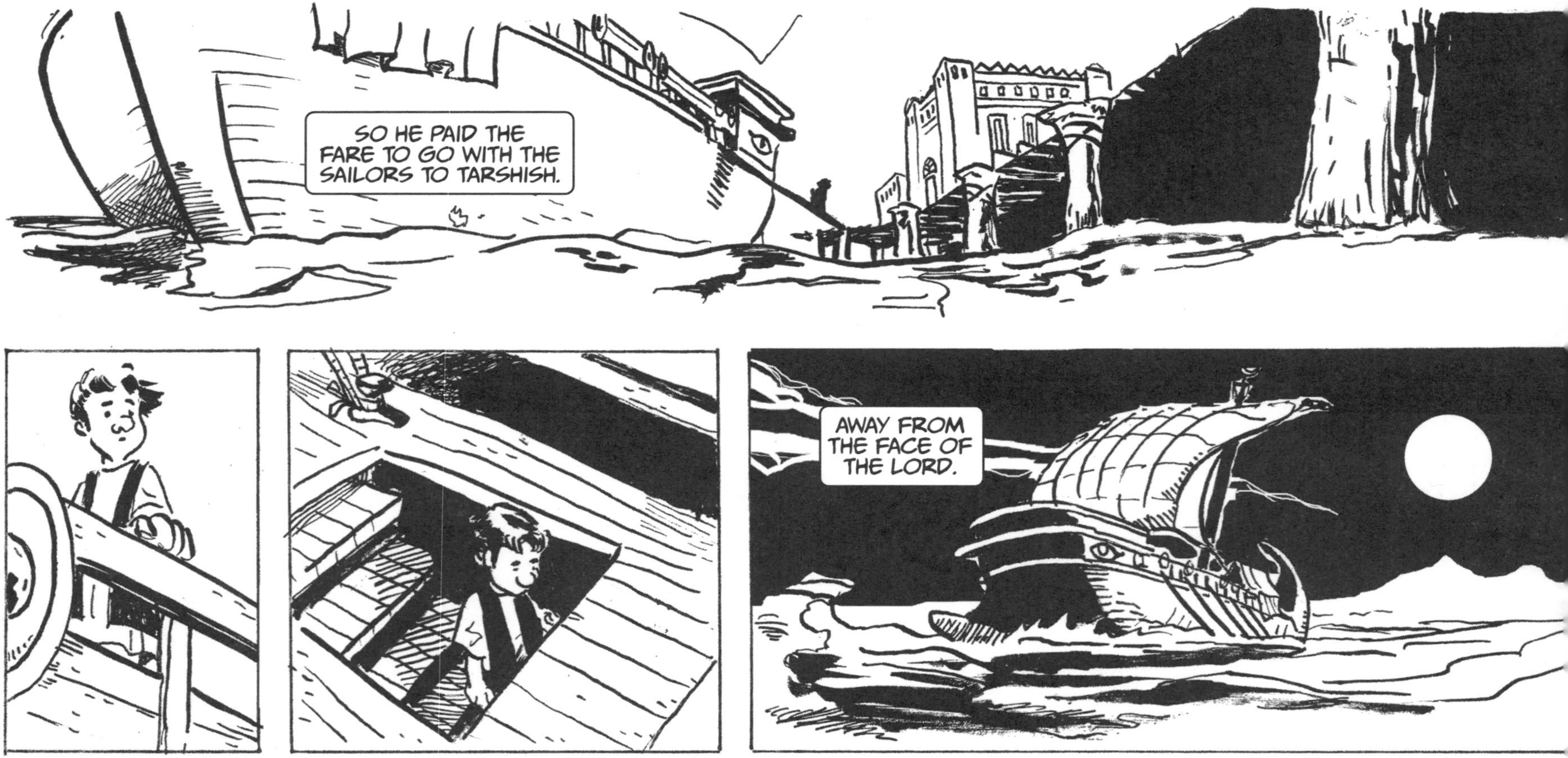
SO HE PAID THE FARE TO GO WITH THE SAILORS TO TARSHISH.
AWAY FROM THE FACE OF THE LORD.

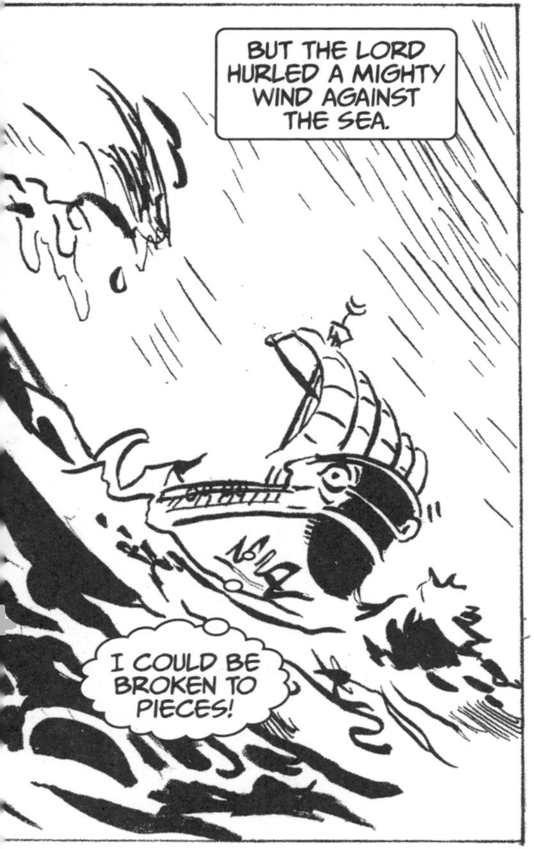
BUT THE LORD HURLED A MIGHTY WIND AGAINST THE SEA.
I COULD BE BROKEN TO PIECES!

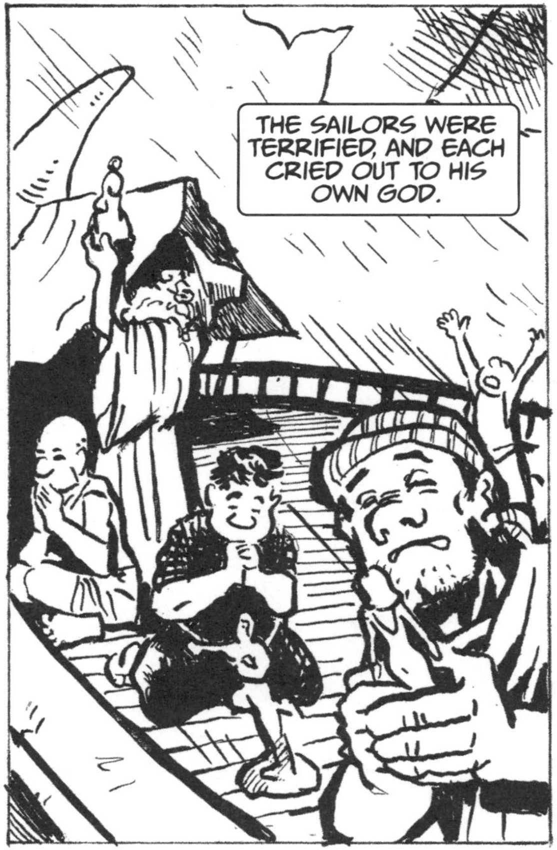
THE SAILORS WERE TERRIFIED, AND EACH CRIED OUT TO HIS OWN GOD.

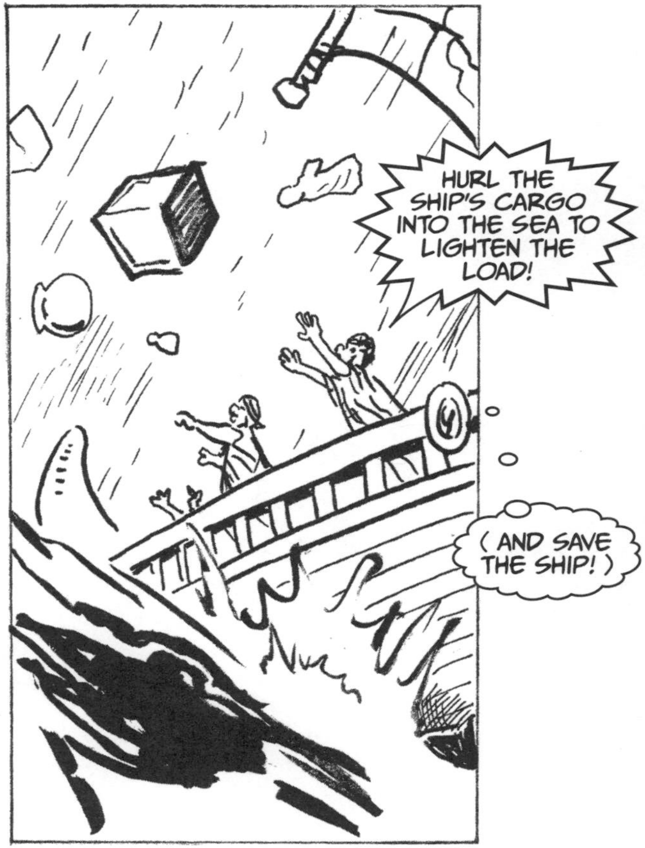
HURL THE SHIP'S CARGO INTO THE SEA TO LIGHTEN THE LOAD!
(AND SAVE THE SHIP!)

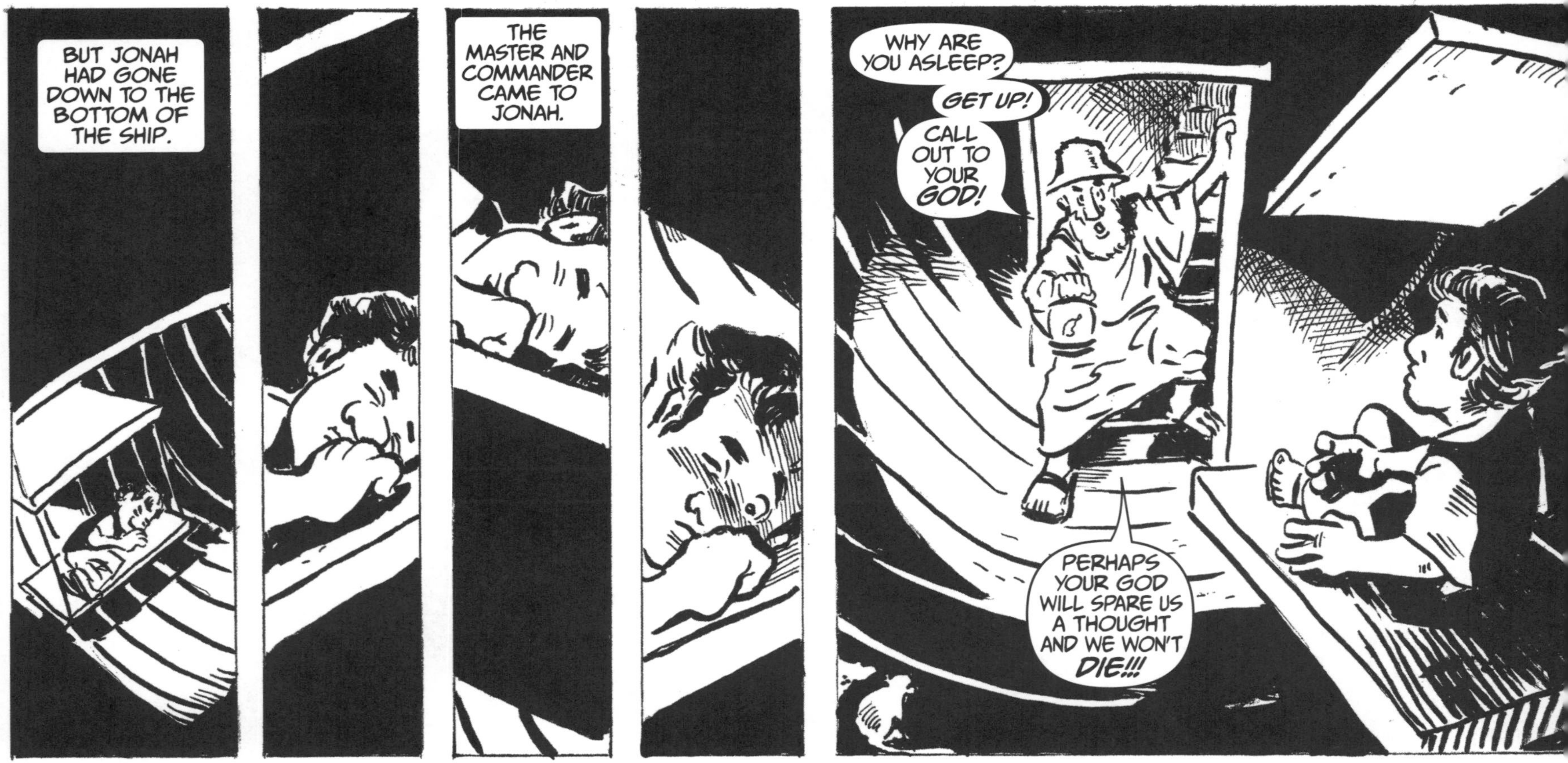
BUT JONAH HAD GONE DOWN TO THE BOTTOM OF THE SHIP.
THE MASTER AND COMMANDER CAME TO JONAH.
WHY ARE YOU ASLEEP?
GET UP!
CALL OUT TO YOUR GOD!
PERHAPS YOUR GOD WILL SPARE US A THOUGHT AND WE WON'T DIE!!!

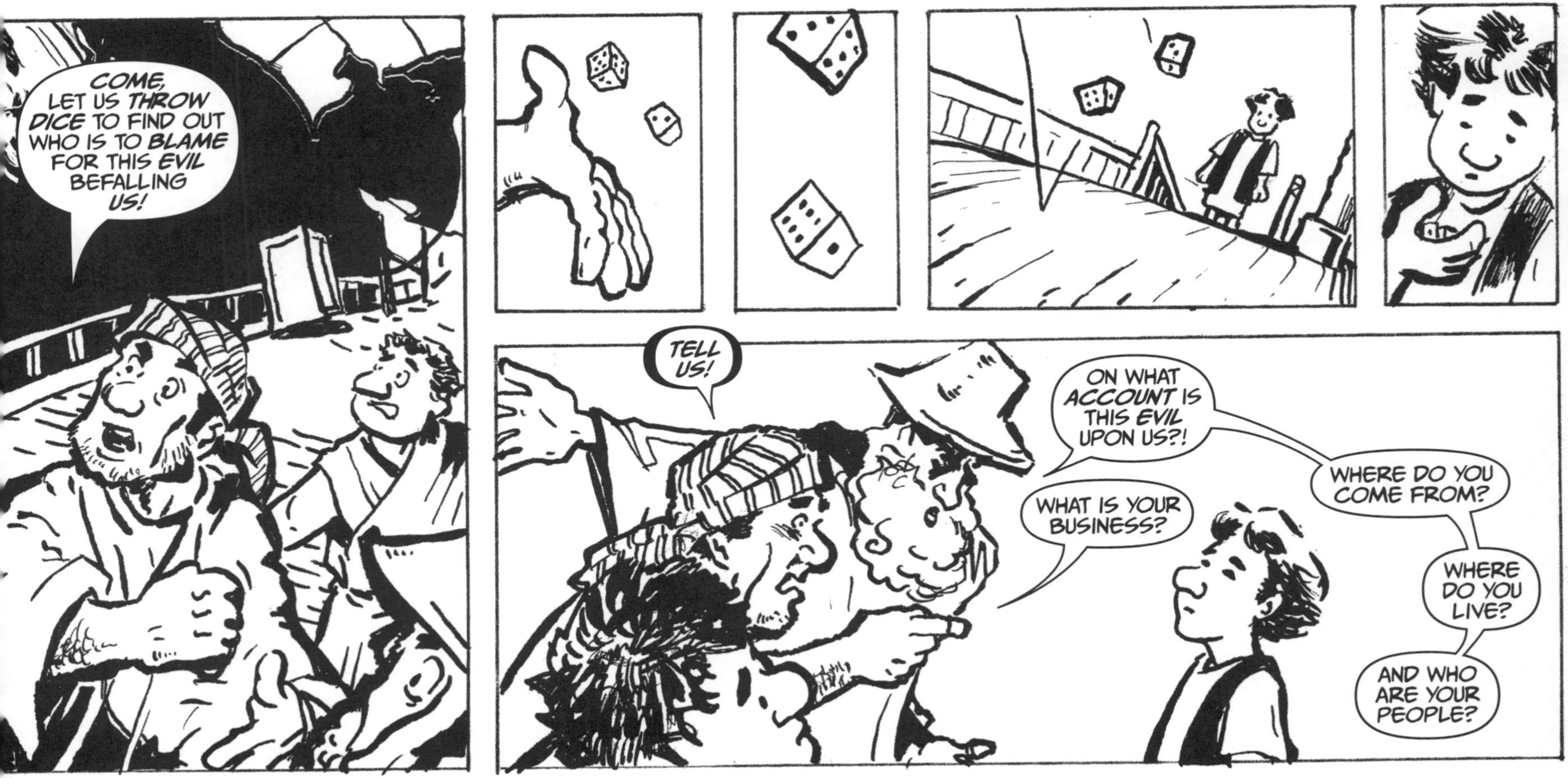

COME, LET US THROW DICE TO FIND OUT WHO IS TO BLAME FOR THIS EVIL BEFALLING US!
TELL US!
ON WHAT ACCOUNT IS THIS EVIL UPON US?!
WHAT IS YOUR BUSINESS?
WHERE DO YOU COME FROM?
WHERE DO YOU LIVE?
AND WHO ARE YOUR PEOPLE?

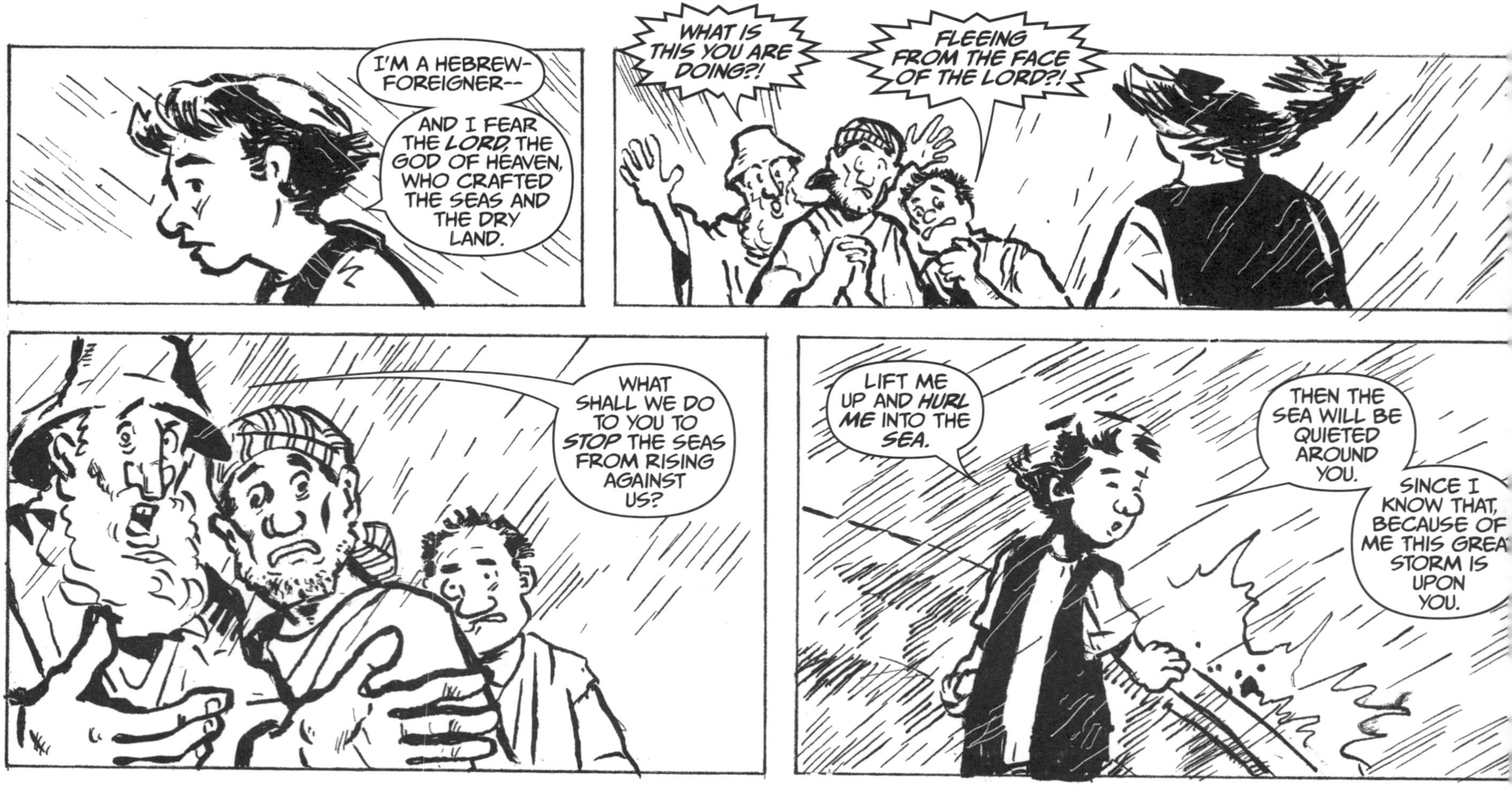
I'M A HEBREW-FOREIGNER--
AND I FEAR THE LORD, THE GOD OF HEAVEN, WHO CRAFTED THE SEAS AND THE DRY LAND.
WHAT IS THIS YOU ARE DOING?!
FLEEING FROM THE FACE OF THE LORD?!
WHAT SHALL WE DO TO YOU TO STOP THE SEAS FROM RISING AGAINST US?
LIFT ME UP AND HURL ME INTO THE SEA.
THEN THE SEA WILL BE QUIETED AROUND YOU.
SINCE I KNOW THAT, BECAUSE OF ME THIS GREA STORM IS UPON YOU.

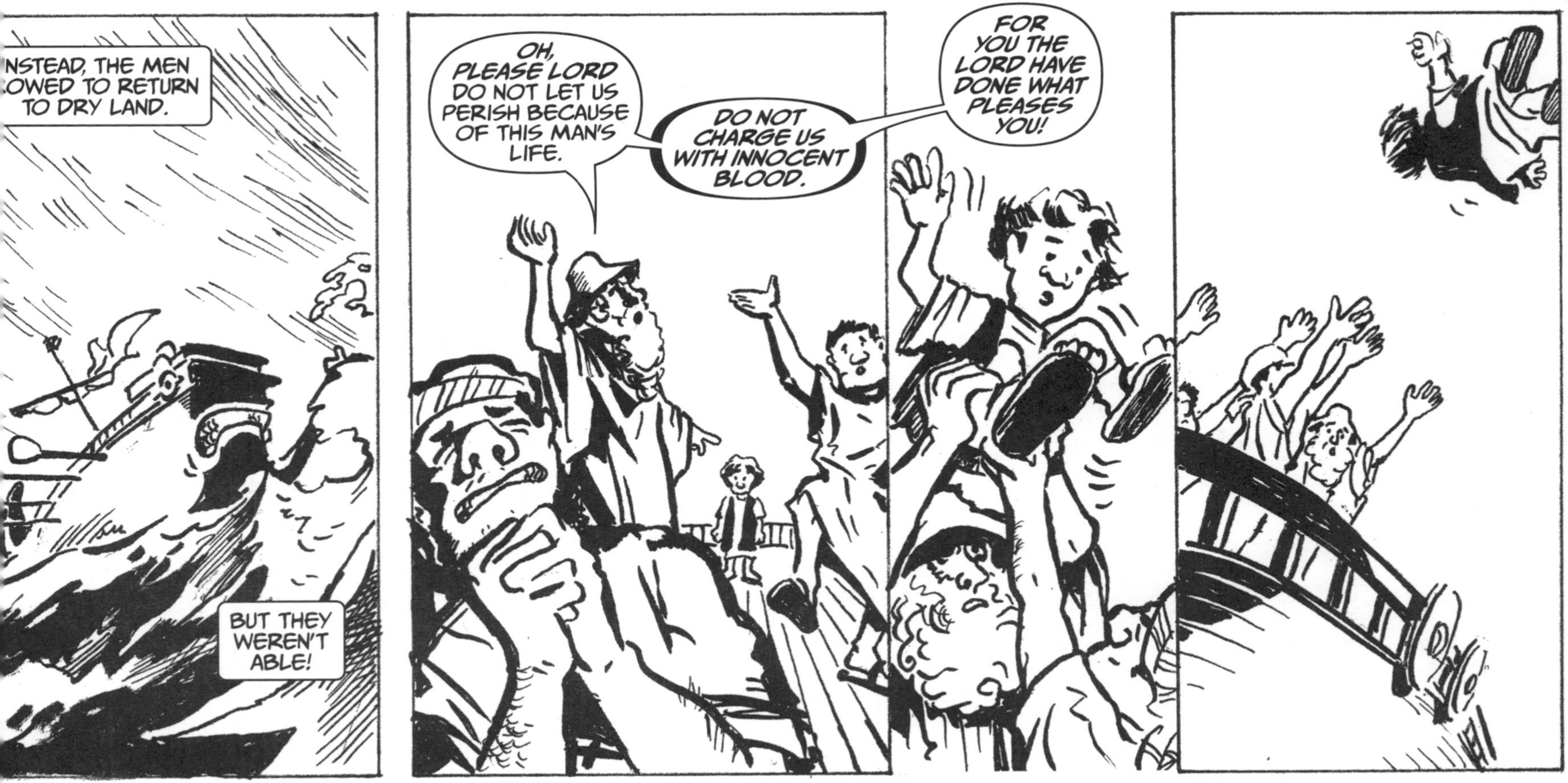
NSTEAD, THE MEN
OWED TO RETURN
TO DRY LAND.
BUT THEY WEREN'T ABLE!
OH, PLEASE LORD DO NOT LET US PERISH BECAUSE OF THIS MAN'S LIFE.
DO NOT CHARGE US WITH INNOCENT BLOOD.
FOR YOU THE LORD HAVE DONE WHAT PLEASES YOU!

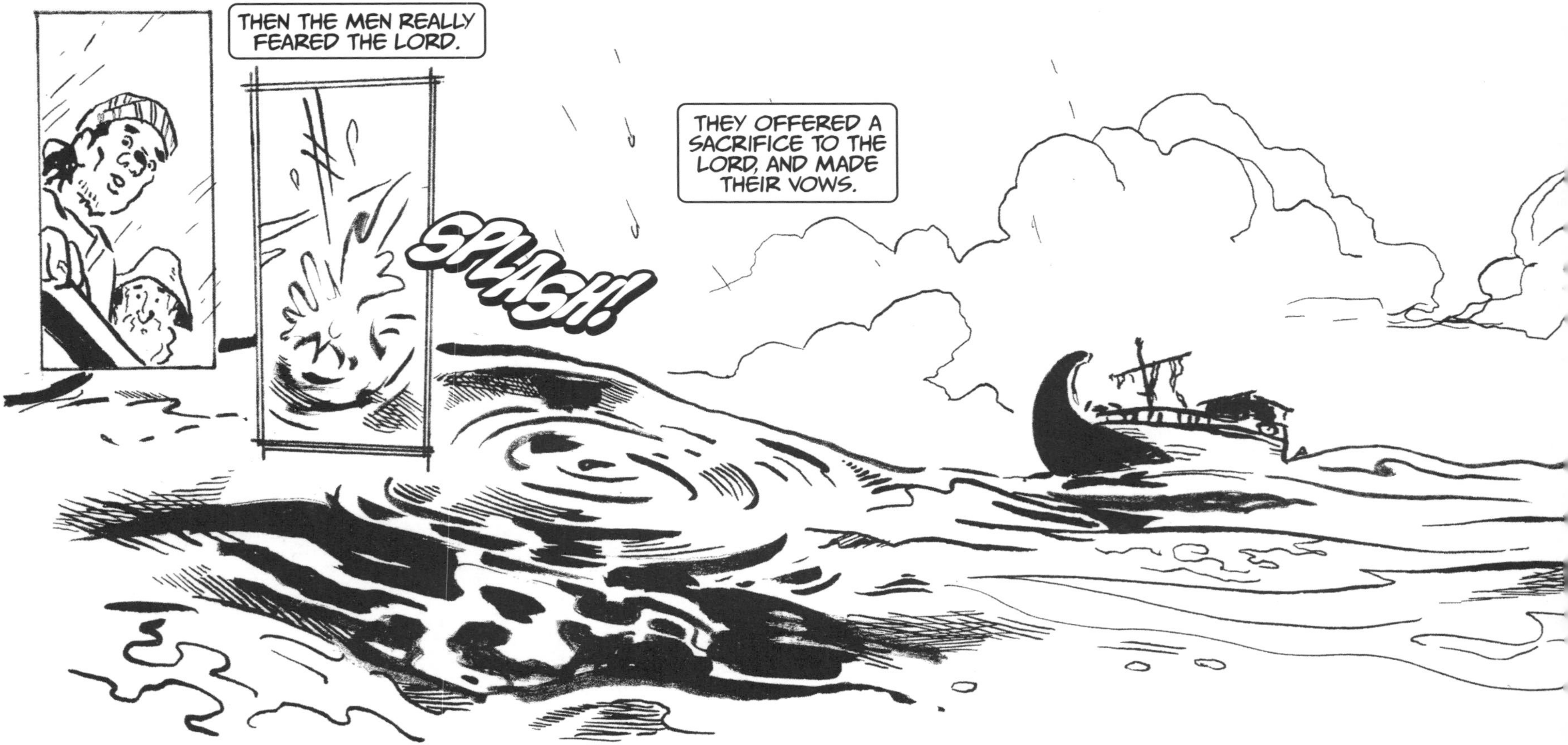
THEN THE MEN REALLY FEARED THE LORD.
SPLASH!
THEY OFFERED A SACRIFICE TO THE LORD, AND MADE THEIR VOWS.

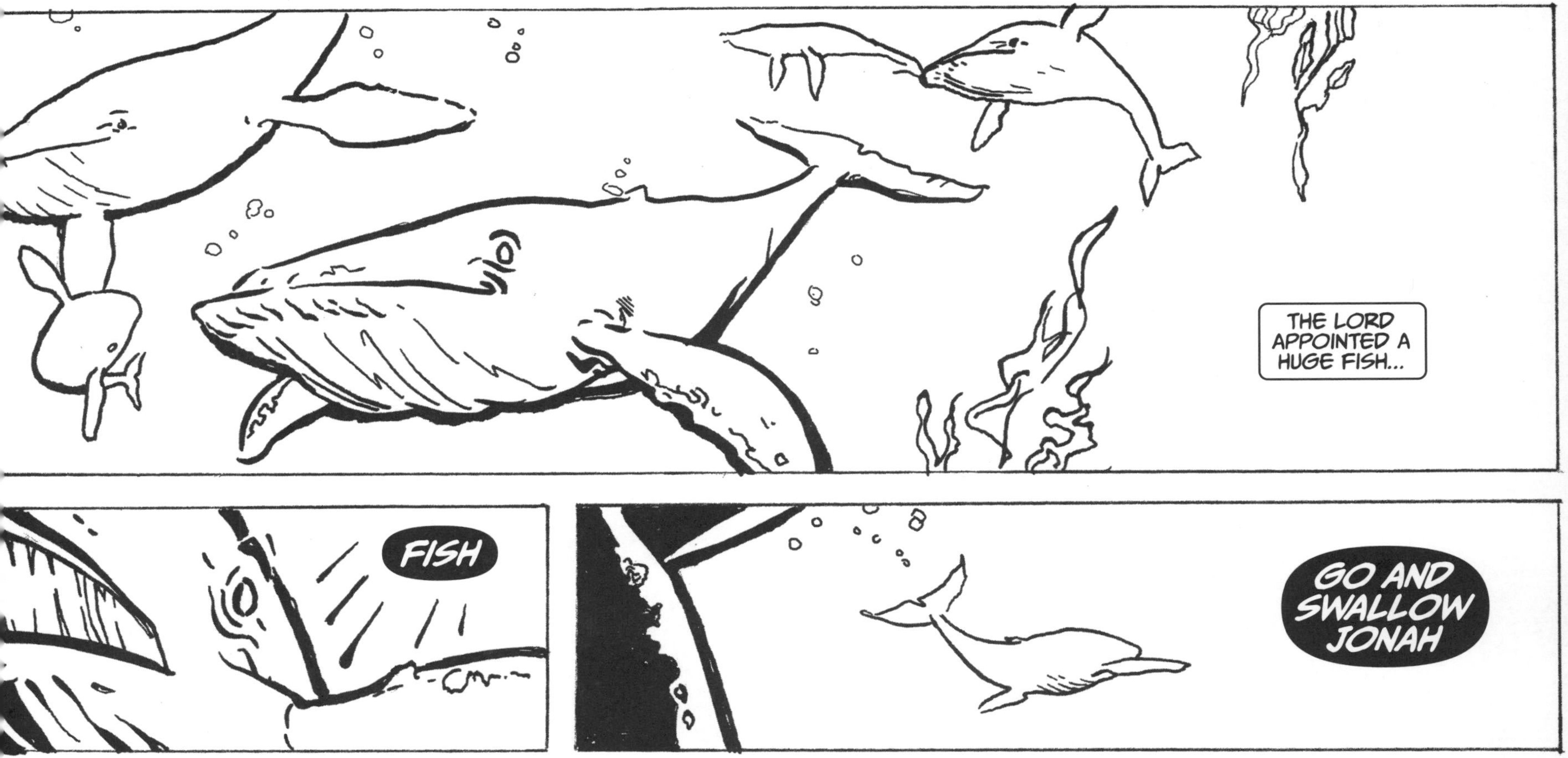
THE LORD APPOINTED A HUGE FISH...
FISH
GO AND SWALLOW JONAH

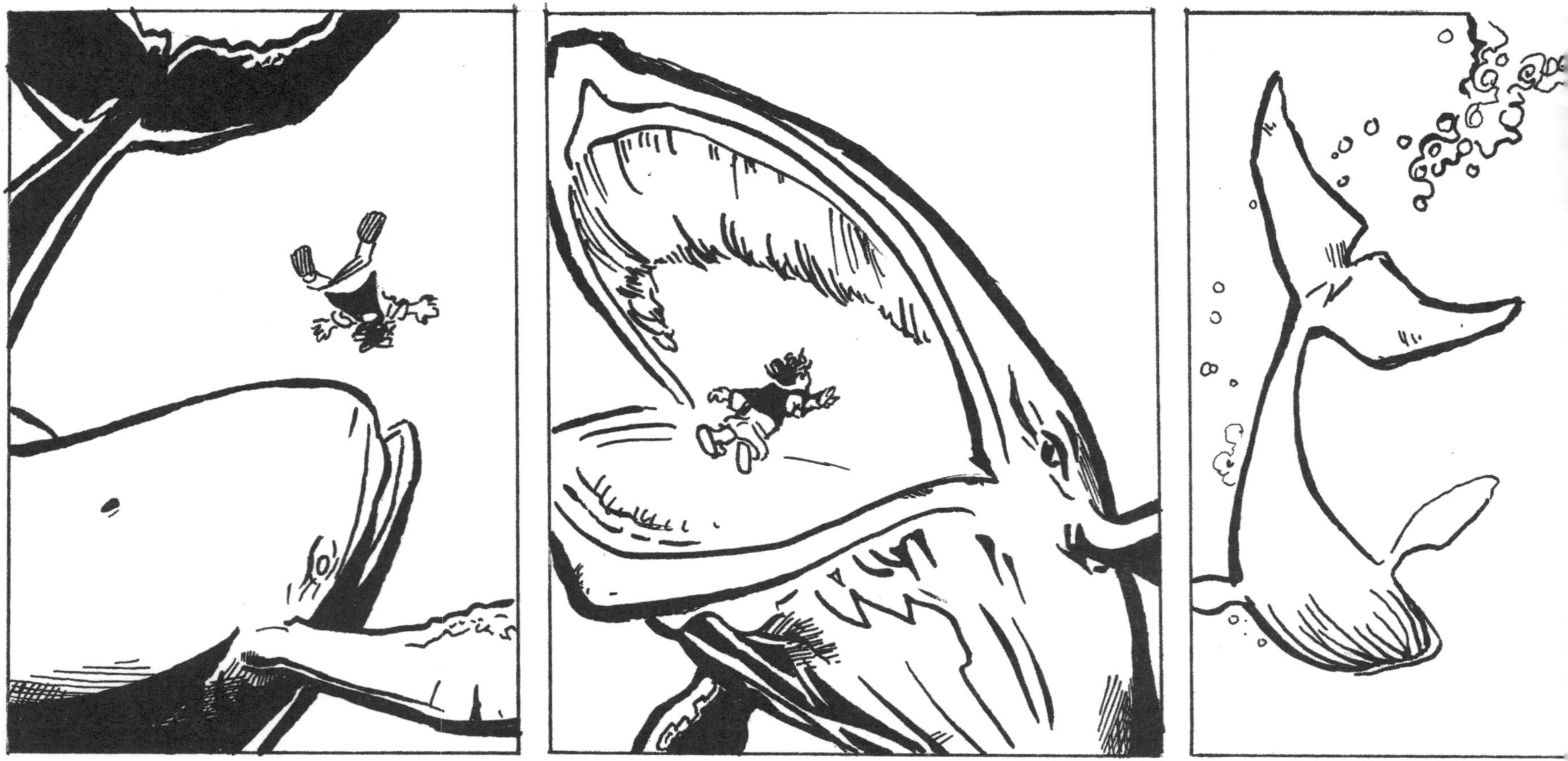

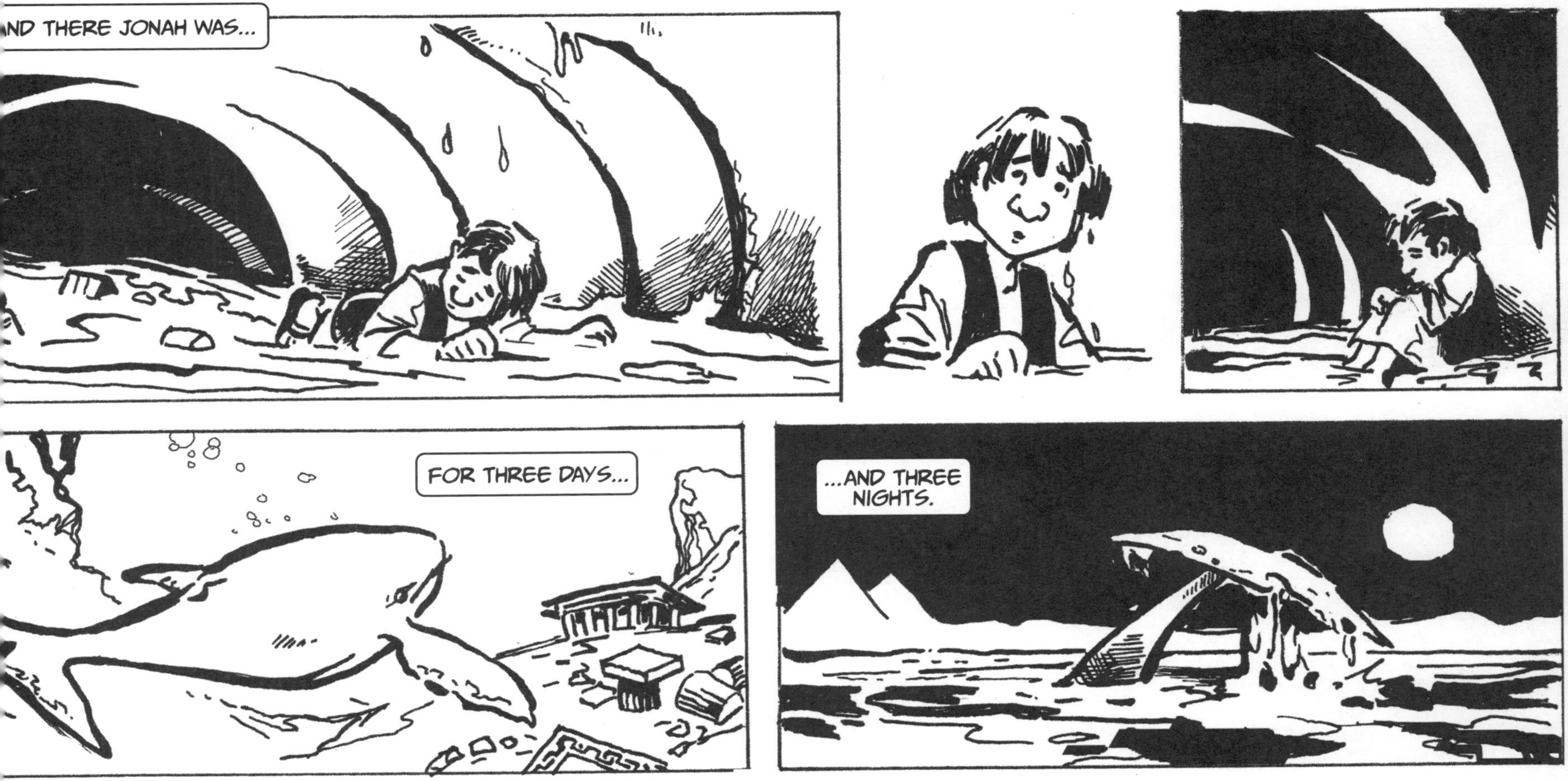
ND THERE JONAH WAS...
FOR THREE DAYS...
...AND THREE NIGHTS.

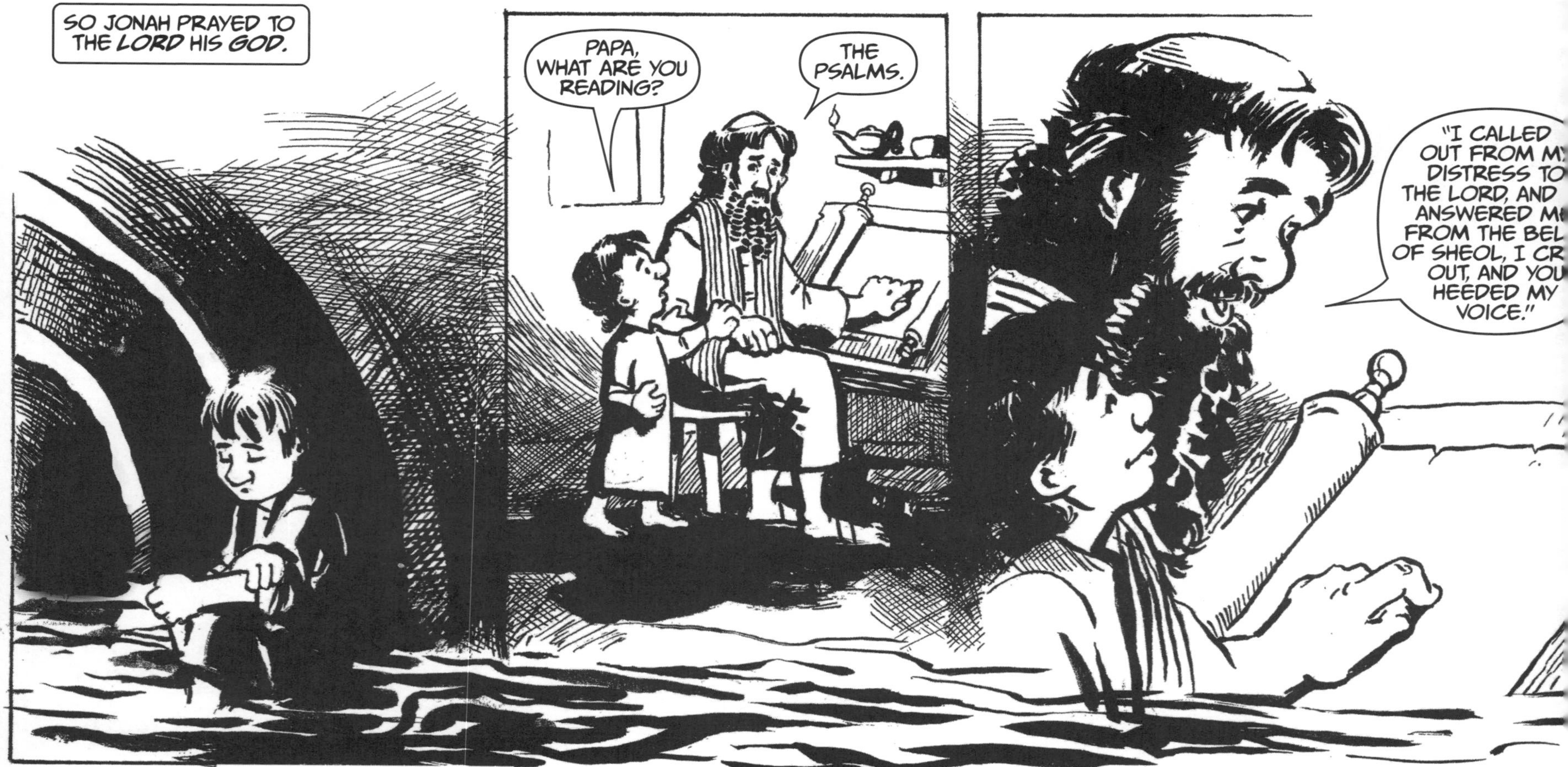
SO JONAH PRAYED TO THE *LORD* HIS *GOD.*
PAPA, WHAT ARE YOU READING?
THE PSALMS.
"I CALLED OUT FROM MY DISTRESS TO THE LORD, AND ANSWERED ME FROM THE BEL OF SHEOL, I CR OUT, AND YOU HEEDED MY VOICE."

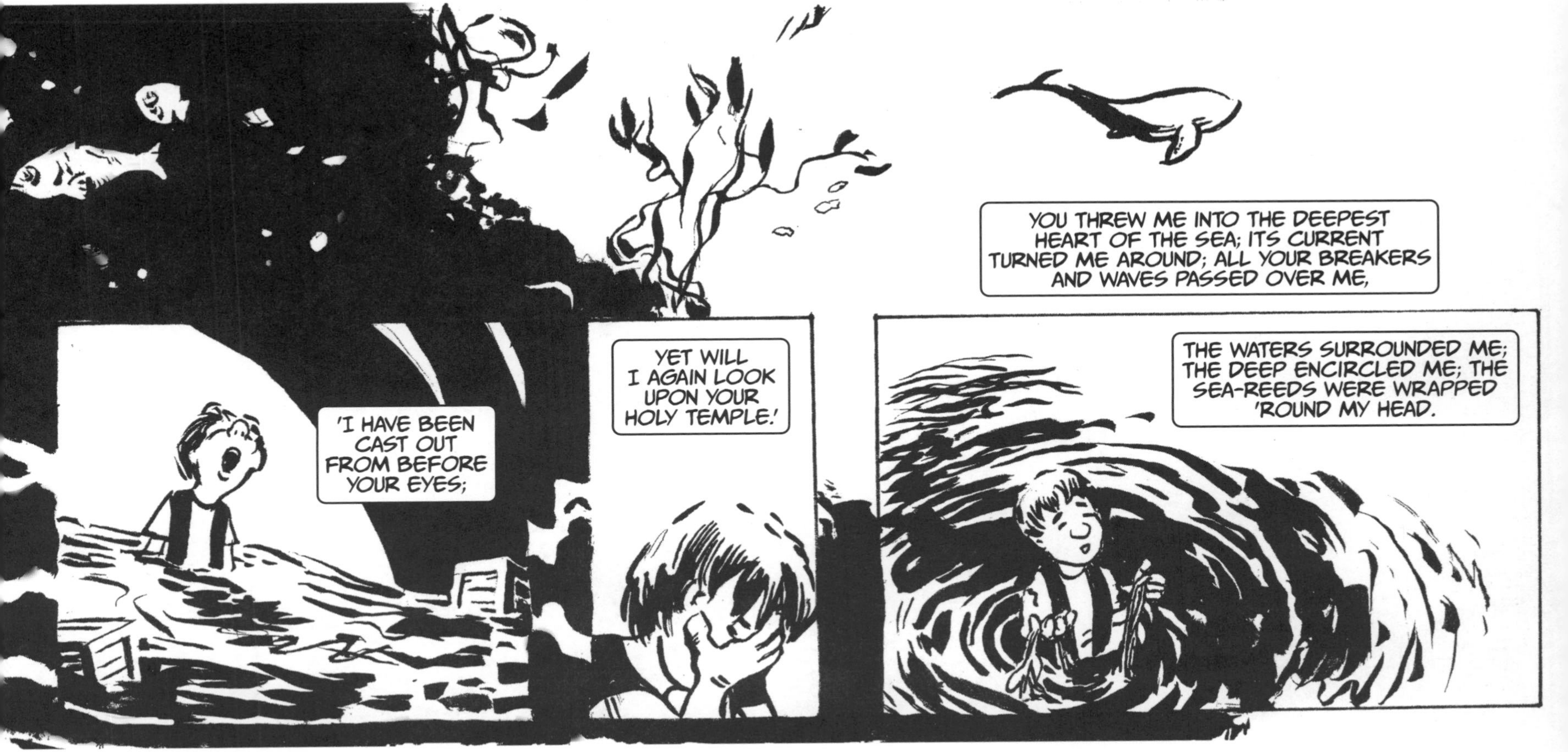
YOU THREW ME INTO THE DEEPEST HEART OF THE SEA; ITS CURRENT TURNED ME AROUND; ALL YOUR BREAKERS AND WAVES PASSED OVER ME,
'I HAVE BEEN CAST OUT FROM BEFORE YOUR EYES;
YET WILL I AGAIN LOOK UPON YOUR HOLY TEMPLE.'
THE WATERS SURROUNDED ME; THE DEEP ENCIRCLED ME; THE SEA-REEDS WERE WRAPPED 'ROUND MY HEAD.

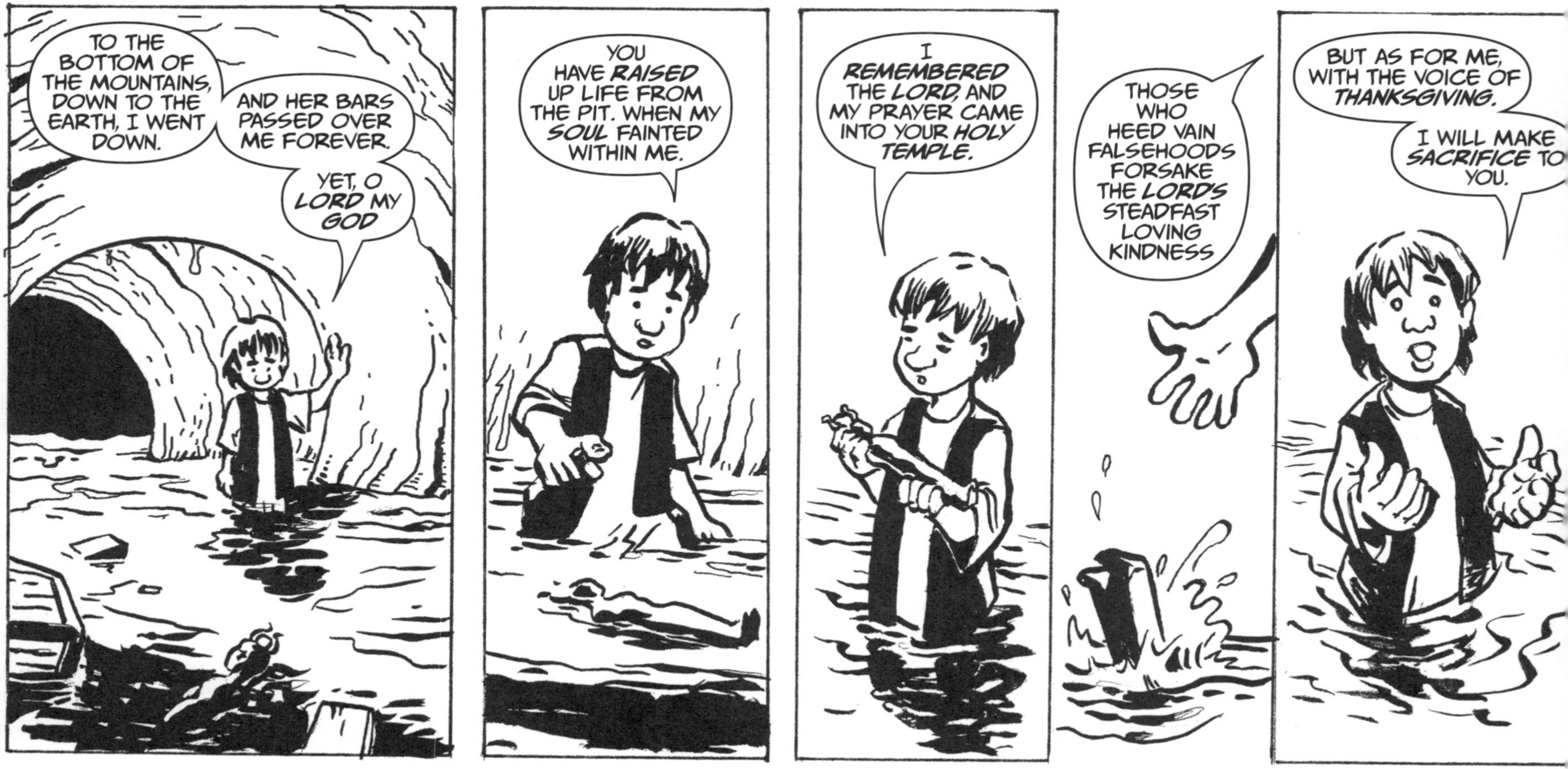

TO THE BOTTOM OF THE MOUNTAINS, DOWN TO THE EARTH, I WENT DOWN.
AND HER BARS PASSED OVER ME FOREVER.
YET, O LORD MY GOD
YOU HAVE RAISED UP LIFE FROM THE PIT. WHEN MY SOUL FAINTED WITHIN ME.
I REMEMBERED THE LORD, AND MY PRAYER CAME INTO YOUR HOLY TEMPLE.
THOSE WHO HEED VAIN FALSEHOODS FORSAKE THE LORD'S STEADFAST LOVING KINDNESS
BUT AS FOR ME, WITH THE VOICE OF THANKSGIVING.
I WILL MAKE SACRIFICE TO YOU.

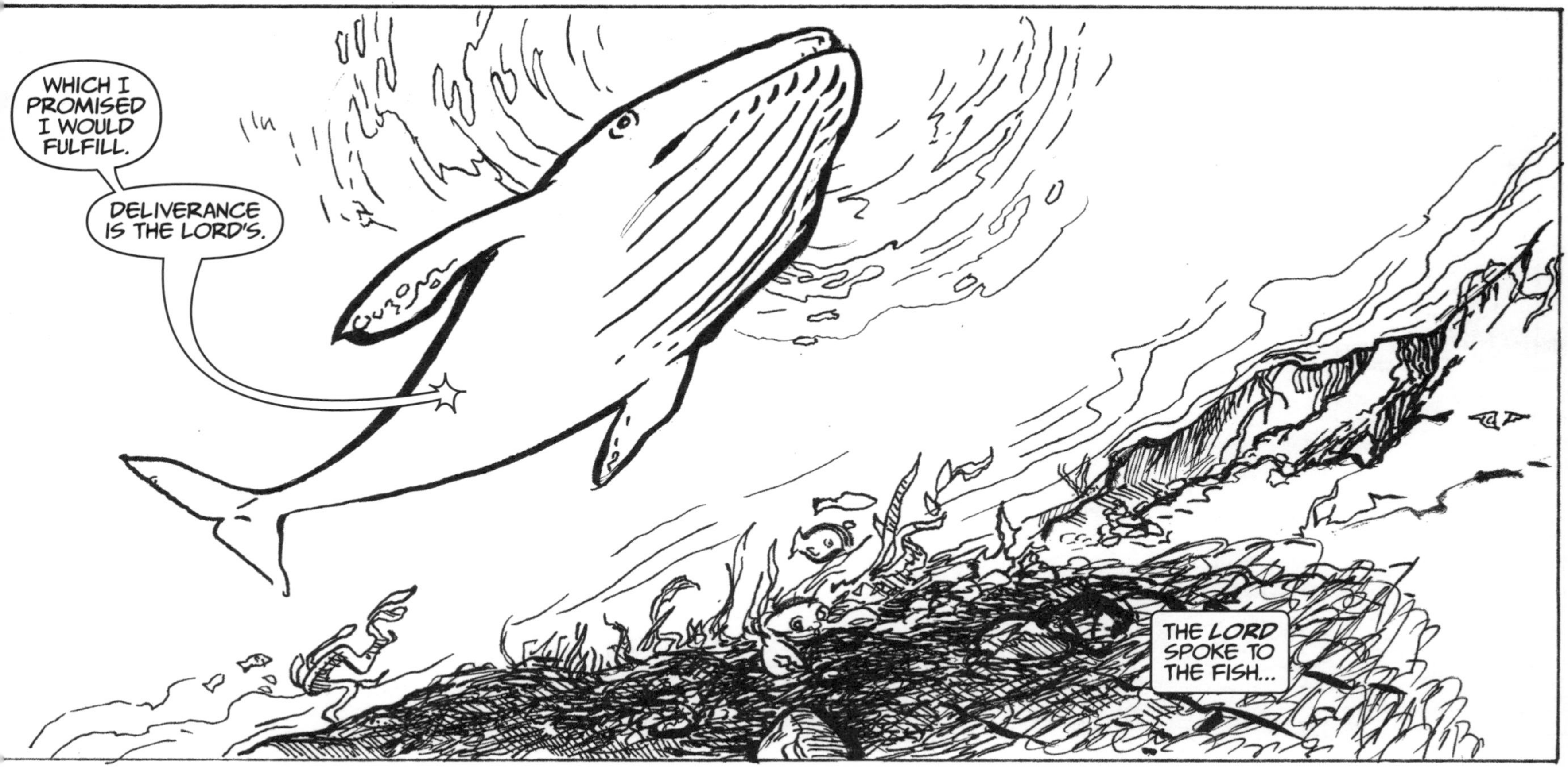
WHICH I PROMISED I WOULD FULFILL.
DELIVERANCE IS THE LORD'S.
THE *LORD* SPOKE TO THE FISH...

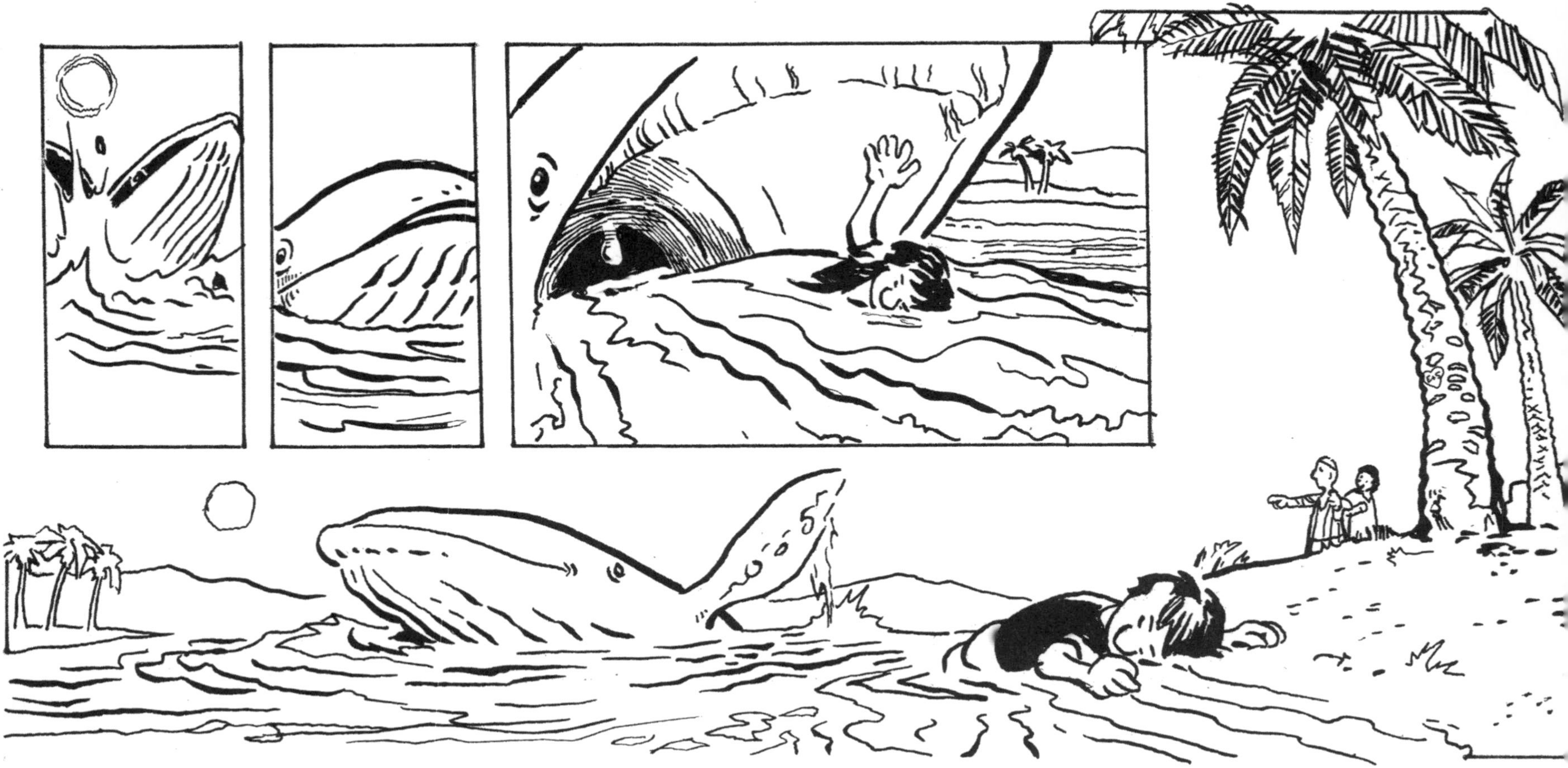

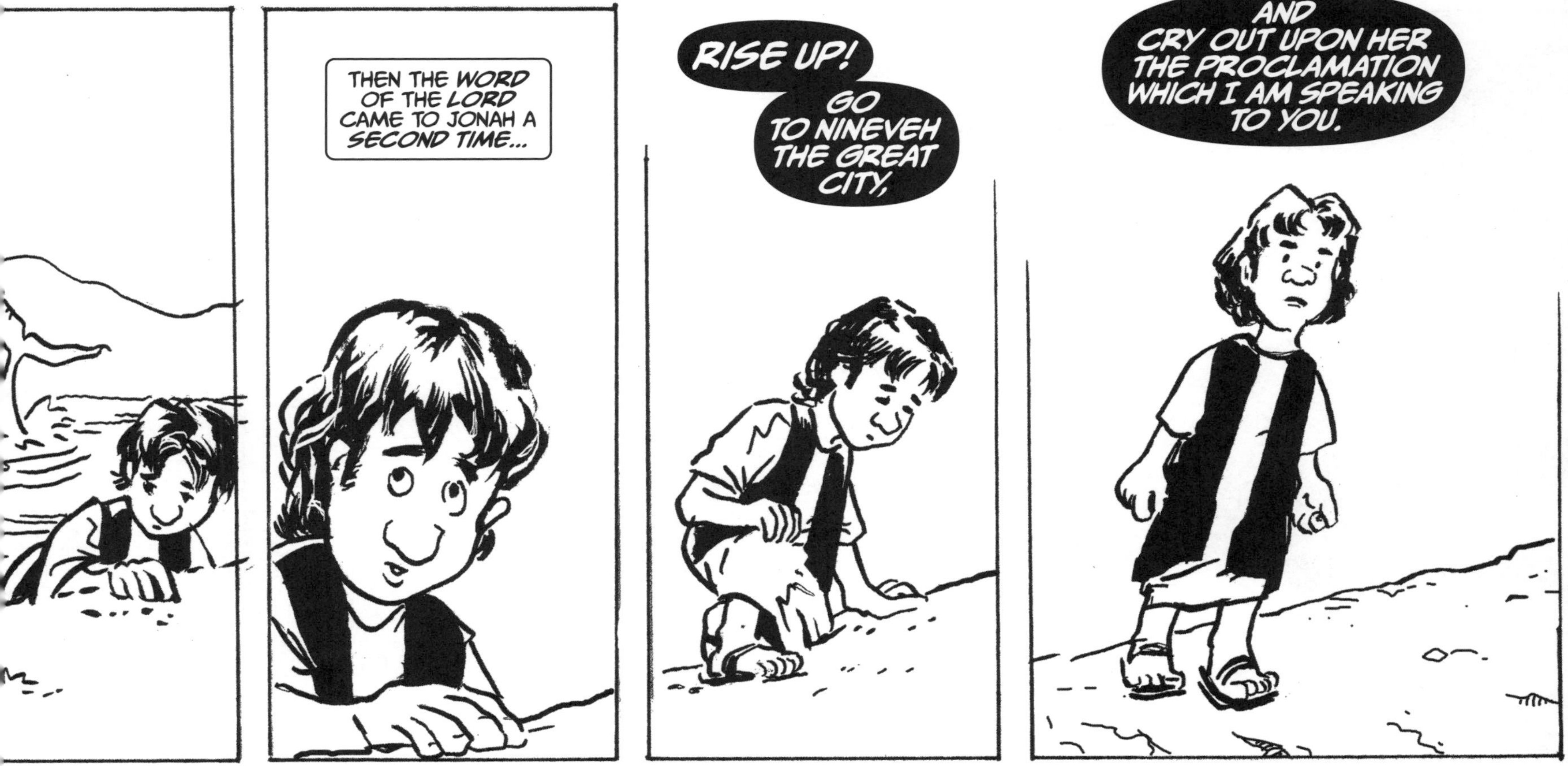
THEN THE WORD OF THE LORD CAME TO JONAH A SECOND TIME...
RISE UP!
GO TO NINEVEH THE GREAT CITY,
AND CRY OUT UPON HER THE PROCLAMATION WHICH I AM SPEAKING TO YOU.

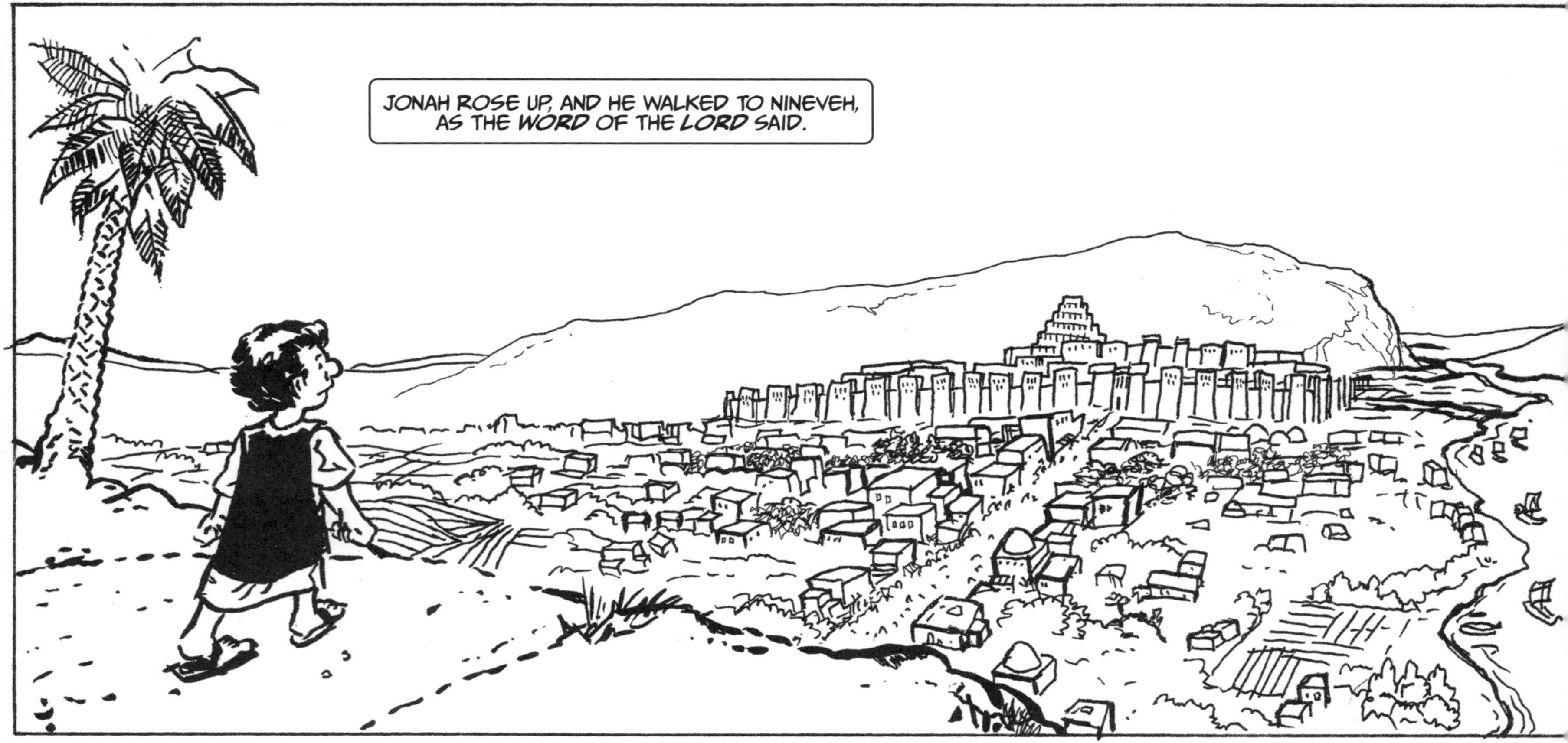
JONAH ROSE UP, AND HE WALKED TO NINEVEH, AS THE *WORD* OF THE *LORD* SAID.

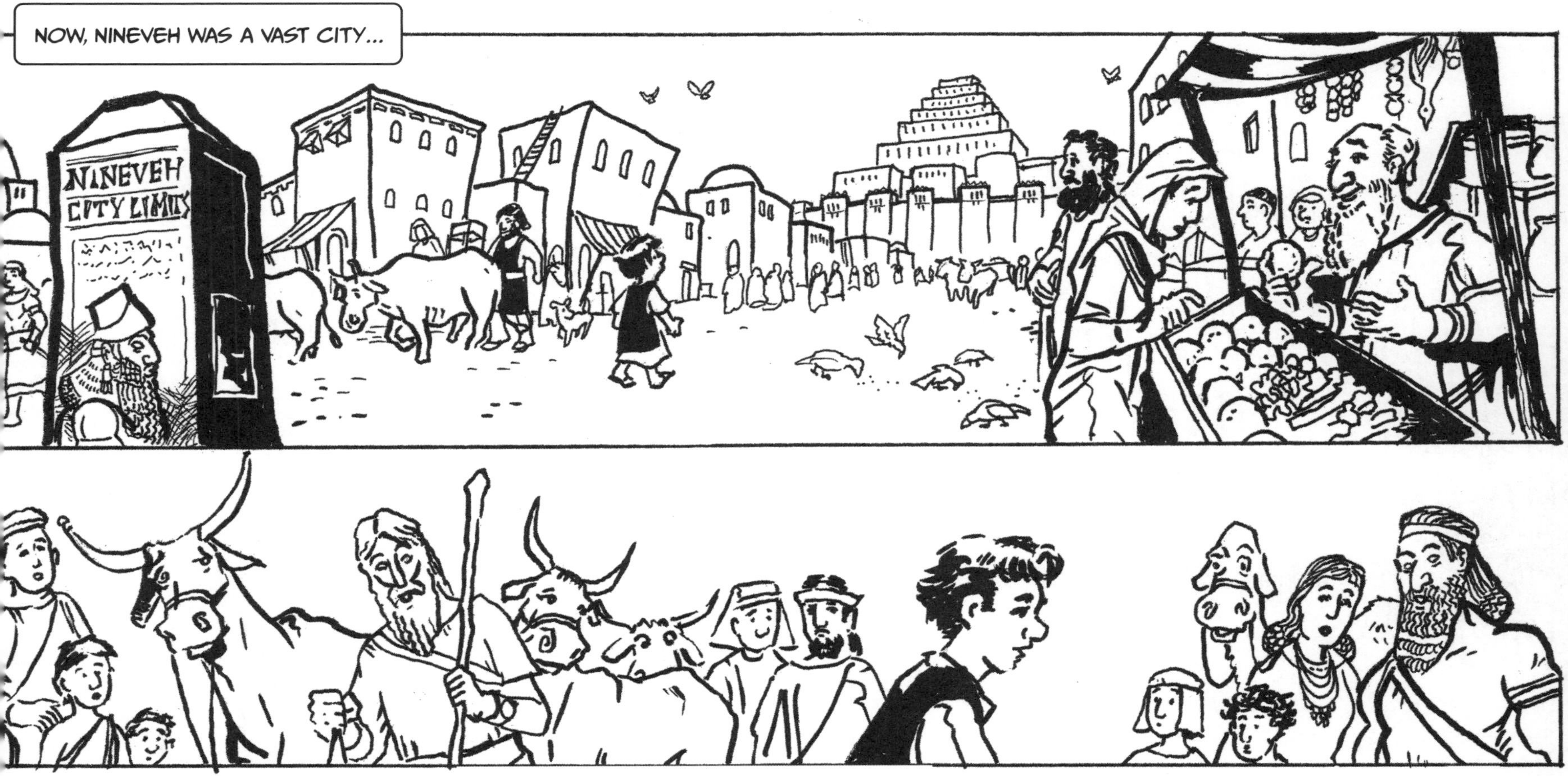
NOW, NINEVEH WAS A VAST CITY...
NINEVEH
CITY LIMITS

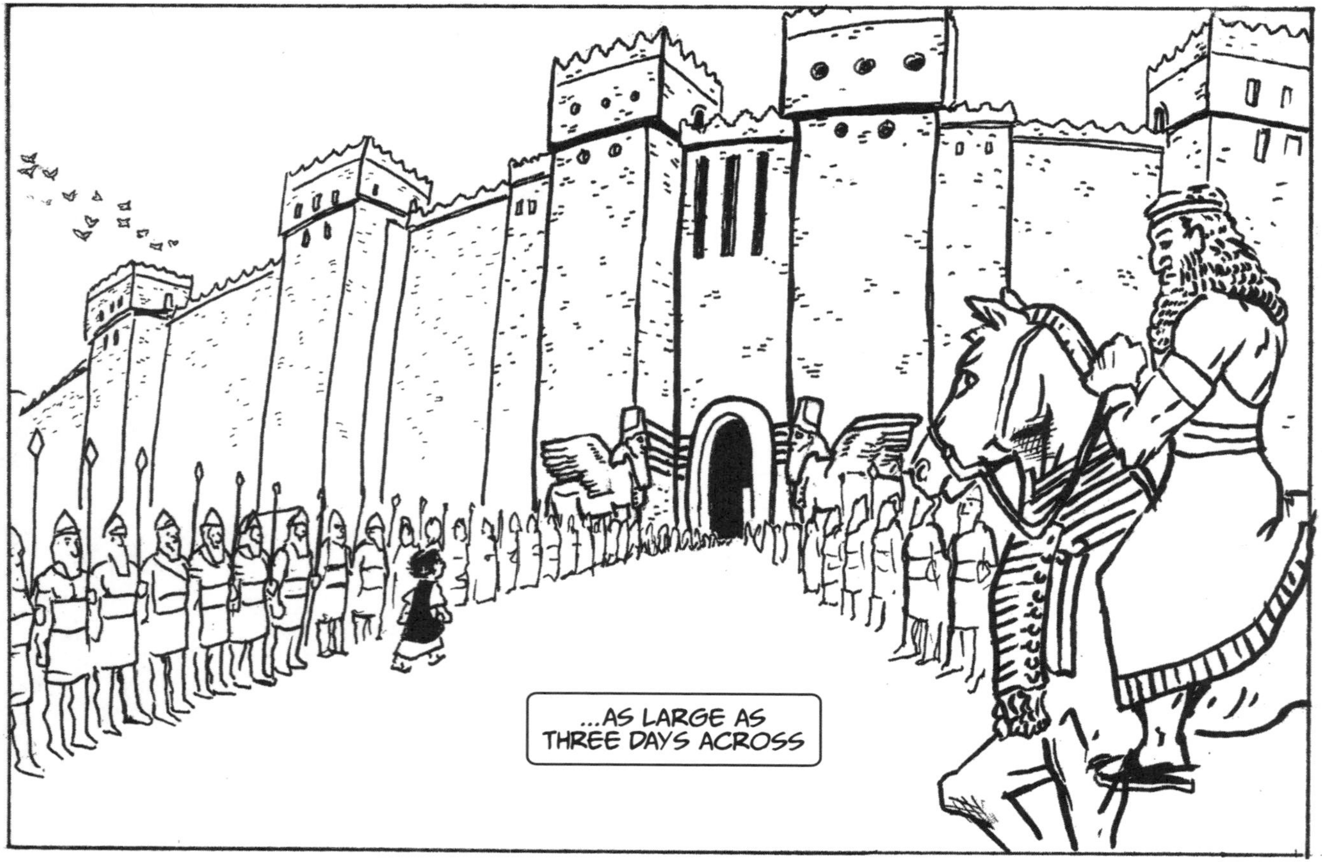
...AS LARGE AS THREE DAYS ACROSS

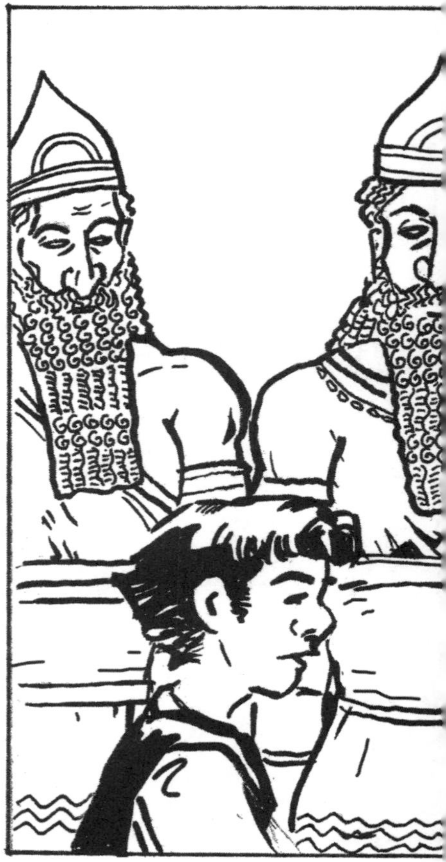

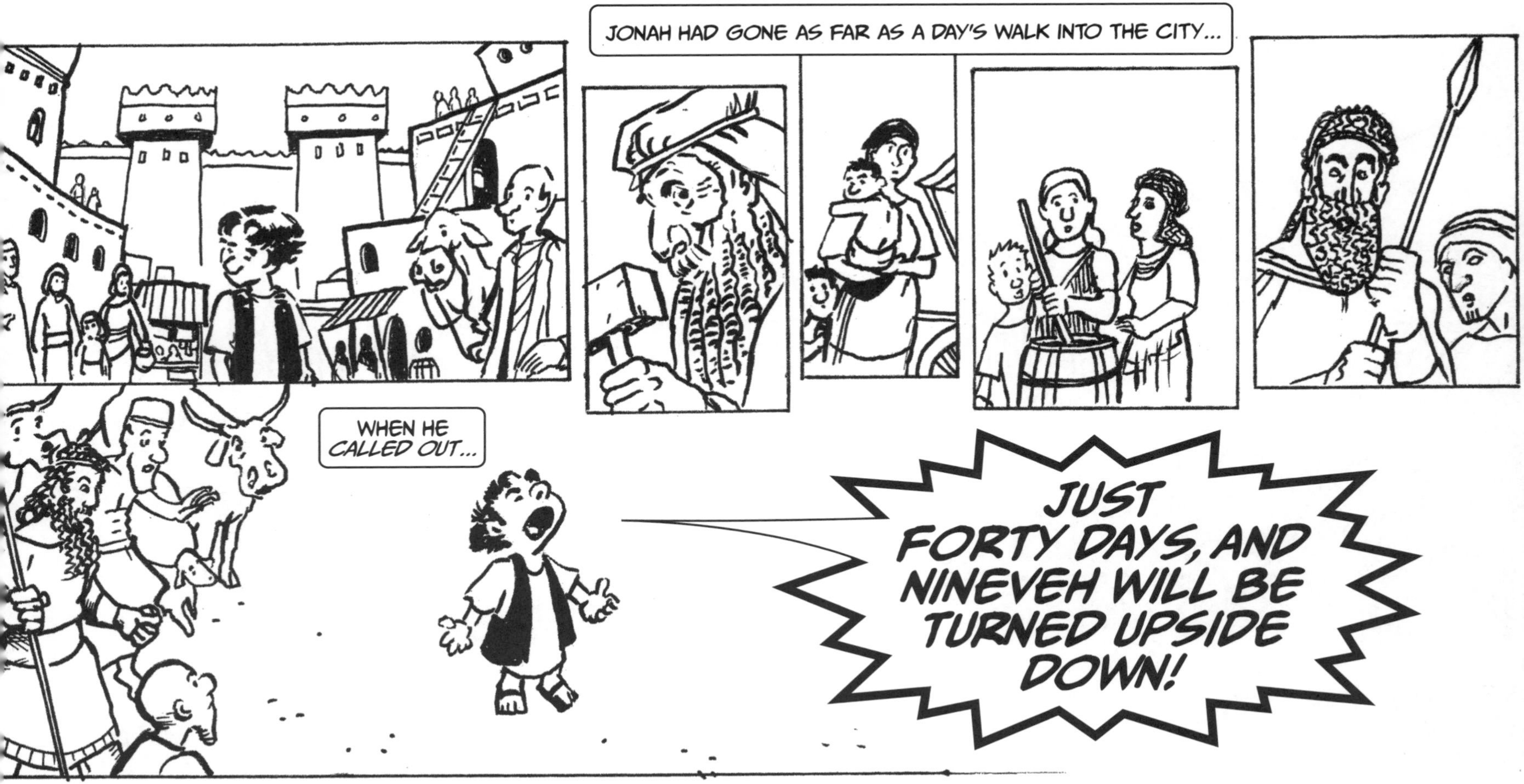
JONAH HAD GONE AS FAR AS A DAY'S WALK INTO THE CITY...
WHEN HE CALLED OUT...
JUST FORTY DAYS, AND NINEVEH WILL BE TURNED UPSIDE DOWN!

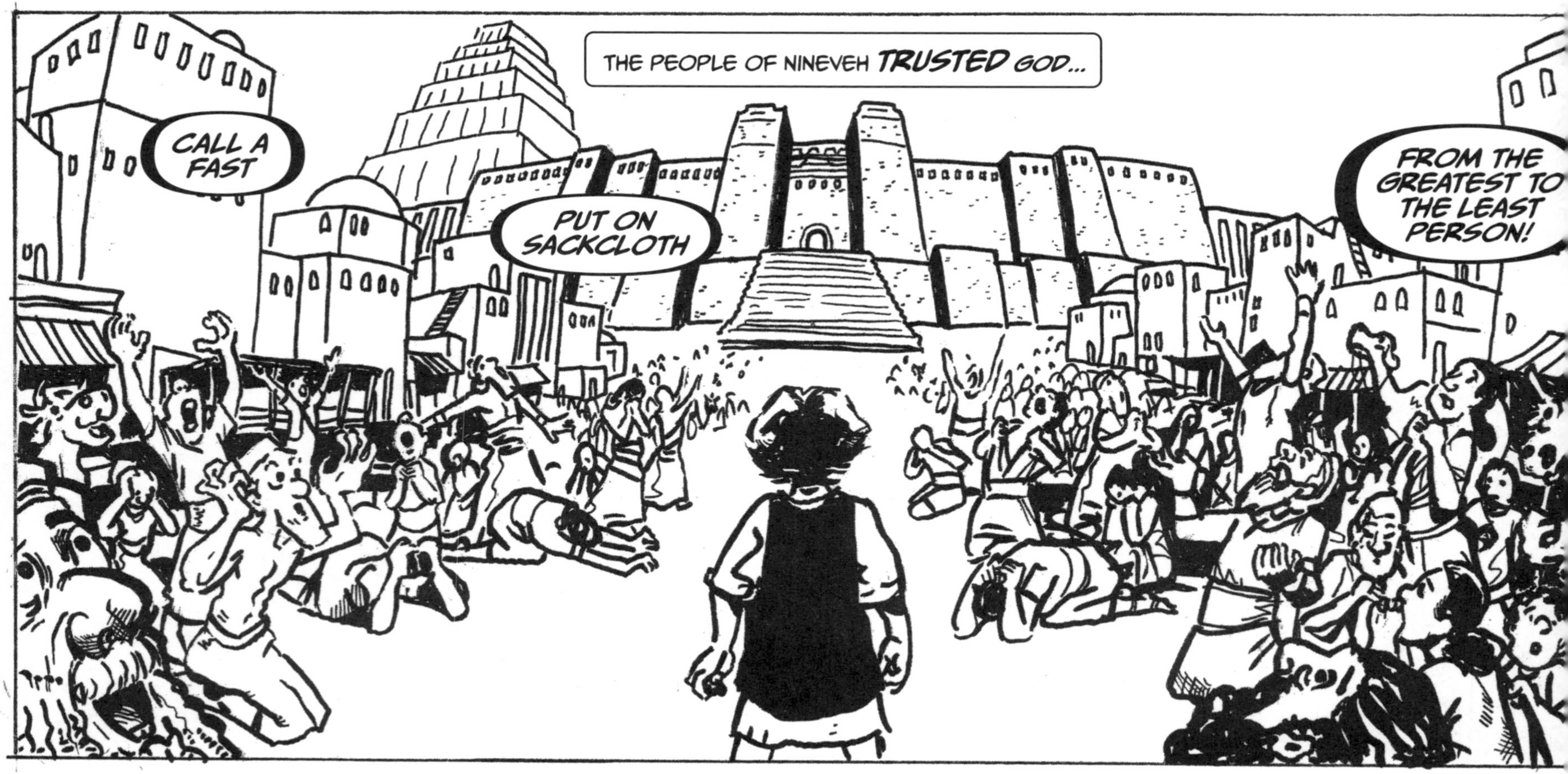
THE PEOPLE OF NINEVEH TRUSTED GOD...
CALL A FAST
PUT ON SACKCLOTH
FROM THE GREATEST TO THE LEAST PERSON!

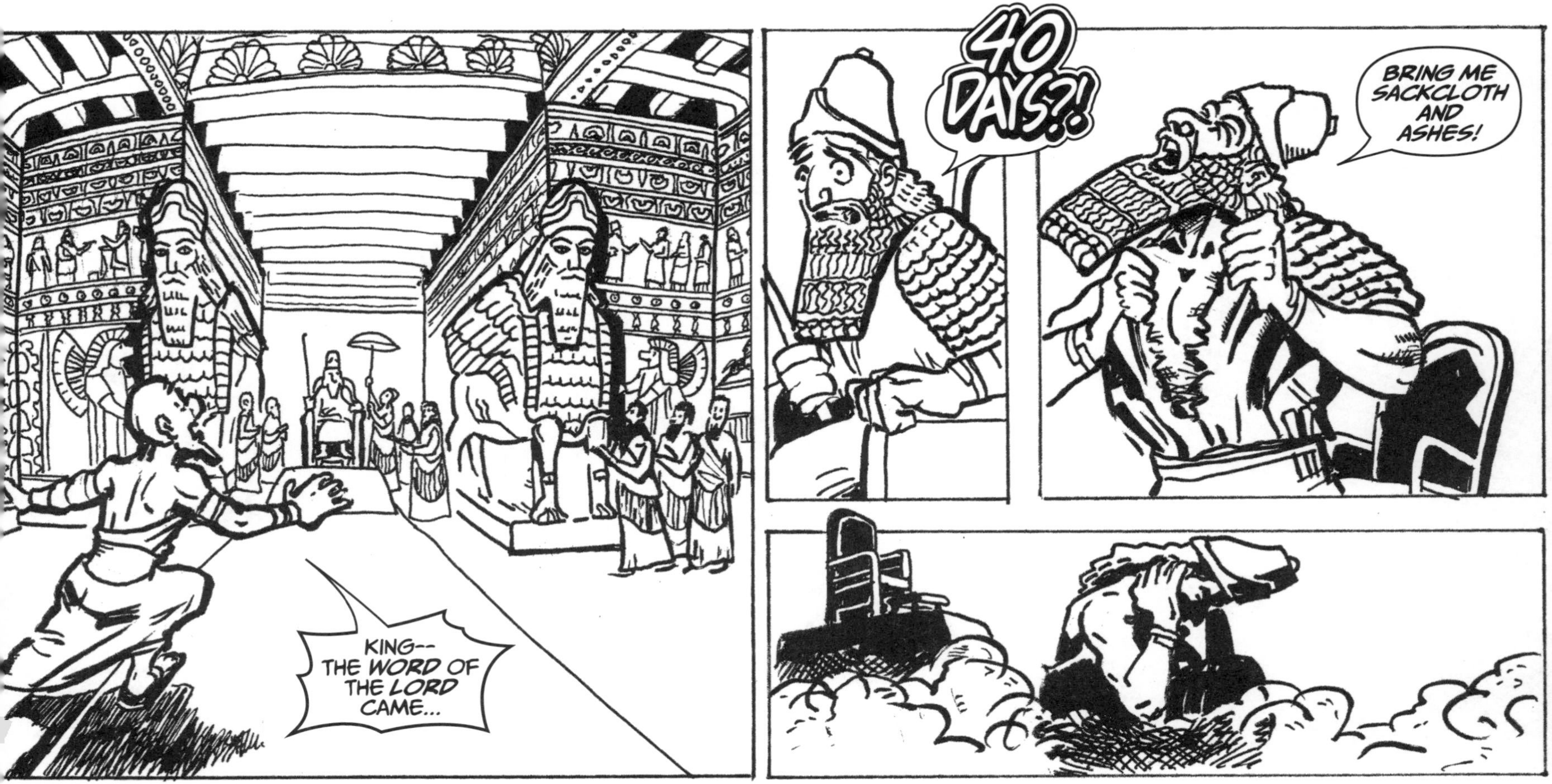
KING-- THE WORD OF THE LORD CAME...
40 DAYS?!
BRING ME SACKCLOTH AND ASHES!

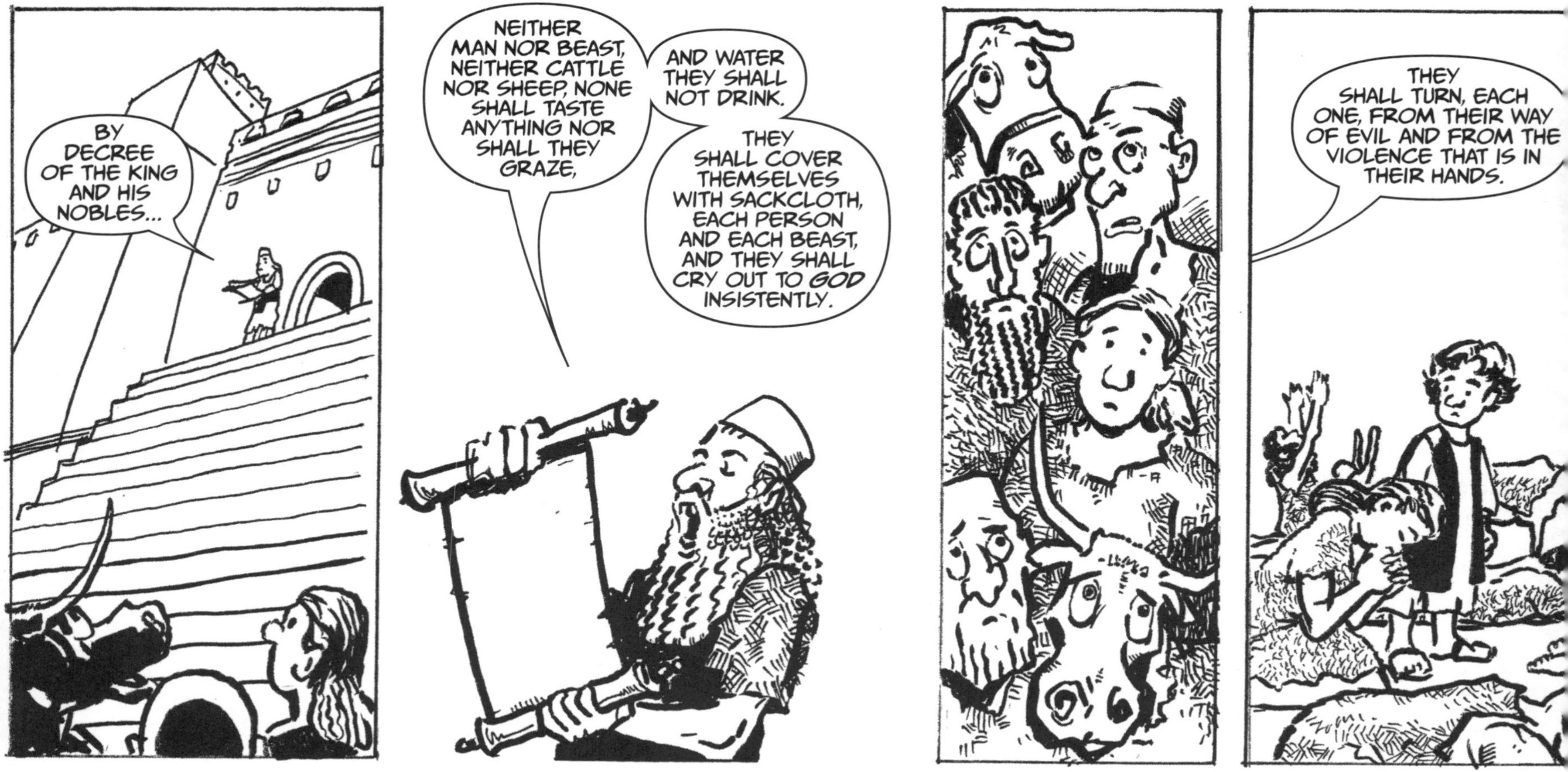

BY DECREE OF THE KING AND HIS NOBLES...
NEITHER MAN NOR BEAST, NEITHER CATTLE NOR SHEEP, NONE SHALL TASTE ANYTHING NOR SHALL THEY GRAZE,
AND WATER THEY SHALL NOT DRINK.
THEY SHALL COVER THEMSELVES WITH SACKCLOTH, EACH PERSON AND EACH BEAST, AND THEY SHALL CRY OUT TO *GOD* INSISTENTLY.
THEY SHALL TURN, EACH ONE, FROM THEIR WAY OF EVIL AND FROM THE VIOLENCE THAT IS IN THEIR HANDS.

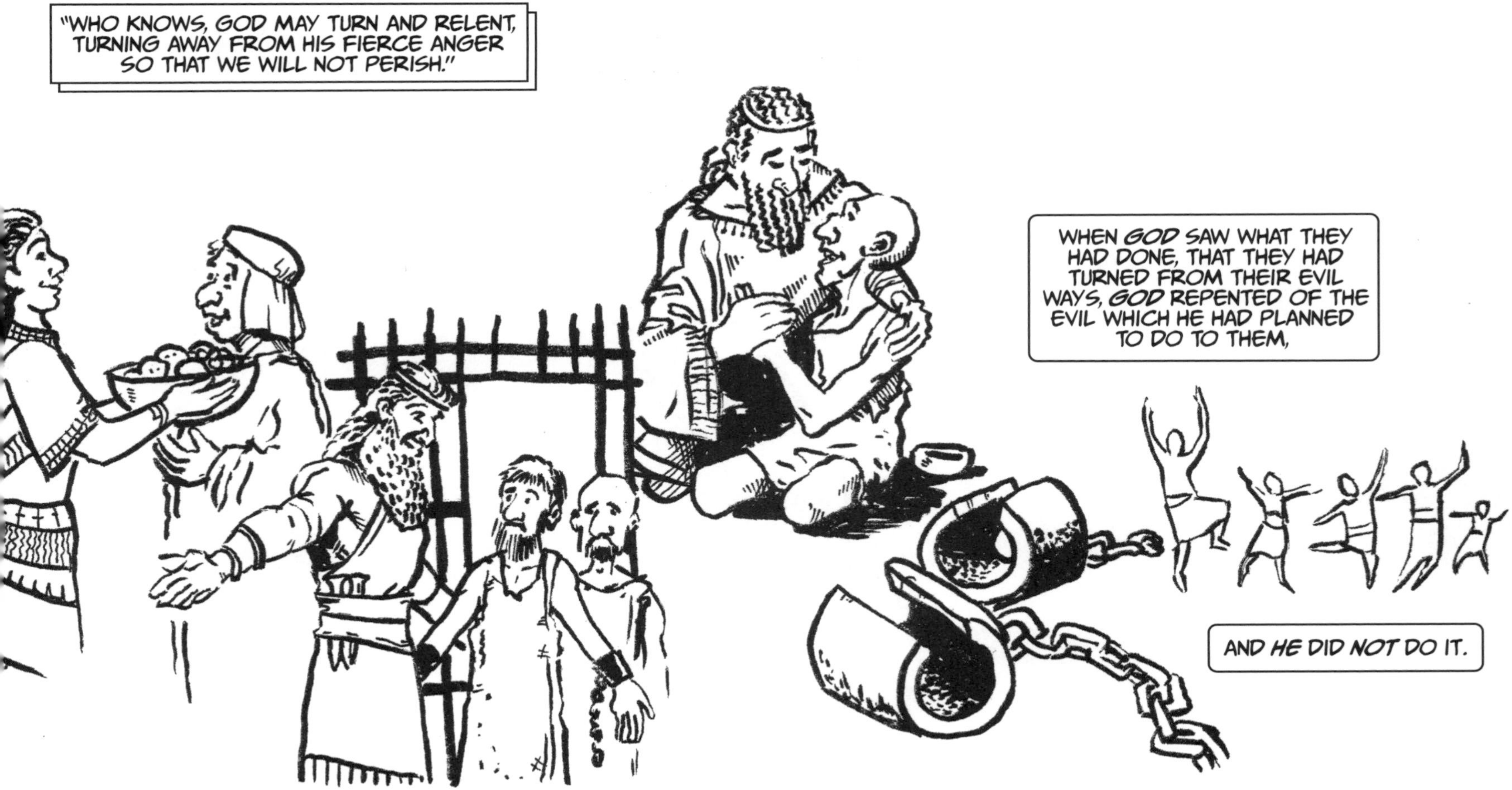
"WHO KNOWS, GOD MAY TURN AND RELENT, TURNING AWAY FROM HIS FIERCE ANGER SO THAT WE WILL NOT PERISH."
WHEN GOD SAW WHAT THEY HAD DONE, THAT THEY HAD TURNED FROM THEIR EVIL WAYS, GOD REPENTED OF THE EVIL WHICH HE HAD PLANNED TO DO TO THEM,
AND HE DID NOT DO IT.

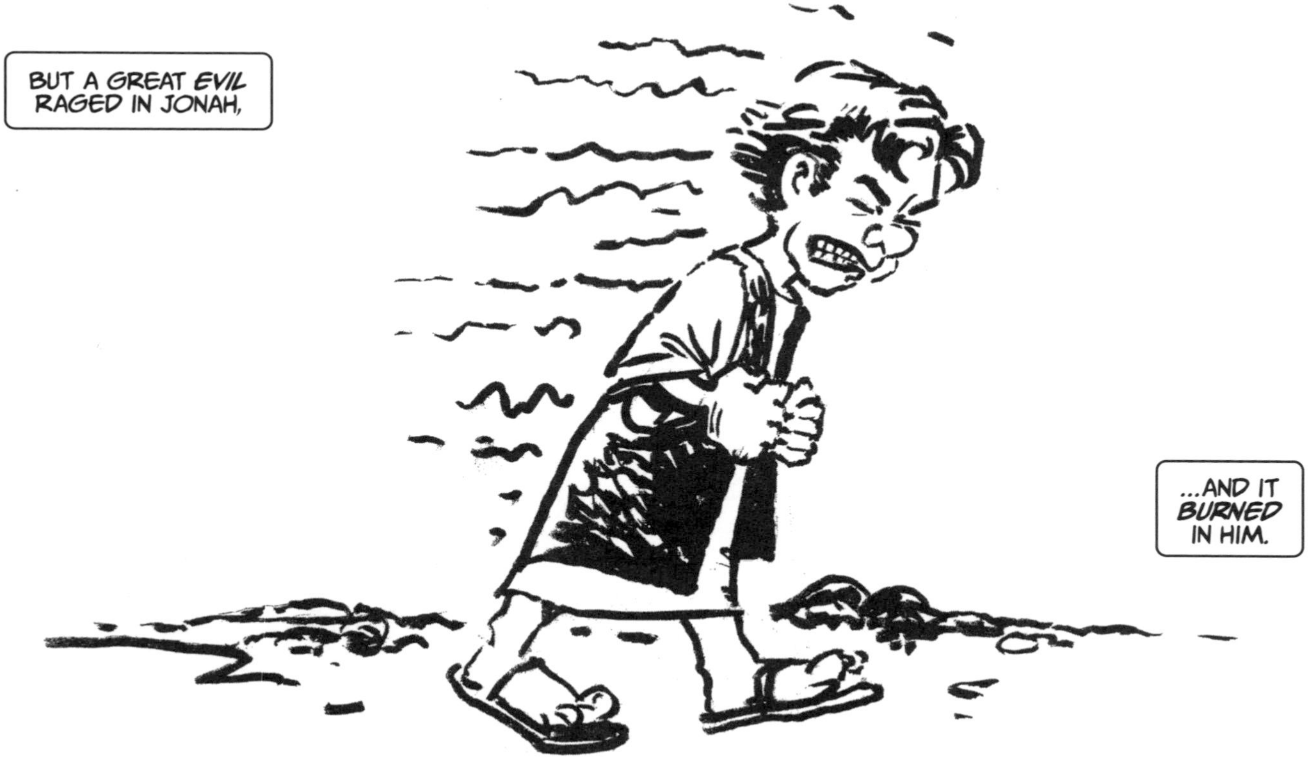
BUT A GREAT EVIL RAGED IN JONAH,
...AND IT BURNED IN HIM.

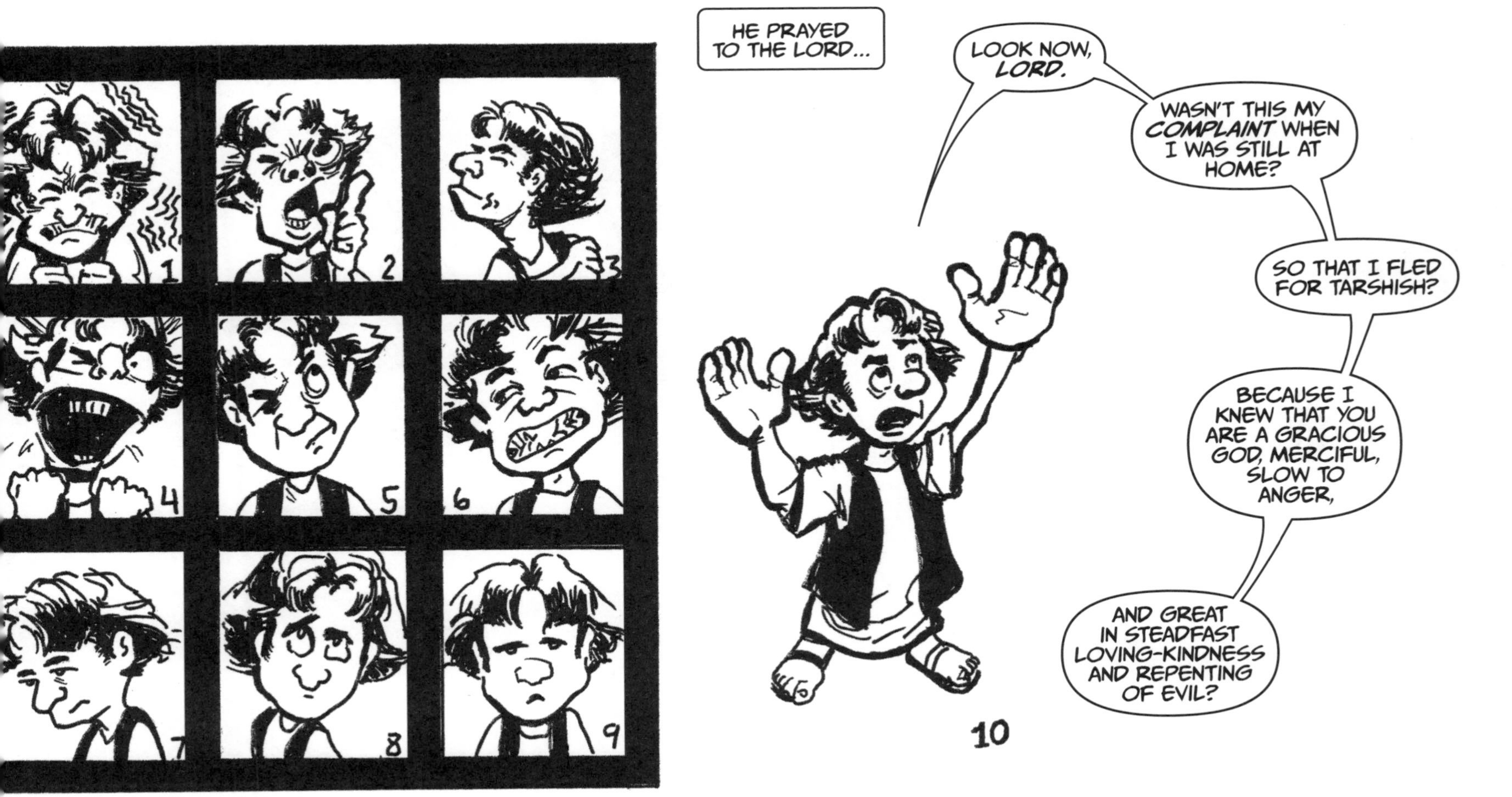

1
2
3
4
5
6
7
8
9
HE PRAYED TO THE LORD...
LOOK NOW, LORD.
WASN'T THIS MY COMPLAINT WHEN I WAS STILL AT HOME?
SO THAT I FLED FOR TARSHISH?
BECAUSE I KNEW THAT YOU ARE A GRACIOUS GOD, MERCIFUL, SLOW TO ANGER,
AND GREAT IN STEADFAST LOVING-KINDNESS AND REPENTING OF EVIL?
10

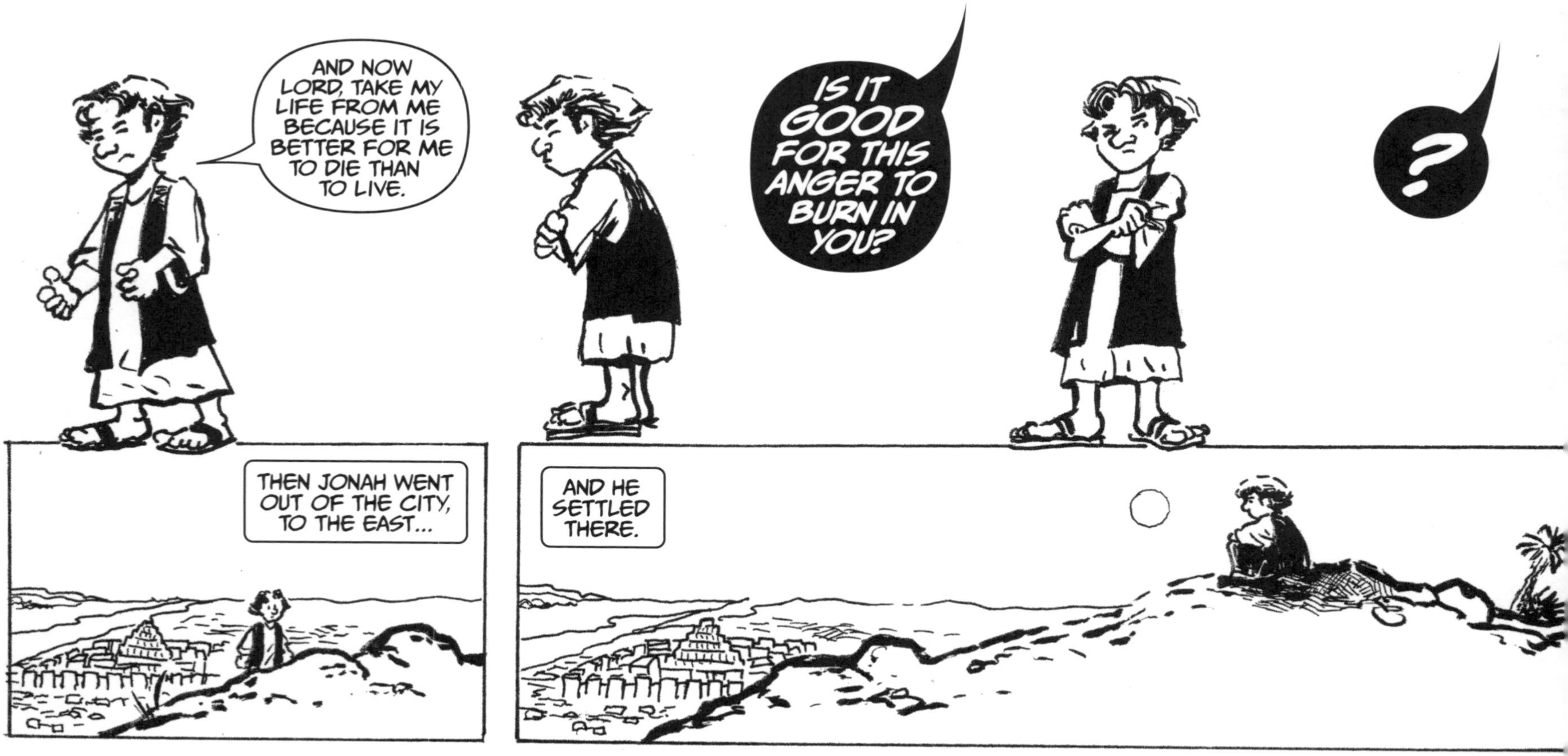

AND NOW LORD, TAKE MY LIFE FROM ME BECAUSE IT IS BETTER FOR ME TO DIE THAN TO LIVE.
IS IT GOOD FOR THIS ANGER TO BURN IN YOU?
?
THEN JONAH WENT OUT OF THE CITY, TO THE EAST...
AND HE SETTLED THERE.

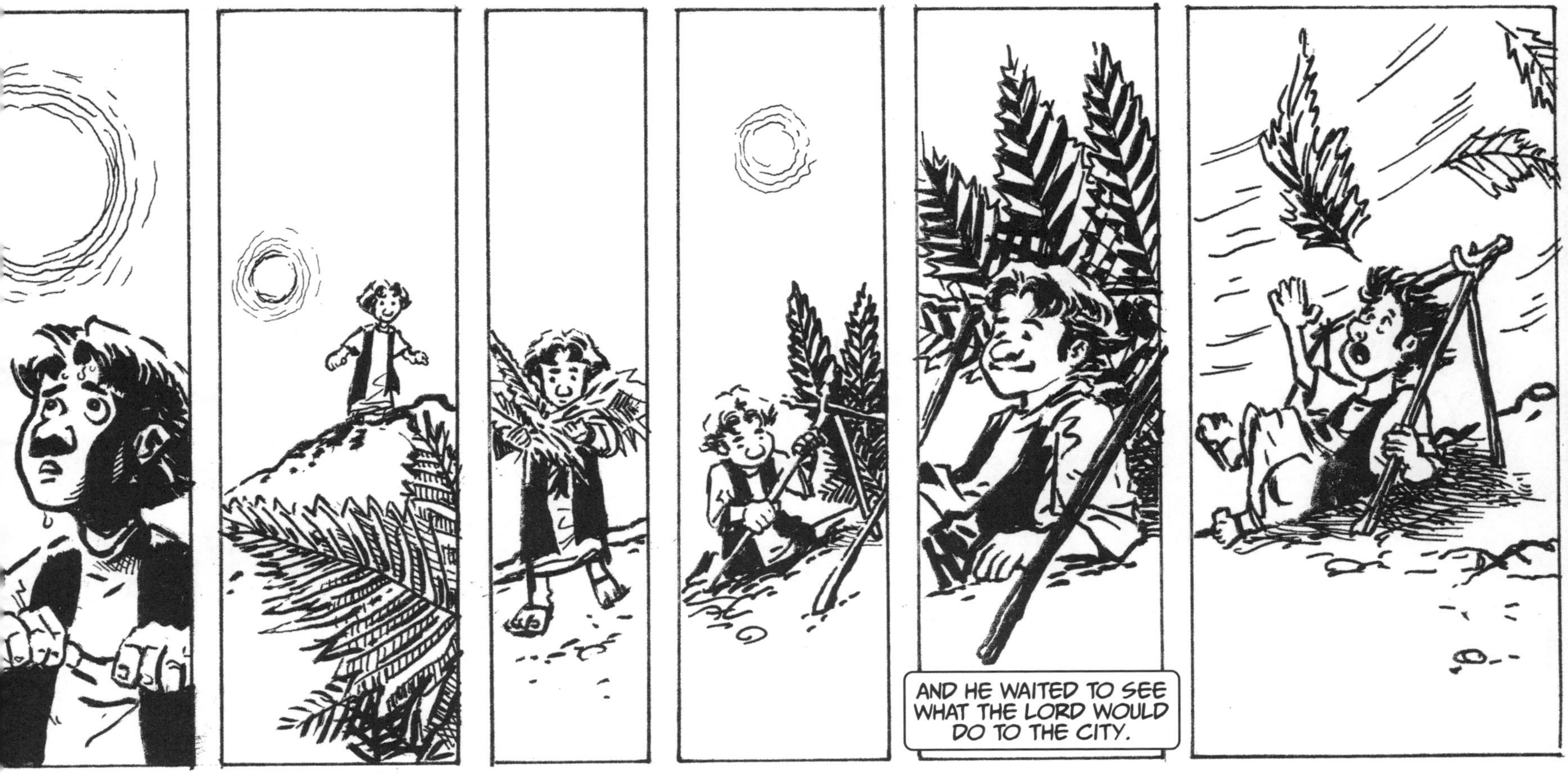
AND HE WAITED TO SEE WHAT THE LORD WOULD DO TO THE CITY.

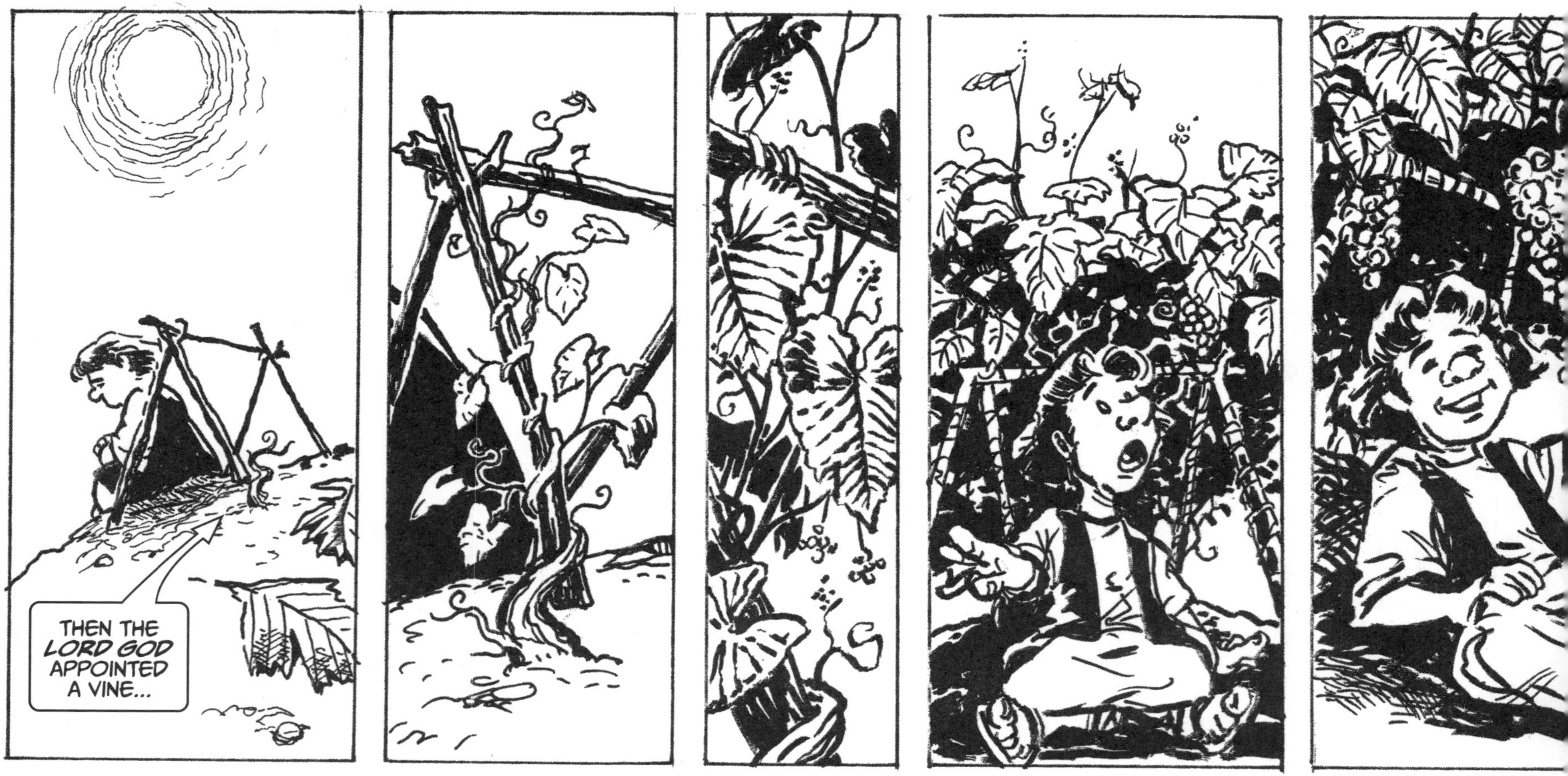
THEN THE LORD GOD APPOINTED A VINE...

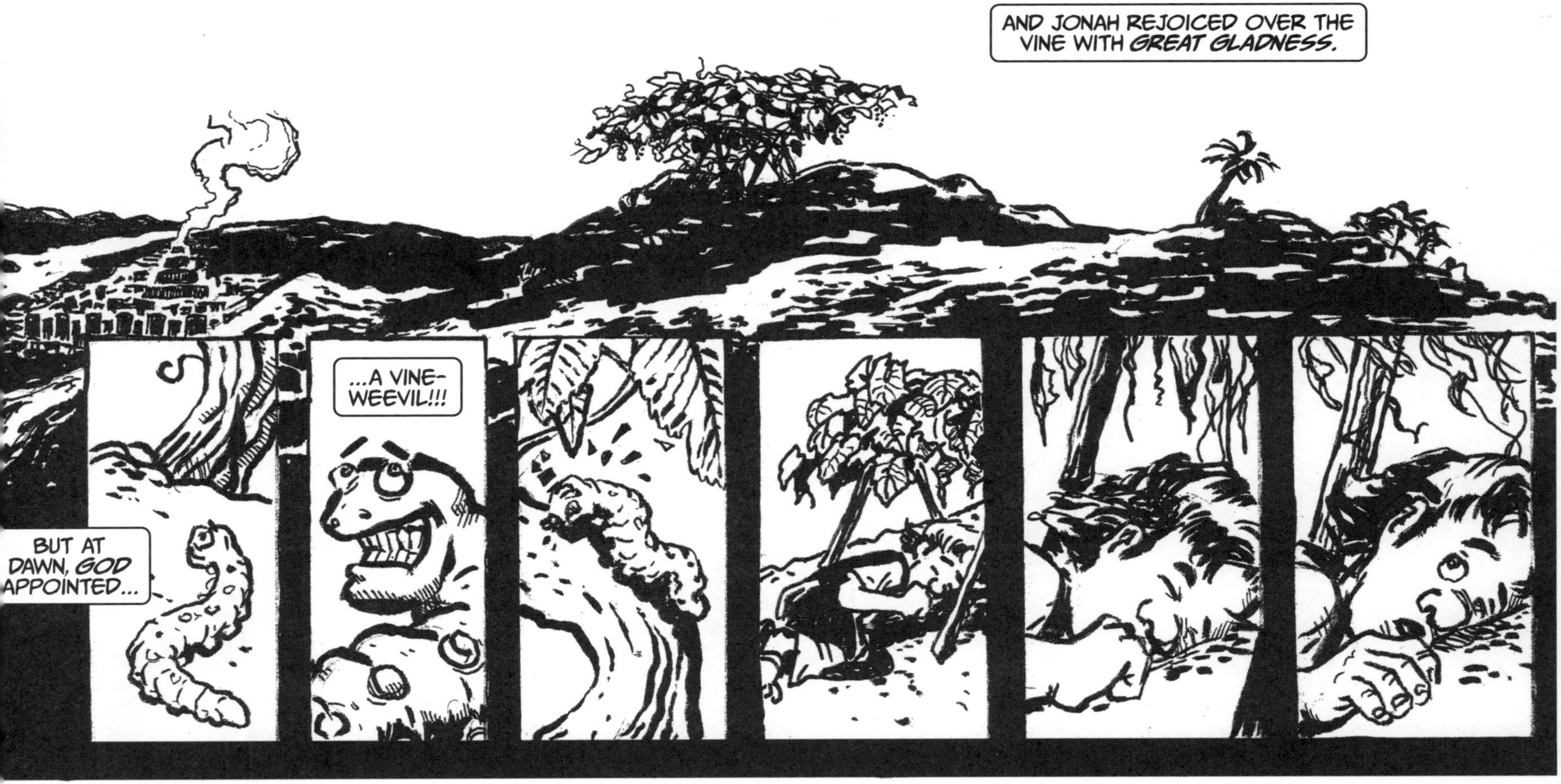
AND JONAH REJOICED OVER THE VINE WITH *GREAT GLADNESS.*
BUT AT DAWN, *GOD* APPOINTED...
...A VINE-WEEVIL!!!

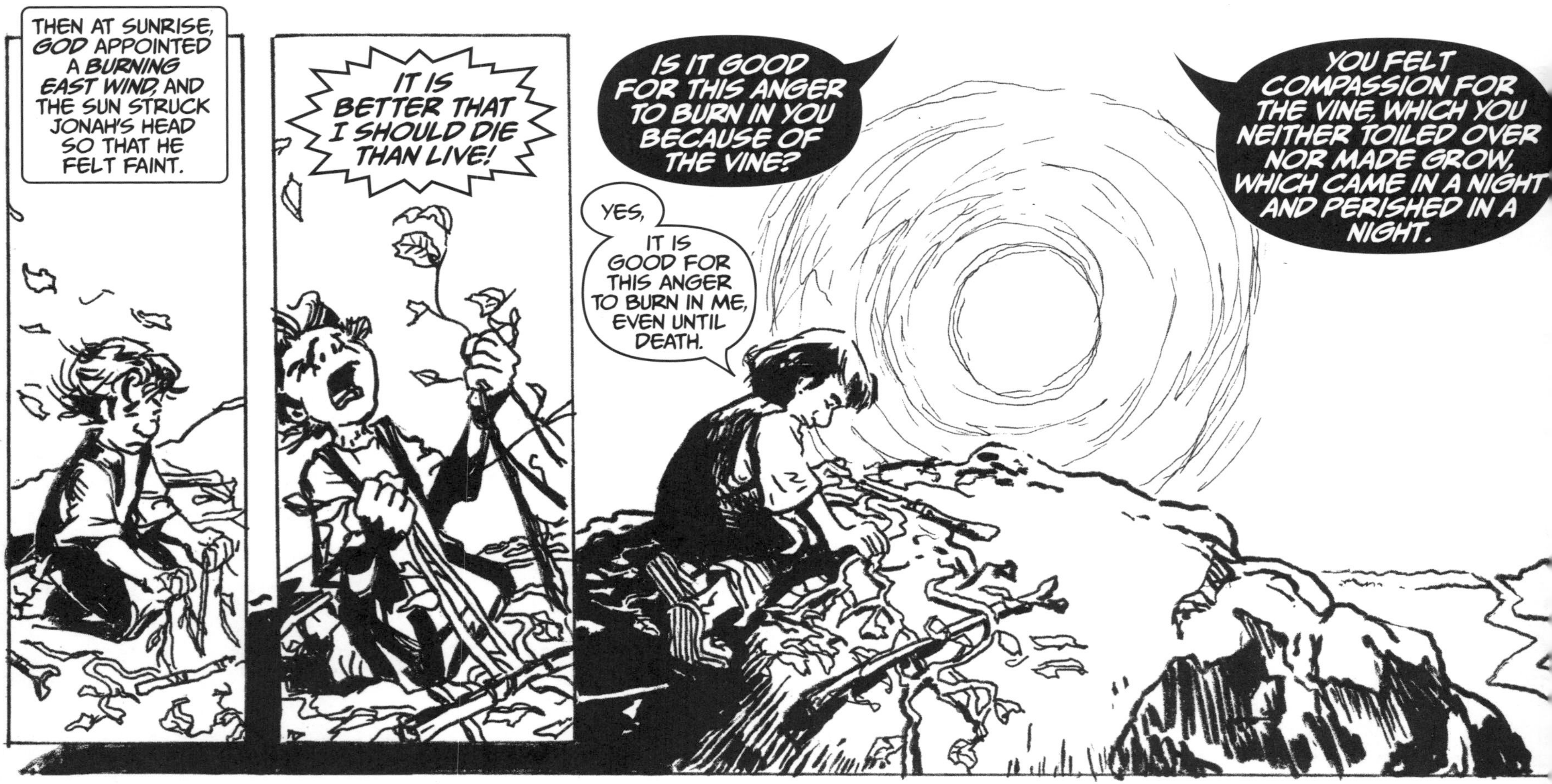
THEN AT SUNRISE, GOD APPOINTED A BURNING EAST WIND, AND THE SUN STRUCK JONAH'S HEAD SO THAT HE FELT FAINT.
IT IS BETTER THAT I SHOULD DIE THAN LIVE!
IS IT GOOD FOR THIS ANGER TO BURN IN YOU BECAUSE OF THE VINE?
YES,
IT IS GOOD FOR THIS ANGER TO BURN IN ME, EVEN UNTIL DEATH.
YOU FELT COMPASSION FOR THE VINE, WHICH YOU NEITHER TOILED OVER NOR MADE GROW, WHICH CAME IN A NIGHT AND PERISHED IN A NIGHT.

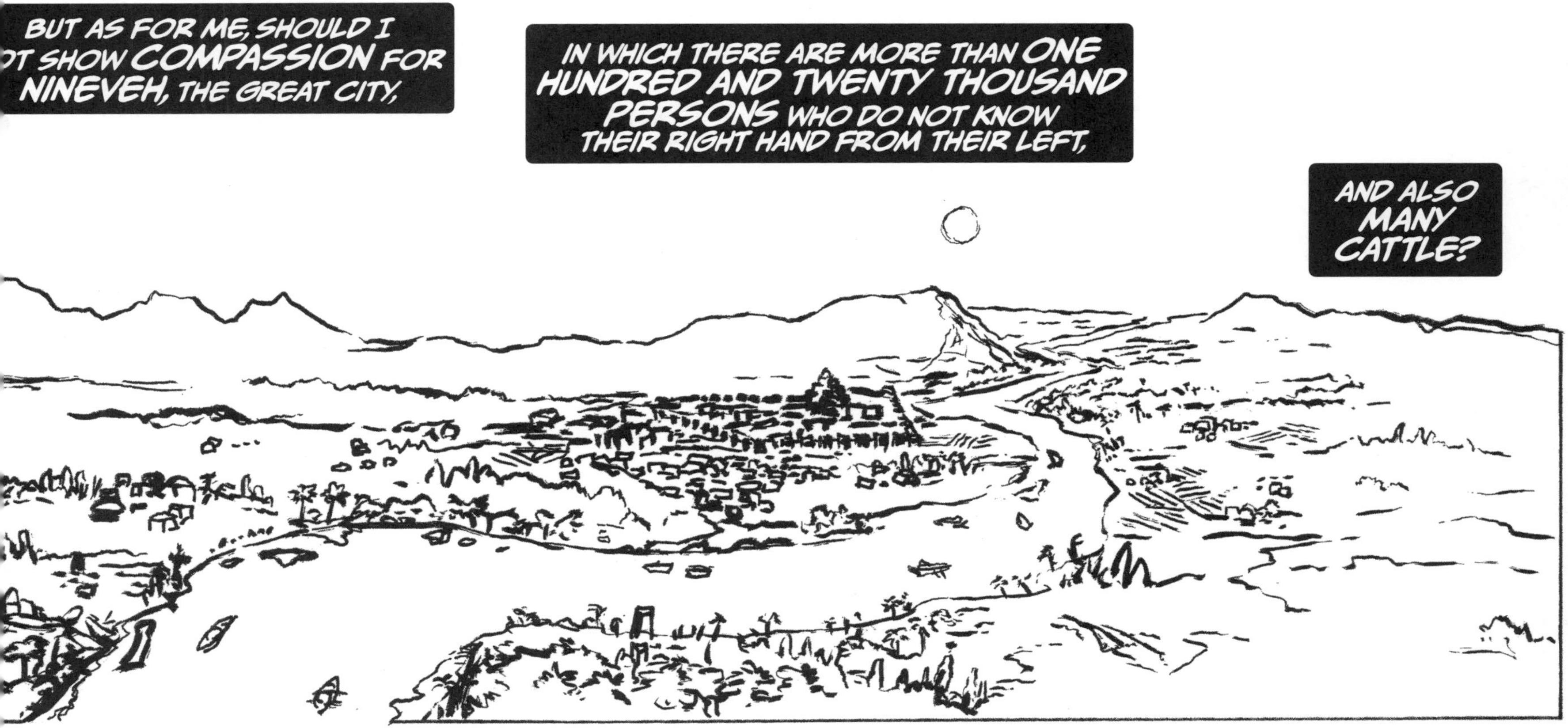
BUT AS FOR ME, SHOULD I
OT SHOW COMPASSION FOR
NINEVEH, THE GREAT CITY,
IN WHICH THERE ARE MORE THAN ONE HUNDRED AND TWENTY THOUSAND PERSONS WHO DO NOT KNOW THEIR RIGHT HAND FROM THEIR LEFT,
AND ALSO MANY CATTLE?

ESTHER

CHAPTER 1

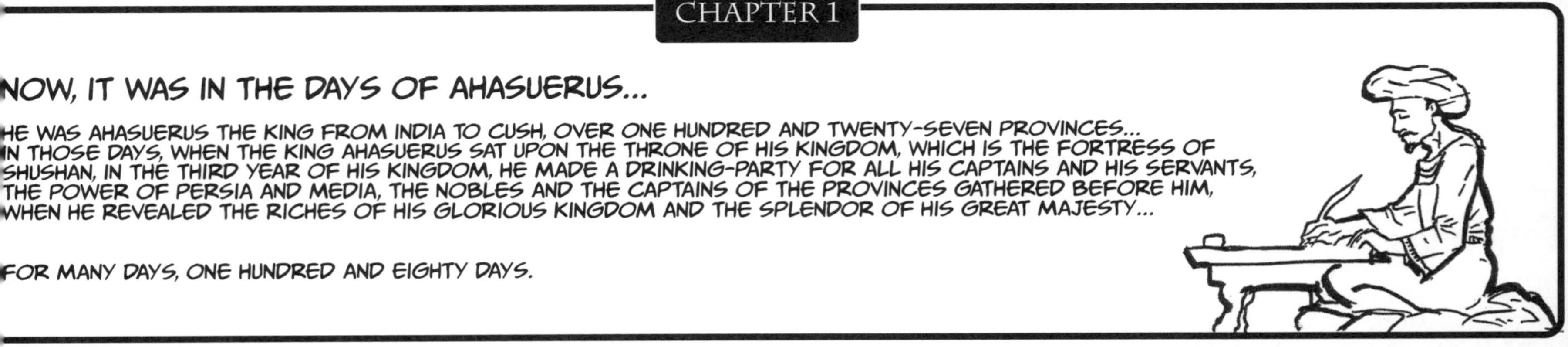
NOW, IT WAS IN THE DAYS OF AHASUERUS...
HE WAS AHASUERUS THE KING FROM INDIA TO CUSH, OVER ONE HUNDRED AND TWENTY-SEVEN PROVINCES... IN THOSE DAYS, WHEN THE KING AHASUERUS SAT UPON THE THRONE OF HIS KINGDOM, WHICH IS THE FORTRESS OF SHUSHAN, IN THE THIRD YEAR OF HIS KINGDOM, HE MADE A DRINKING-PARTY FOR ALL HIS CAPTAINS AND HIS SERVANTS, THE POWER OF PERSIA AND MEDIA, THE NOBLES AND THE CAPTAINS OF THE PROVINCES GATHERED BEFORE HIM, WHEN HE REVEALED THE RICHES OF HIS GLORIOUS KINGDOM AND THE SPLENDOR OF HIS GREAT MAJESTY...
FOR MANY DAYS, ONE HUNDRED AND EIGHTY DAYS.

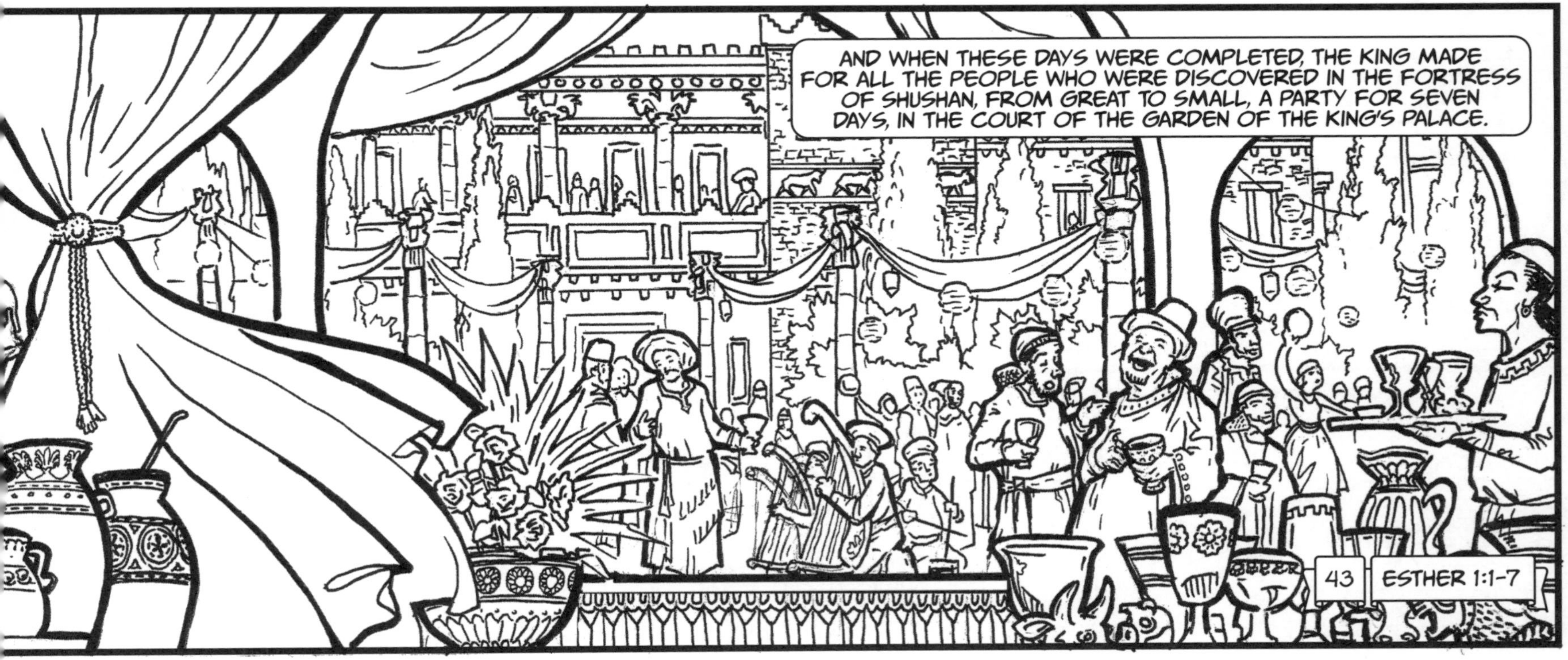
AND WHEN THESE DAYS WERE COMPLETED, THE KING MADE FOR ALL THE PEOPLE WHO WERE DISCOVERED IN THE FORTRESS OF SHUSHAN, FROM GREAT TO SMALL, A PARTY FOR SEVEN DAYS, IN THE COURT OF THE GARDEN OF THE KING'S PALACE.

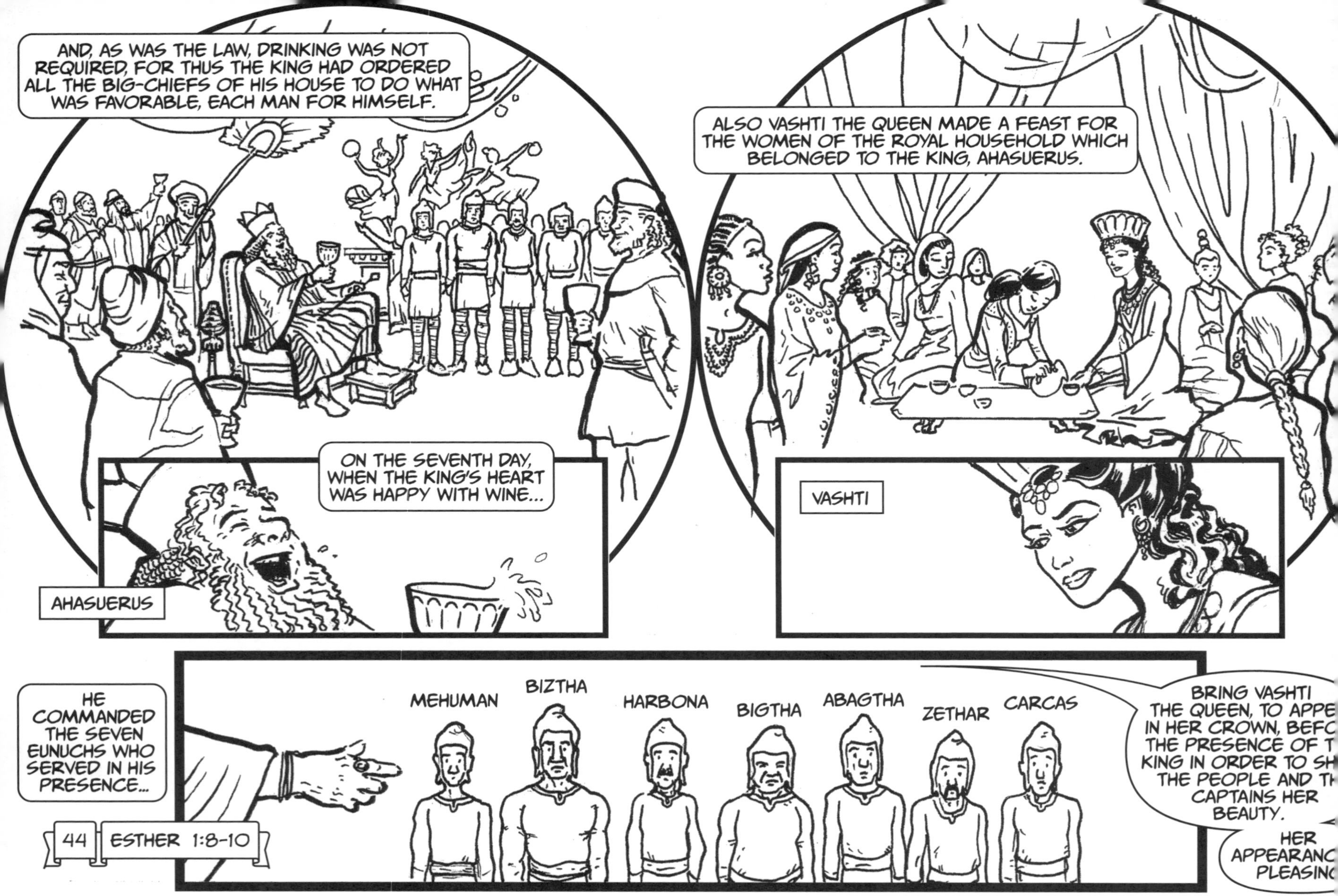

AND, AS WAS THE LAW, DRINKING WAS NOT REQUIRED, FOR THUS THE KING HAD ORDERED ALL THE BIG-CHIEFS OF HIS HOUSE TO DO WHAT WAS FAVORABLE, EACH MAN FOR HIMSELF.
ALSO VASHTI THE QUEEN MADE A FEAST FOR THE WOMEN OF THE ROYAL HOUSEHOLD WHICH BELONGED TO THE KING, AHASUERUS.
ON THE SEVENTH DAY, WHEN THE KING'S HEART WAS HAPPY WITH WINE...
AHASUERUS
VASHTI
HE COMMANDED THE SEVEN EUNUCHS WHO SERVED IN HIS PRESENCE...
MEHUMAN
BIZTHA
HARBONA
BIGTHA
ABAGTHA
ZETHAR
CARCAS
BRING VASHTI THE QUEEN, TO APPE IN HER CROWN, BEFO THE PRESENCE OF T KING IN ORDER TO SH THE PEOPLE AND T CAPTAINS HER BEAUTY.
HER APPEARANC PLEASIN

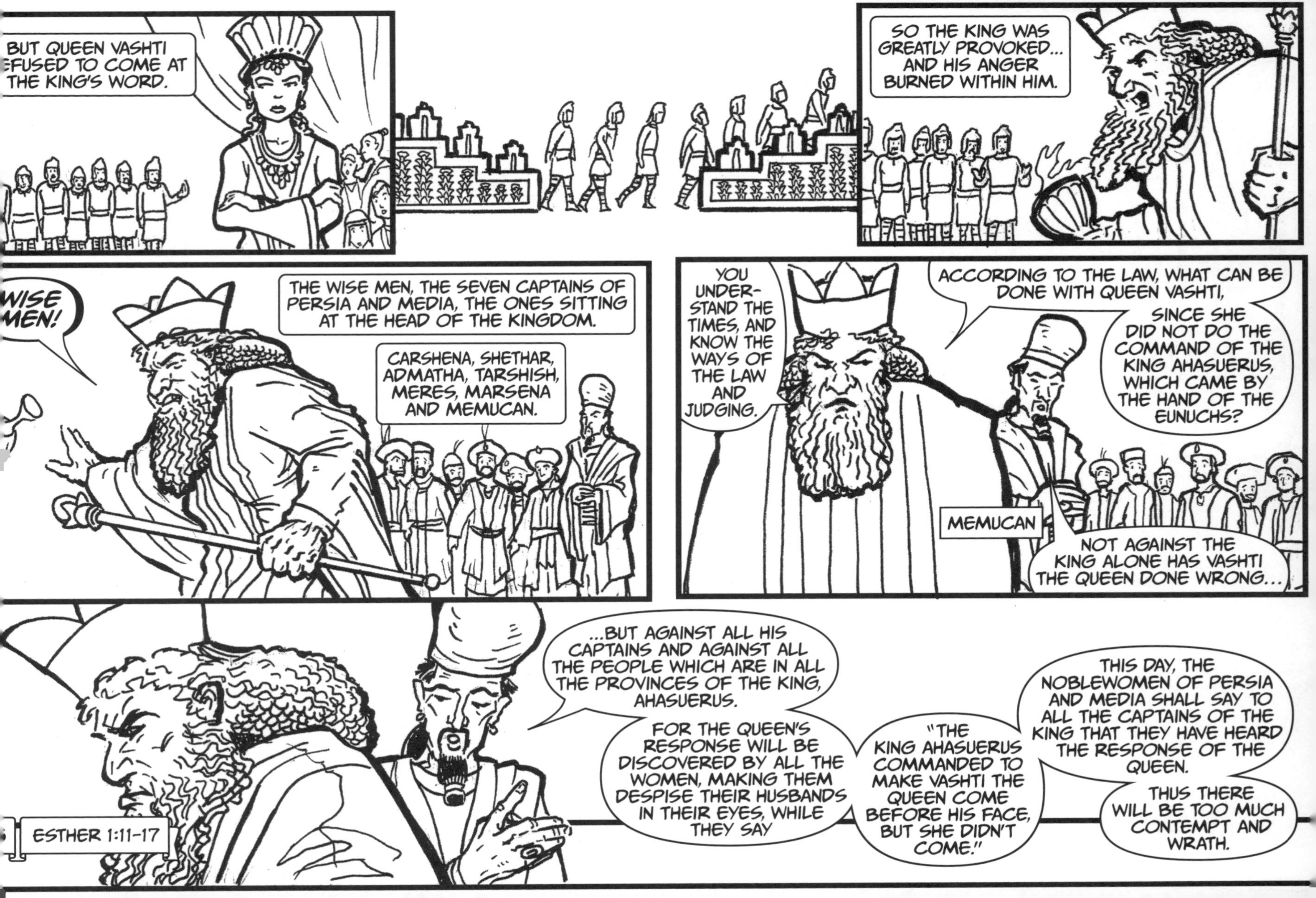

BUT QUEEN VASHTI EFUSED TO COME AT THE KING'S WORD.
SO THE KING WAS GREATLY PROVOKED... AND HIS ANGER BURNED WITHIN HIM.
WISE MEN!
THE WISE MEN, THE SEVEN CAPTAINS OF PERSIA AND MEDIA, THE ONES SITTING AT THE HEAD OF THE KINGDOM.
CARSHENA, SHETHAR, ADMATHA, TARSHISH, MERES, MARSENA AND MEMUCAN.
YOU UNDERSTAND THE TIMES, AND KNOW THE WAYS OF THE LAW AND JUDGING.
ACCORDING TO THE LAW, WHAT CAN BE DONE WITH QUEEN VASHTI,
SINCE SHE DID NOT DO THE COMMAND OF THE KING AHASUERUS, WHICH CAME BY THE HAND OF THE EUNUCHS?
MEMUCAN
NOT AGAINST THE KING ALONE HAS VASHTI THE QUEEN DONE WRONG...
...BUT AGAINST ALL HIS CAPTAINS AND AGAINST ALL THE PEOPLE WHICH ARE IN ALL THE PROVINCES OF THE KING, AHASUERUS.
FOR THE QUEEN'S RESPONSE WILL BE DISCOVERED BY ALL THE WOMEN, MAKING THEM DESPISE THEIR HUSBANDS IN THEIR EYES, WHILE THEY SAY
"THE KING AHASUERUS COMMANDED TO MAKE VASHTI THE QUEEN COME BEFORE HIS FACE, BUT SHE DIDN'T COME."
THIS DAY, THE NOBLEWOMEN OF PERSIA AND MEDIA SHALL SAY TO ALL THE CAPTAINS OF THE KING THAT THEY HAVE HEARD THE RESPONSE OF THE QUEEN.
THUS THERE WILL BE TOO MUCH CONTEMPT AND WRATH.
ESTHER 1:11–17

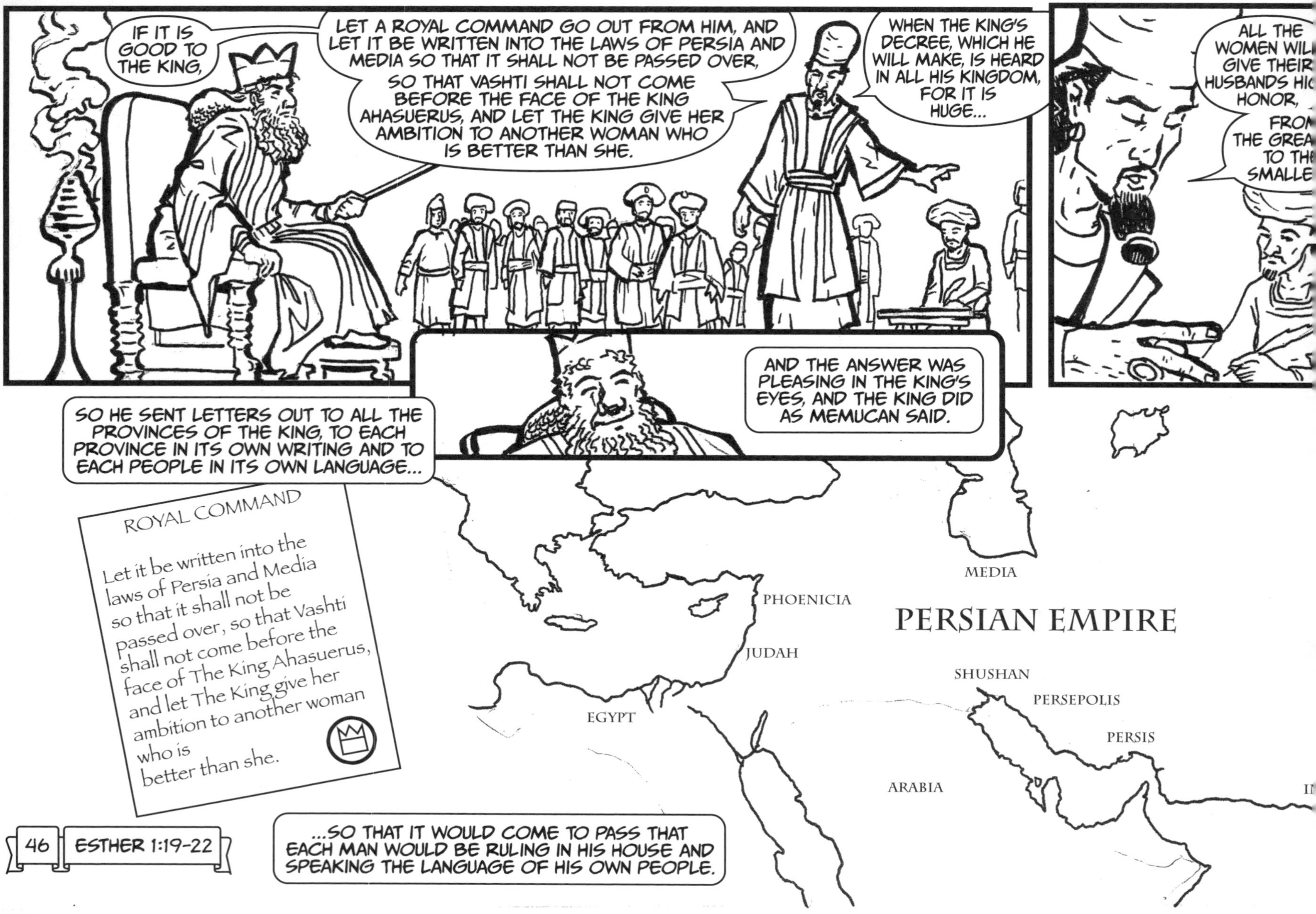

IF IT IS GOOD TO THE KING,
LET A ROYAL COMMAND GO OUT FROM HIM, AND LET IT BE WRITTEN INTO THE LAWS OF PERSIA AND MEDIA SO THAT IT SHALL NOT BE PASSED OVER,
SO THAT VASHTI SHALL NOT COME BEFORE THE FACE OF THE KING AHASUERUS, AND LET THE KING GIVE HER AMBITION TO ANOTHER WOMAN WHO IS BETTER THAN SHE.
WHEN THE KING'S DECREE, WHICH HE WILL MAKE, IS HEARD IN ALL HIS KINGDOM, FOR IT IS HUGE...
ALL THE WOMEN WIL GIVE THEIR HUSBANDS HI HONOR,
FRO THE GREA TO TH SMALLE
AND THE ANSWER WAS PLEASING IN THE KING'S EYES, AND THE KING DID AS MEMUCAN SAID.
SO HE SENT LETTERS OUT TO ALL THE PROVINCES OF THE KING, TO EACH PROVINCE IN ITS OWN WRITING AND TO EACH PEOPLE IN ITS OWN LANGUAGE...
ROYAL COMMAND
Let it be written into the laws of Persia and Media so that it shall not be passed over, so that Vashti shall not come before the face of The King Ahasuerus, and let The King give her ambition to another woman who is better than she.
MEDIA
PHOENICIA
PERSIAN EMPIRE
JUDAH
SHUSHAN
PERSEPOLIS
EGYPT
PERSIS
ARABIA
...SO THAT IT WOULD COME TO PASS THAT EACH MAN WOULD BE RULING IN HIS HOUSE AND SPEAKING THE LANGUAGE OF HIS OWN PEOPLE.

CHAPTER 2

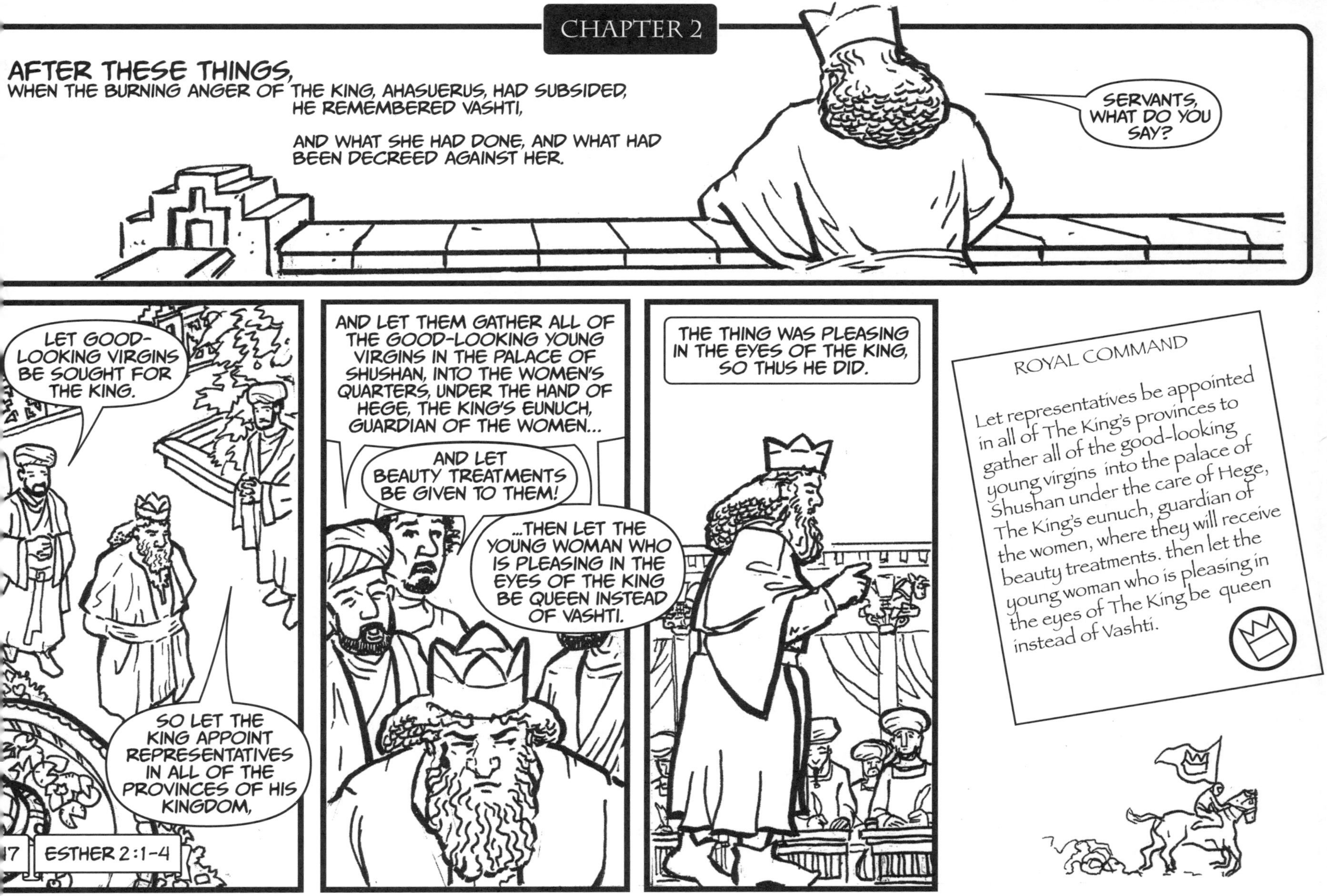
AFTER THESE THINGS,
WHEN THE BURNING ANGER OF THE KING, AHASUERUS, HAD SUBSIDED, HE REMEMBERED VASHTI,
AND WHAT SHE HAD DONE, AND WHAT HAD BEEN DECREED AGAINST HER.
SERVANTS, WHAT DO YOU SAY?
LET GOOD-LOOKING VIRGINS BE SOUGHT FOR THE KING.
SO LET THE KING APPOINT REPRESENTATIVES IN ALL OF THE PROVINCES OF HIS KINGDOM,
AND LET THEM GATHER ALL OF THE GOOD-LOOKING YOUNG VIRGINS IN THE PALACE OF SHUSHAN, INTO THE WOMEN'S QUARTERS, UNDER THE HAND OF HEGE, THE KING'S EUNUCH, GUARDIAN OF THE WOMEN...
AND LET BEAUTY TREATMENTS BE GIVEN TO THEM!
...THEN LET THE YOUNG WOMAN WHO IS PLEASING IN THE EYES OF THE KING BE QUEEN INSTEAD OF VASHTI.
THE THING WAS PLEASING IN THE EYES OF THE KING, SO THUS HE DID.
ROYAL COMMAND
Let representatives be appointed in all of The King's provinces to gather all of the good-looking young virgins into the palace of Shushan under the care of Hege, The King's eunuch, guardian of the women, where they will receive beauty treatments. then let the young woman who is pleasing in the eyes of The King be queen instead of Vashti.
ESTHER 2:1-4

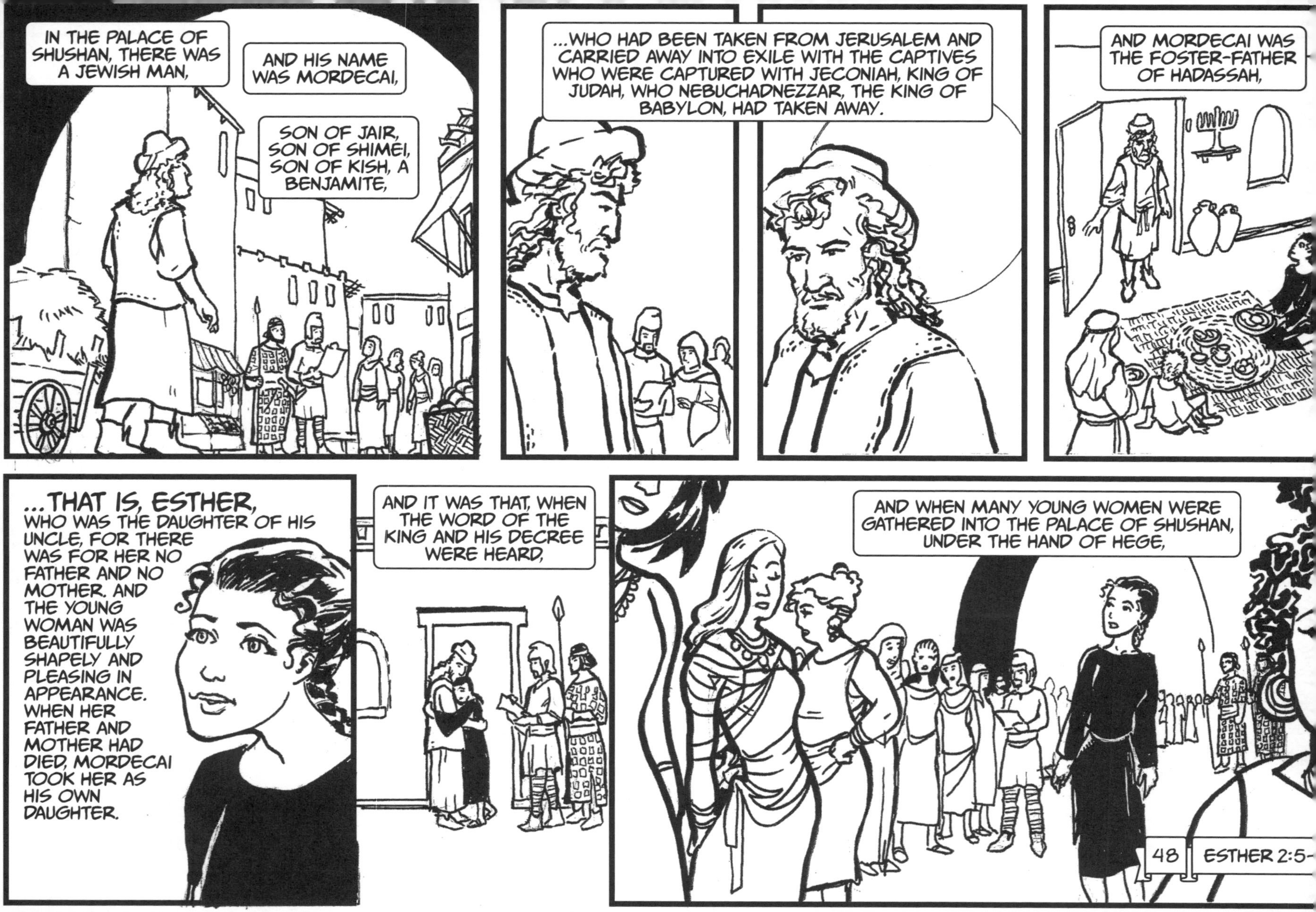
IN THE PALACE OF SHUSHAN, THERE WAS A JEWISH MAN,
AND HIS NAME WAS MORDECAI,
SON OF JAIR, SON OF SHIMEI, SON OF KISH, A BENJAMITE,
...WHO HAD BEEN TAKEN FROM JERUSALEM AND CARRIED AWAY INTO EXILE WITH THE CAPTIVES WHO WERE CAPTURED WITH JECONIAH, KING OF JUDAH, WHO NEBUCHADNEZZAR, THE KING OF BABYLON, HAD TAKEN AWAY.
AND MORDECAI WAS THE FOSTER-FATHER OF HADASSAH,
...THAT IS, ESTHER, WHO WAS THE DAUGHTER OF HIS UNCLE, FOR THERE WAS FOR HER NO FATHER AND NO MOTHER. AND THE YOUNG WOMAN WAS BEAUTIFULLY SHAPELY AND PLEASING IN APPEARANCE. WHEN HER FATHER AND MOTHER HAD DIED, MORDECAI TOOK HER AS HIS OWN DAUGHTER.
AND IT WAS THAT, WHEN THE WORD OF THE KING AND HIS DECREE WERE HEARD,
AND WHEN MANY YOUNG WOMEN WERE GATHERED INTO THE PALACE OF SHUSHAN, UNDER THE HAND OF HEGE,

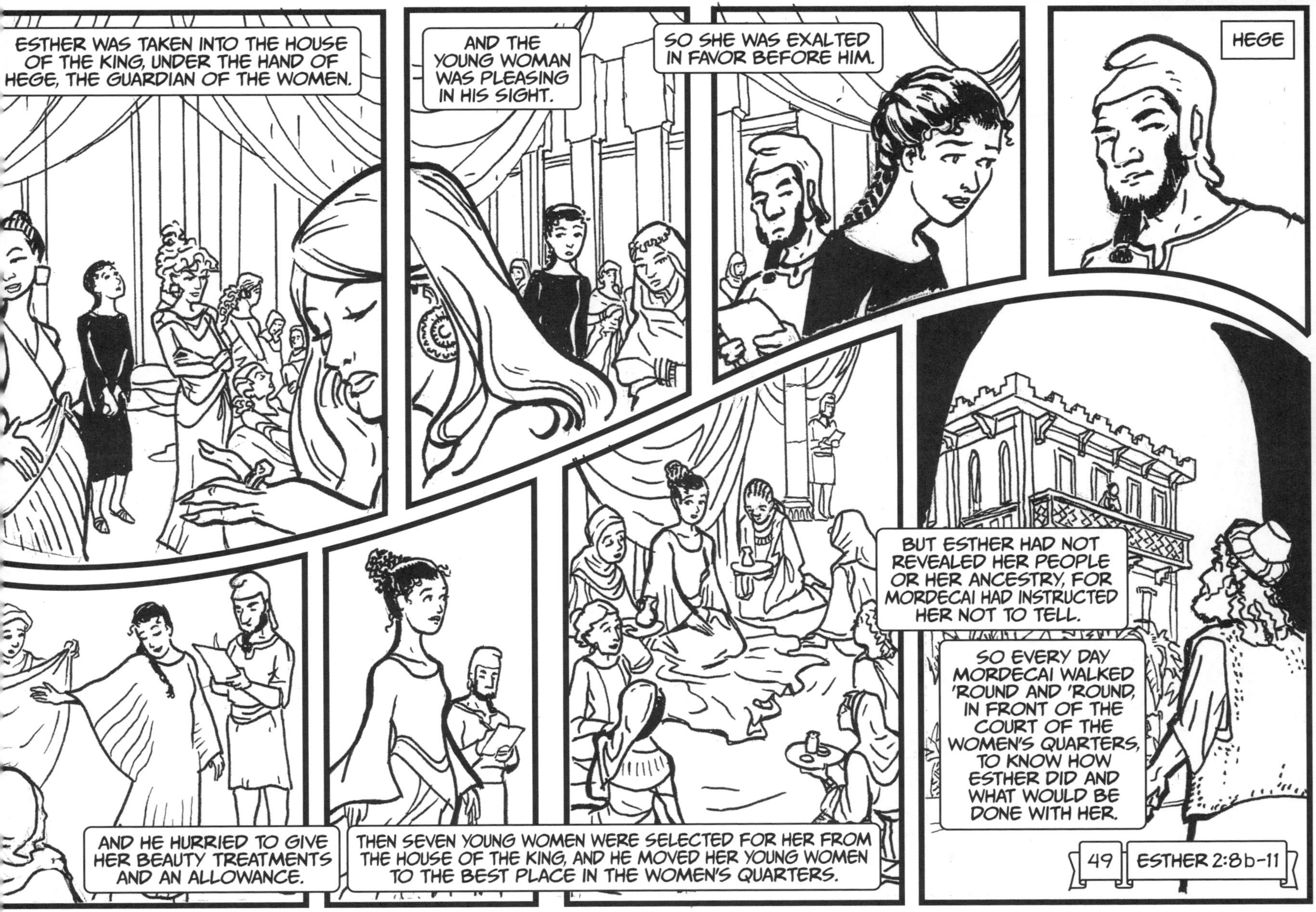
ESTHER WAS TAKEN INTO THE HOUSE OF THE KING, UNDER THE HAND OF HEGE, THE GUARDIAN OF THE WOMEN.
AND THE YOUNG WOMAN WAS PLEASING IN HIS SIGHT.
SO SHE WAS EXALTED IN FAVOR BEFORE HIM.
HEGE
AND HE HURRIED TO GIVE HER BEAUTY TREATMENTS AND AN ALLOWANCE.
THEN SEVEN YOUNG WOMEN WERE SELECTED FOR HER FROM THE HOUSE OF THE KING, AND HE MOVED HER YOUNG WOMEN TO THE BEST PLACE IN THE WOMEN'S QUARTERS.
BUT ESTHER HAD NOT REVEALED HER PEOPLE OR HER ANCESTRY, FOR MORDECAI HAD INSTRUCTED HER NOT TO TELL.
SO EVERY DAY MORDECAI WALKED 'ROUND AND 'ROUND, IN FRONT OF THE COURT OF THE WOMEN'S QUARTERS, TO KNOW HOW ESTHER DID AND WHAT WOULD BE DONE WITH HER.

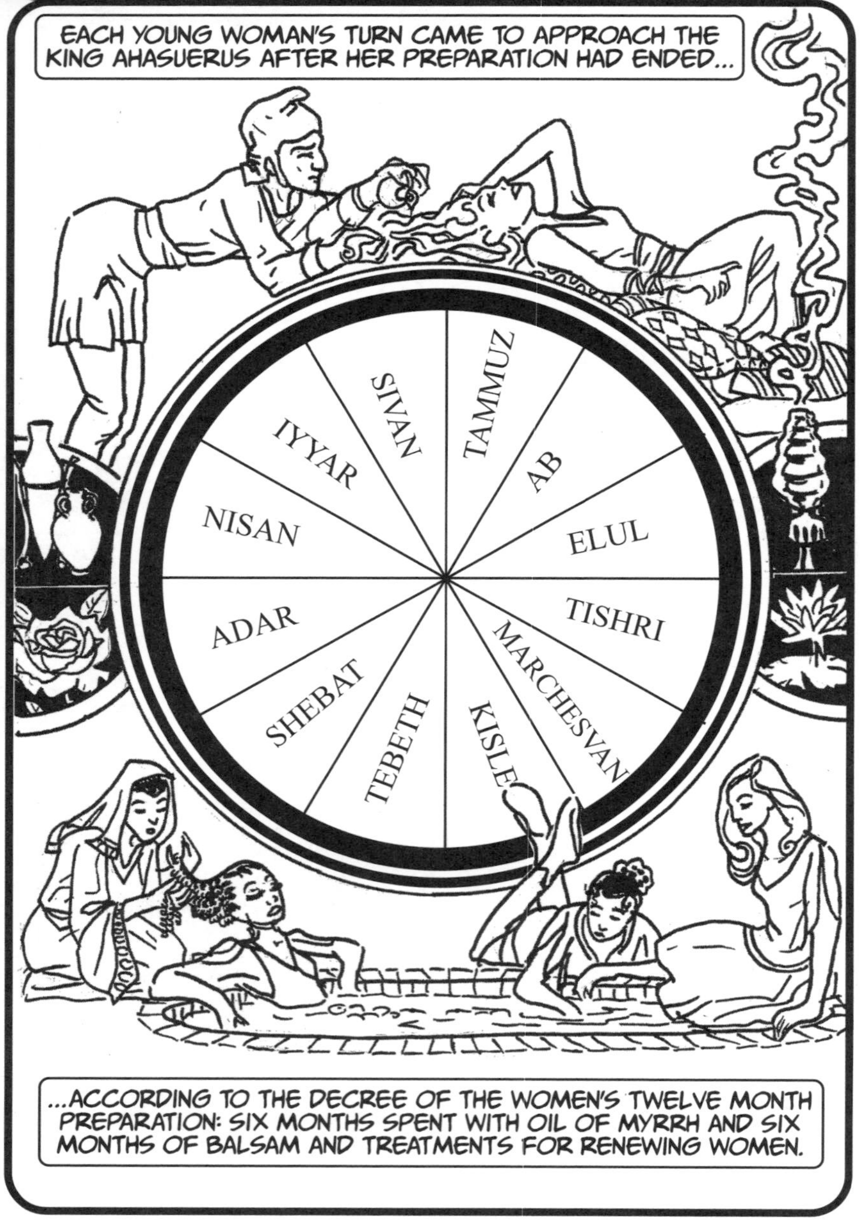
EACH YOUNG WOMAN'S TURN CAME TO APPROACH THE KING AHASUERUS AFTER HER PREPARATION HAD ENDED...
TAMMUZ
SIVAN
IYYAR
AB
NISAN
ELUL
ADAR
TISHRI
SHEBAT
MARCHESVAN
TEBETH
KISLE
...ACCORDING TO THE DECREE OF THE WOMEN'S TWELVE MONTH PREPARATION: SIX MONTHS SPENT WITH OIL OF MYRRH AND SIX MONTHS OF BALSAM AND TREATMENTS FOR RENEWING WOMEN.

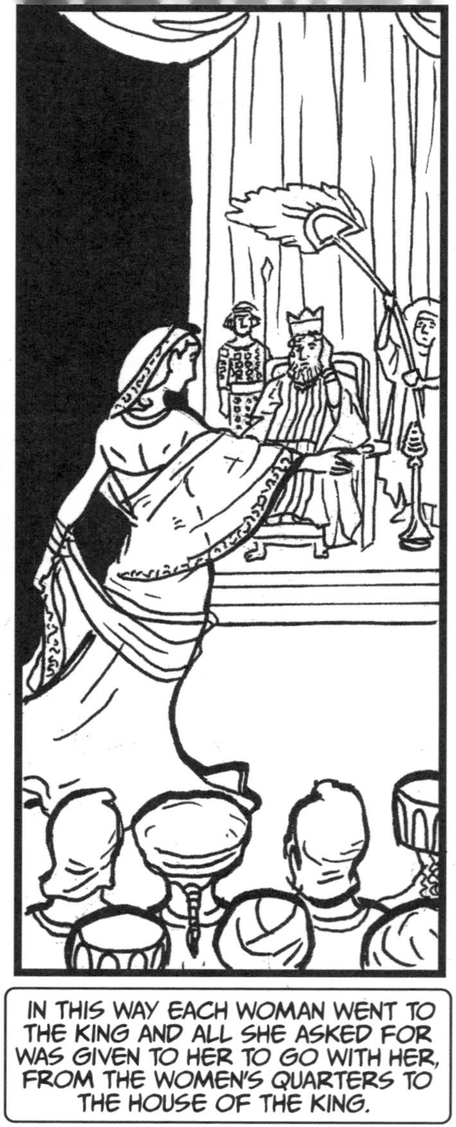
IN THIS WAY EACH WOMAN WENT TO THE KING AND ALL SHE ASKED FOR WAS GIVEN TO HER TO GO WITH HER, FROM THE WOMEN'S QUARTERS TO THE HOUSE OF THE KING.

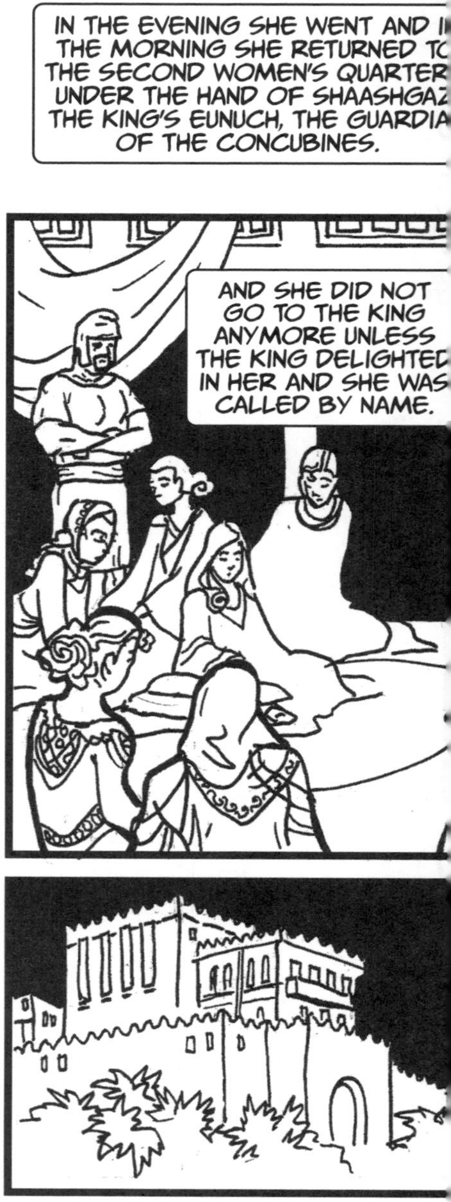
IN THE EVENING SHE WENT AND I
THE MORNING SHE RETURNED TO
THE SECOND WOMEN'S QUARTER
UNDER THE HAND OF SHAASHGAZ
THE KING'S EUNUCH, THE GUARDIA
OF THE CONCUBINES.
AND SHE DID NOT GO TO THE KING ANYMORE UNLESS THE KING DELIGHTED IN HER AND SHE WAS CALLED BY NAME.

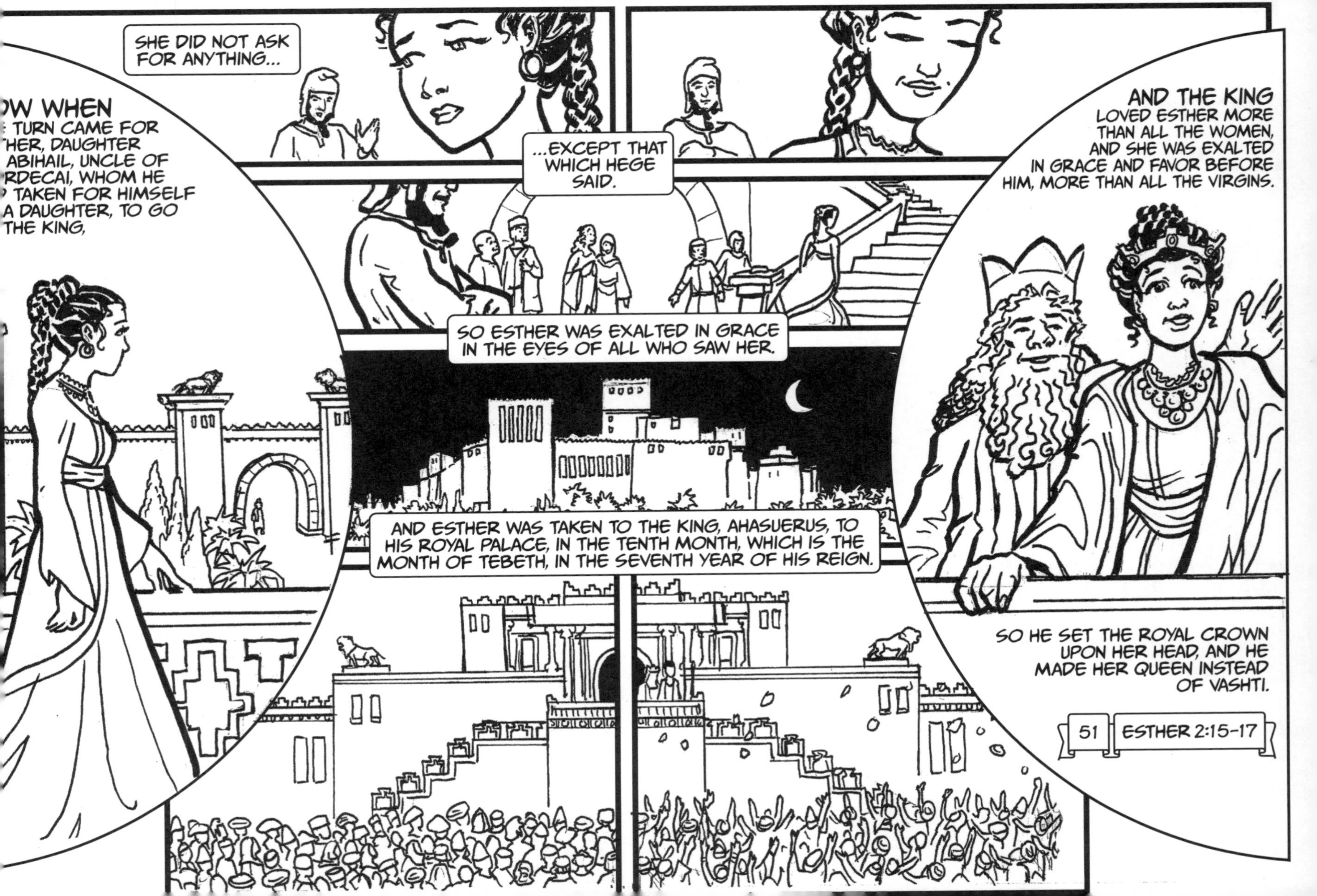

OW WHEN
E TURN CAME FOR
THER, DAUGHTER
ABIHAIL, UNCLE OF
RDECAI, WHOM HE
D TAKEN FOR HIMSELF
A DAUGHTER, TO GO
THE KING,
SHE DID NOT ASK FOR ANYTHING...
...EXCEPT THAT WHICH HEGE SAID.
SO ESTHER WAS EXALTED IN GRACE IN THE EYES OF ALL WHO SAW HER.
AND ESTHER WAS TAKEN TO THE KING, AHASUERUS, TO HIS ROYAL PALACE, IN THE TENTH MONTH, WHICH IS THE MONTH OF TEBETH, IN THE SEVENTH YEAR OF HIS REIGN.
AND THE KING LOVED ESTHER MORE THAN ALL THE WOMEN, AND SHE WAS EXALTED IN GRACE AND FAVOR BEFORE HIM, MORE THAN ALL THE VIRGINS.
SO HE SET THE ROYAL CROWN UPON HER HEAD, AND HE MADE HER QUEEN INSTEAD OF VASHTI.

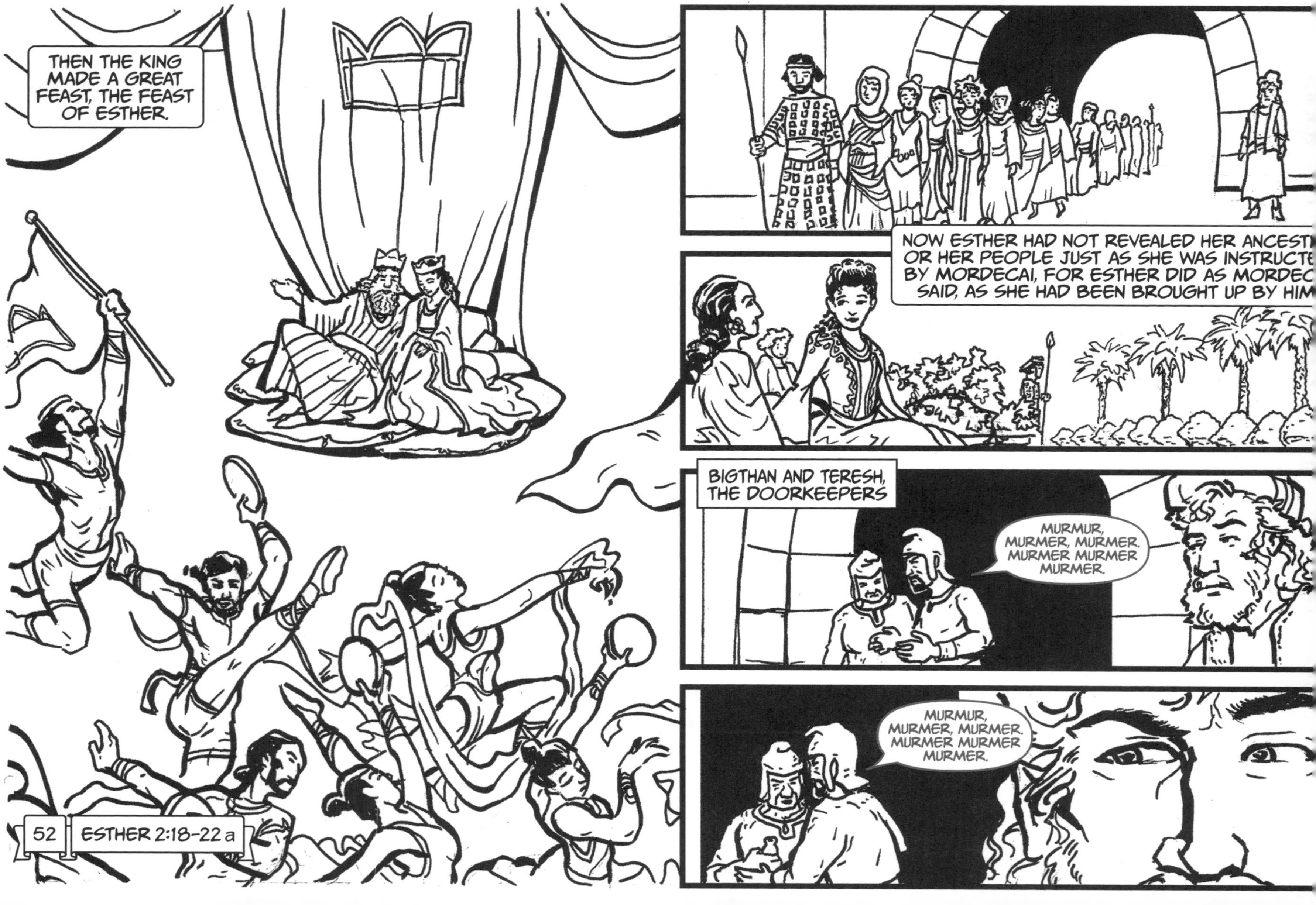
THEN THE KING MADE A GREAT FEAST, THE FEAST OF ESTHER.
NOW ESTHER HAD NOT REVEALED HER ANCEST
OR HER PEOPLE JUST AS SHE WAS INSTRUCTE
BY MORDECAI, FOR ESTHER DID AS MORDEC
SAID, AS SHE HAD BEEN BROUGHT UP BY HIM
BIGTHAN AND TERESH, THE DOORKEEPERS
MURMUR, MURMER, MURMER. MURMER MURMER MURMER.
MURMUR, MURMER, MURMER. MURMER MURMER MURMER.

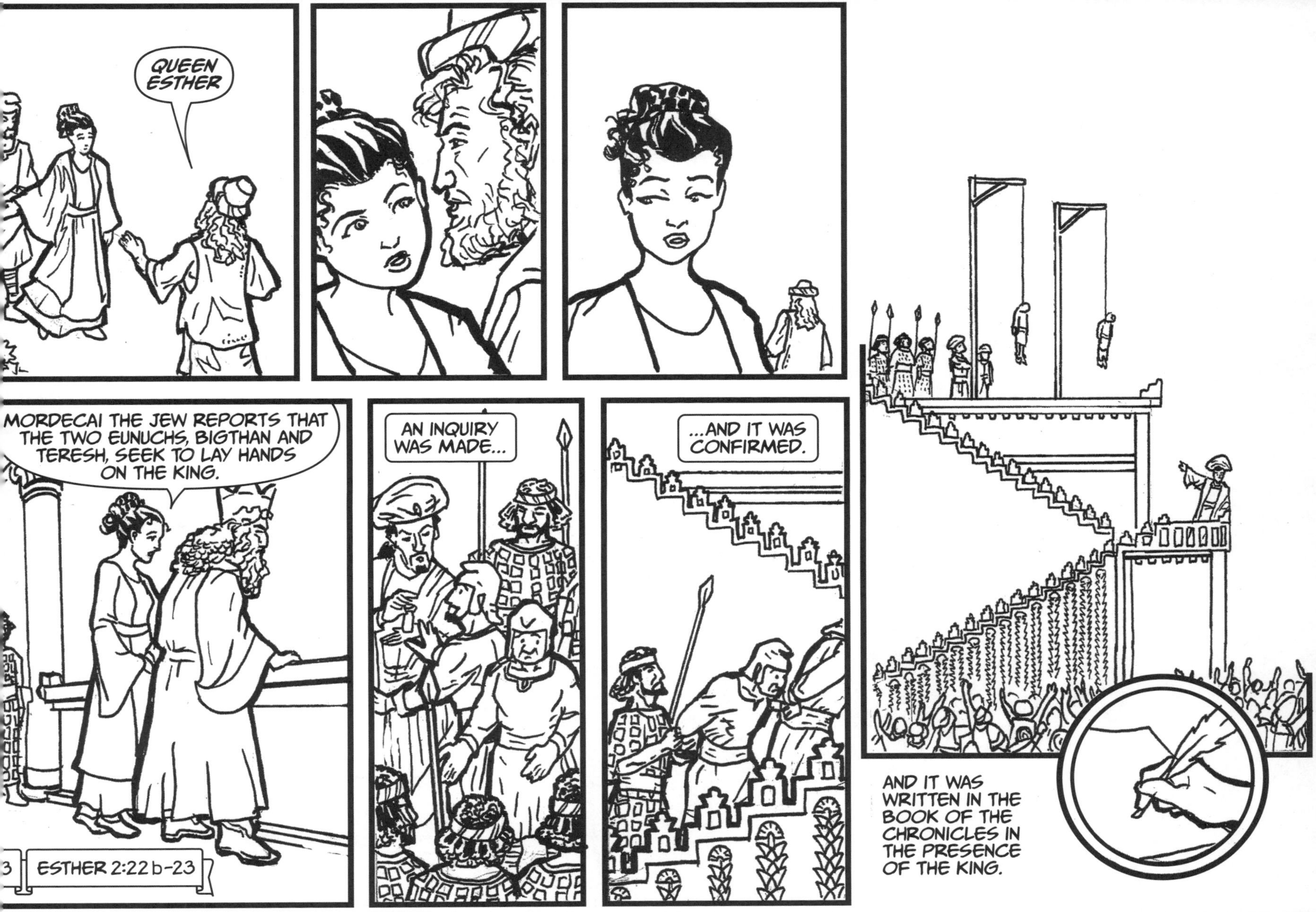
QUEEN ESTHER
MORDECAI THE JEW REPORTS THAT THE TWO EUNUCHS, BIGTHAN AND TERESH, SEEK TO LAY HANDS ON THE KING.
3
ESTHER 2:22b–23
AN INQUIRY WAS MADE...
...AND IT WAS CONFIRMED.
AND IT WAS WRITTEN IN THE BOOK OF THE CHRONICLES IN THE PRESENCE OF THE KING.

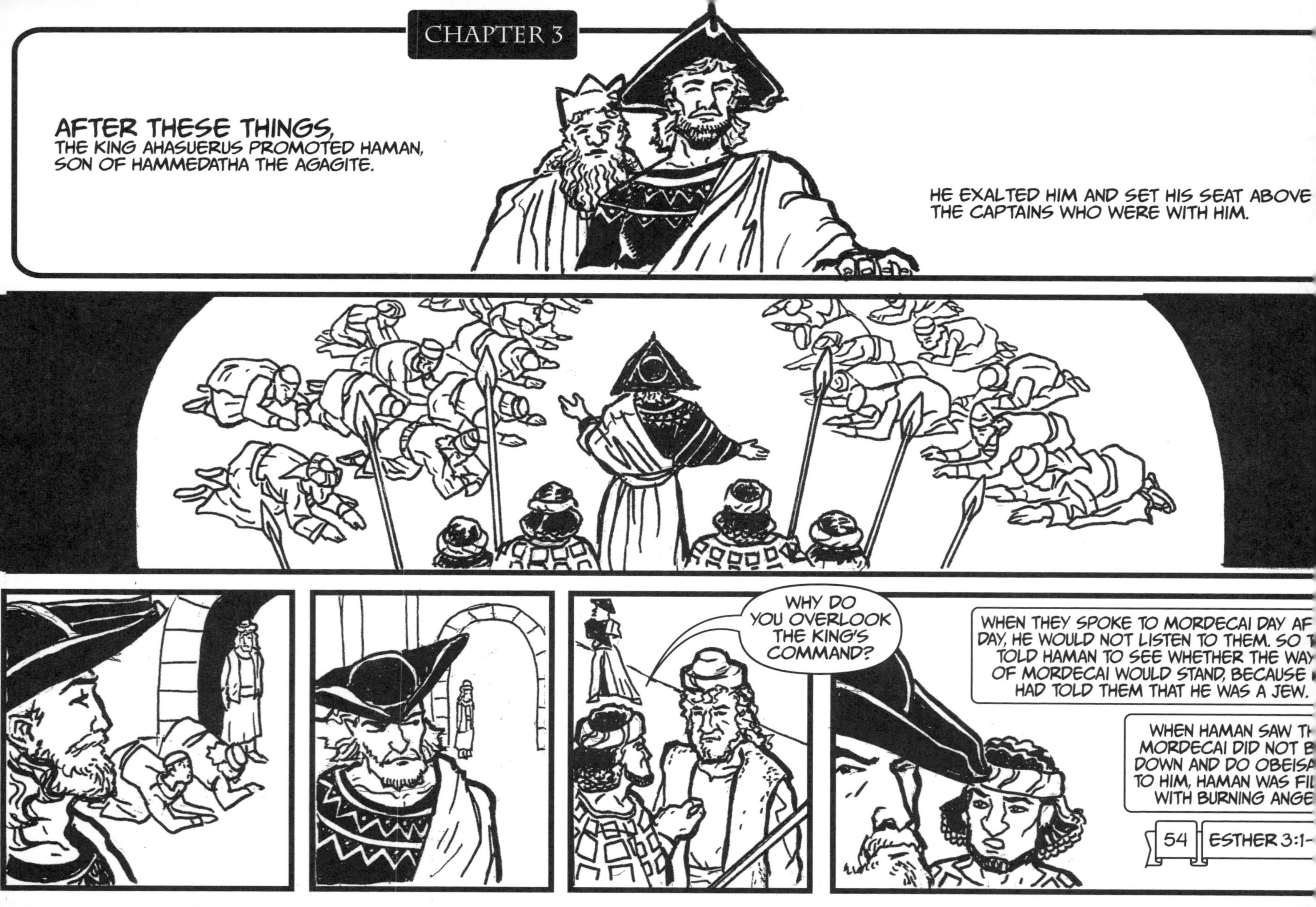
CHAPTER 3
AFTER THESE THINGS,
THE KING AHASUERUS PROMOTED HAMAN, SON OF HAMMEDATHA THE AGAGITE.
HE EXALTED HIM AND SET HIS SEAT ABOVE THE CAPTAINS WHO WERE WITH HIM.
WHY DO YOU OVERLOOK THE KING'S COMMAND?
WHEN THEY SPOKE TO MORDECAI DAY AF
DAY, HE WOULD NOT LISTEN TO THEM. SO T
TOLD HAMAN TO SEE WHETHER THE WAY
OF MORDECAI WOULD STAND, BECAUSE
HAD TOLD THEM THAT HE WAS A JEW.
WHEN HAMAN SAW TH
MORDECAI DID NOT B
DOWN AND DO OBEISA
TO HIM, HAMAN WAS FIL
WITH BURNING ANGE
54
ESTHER 3:1-

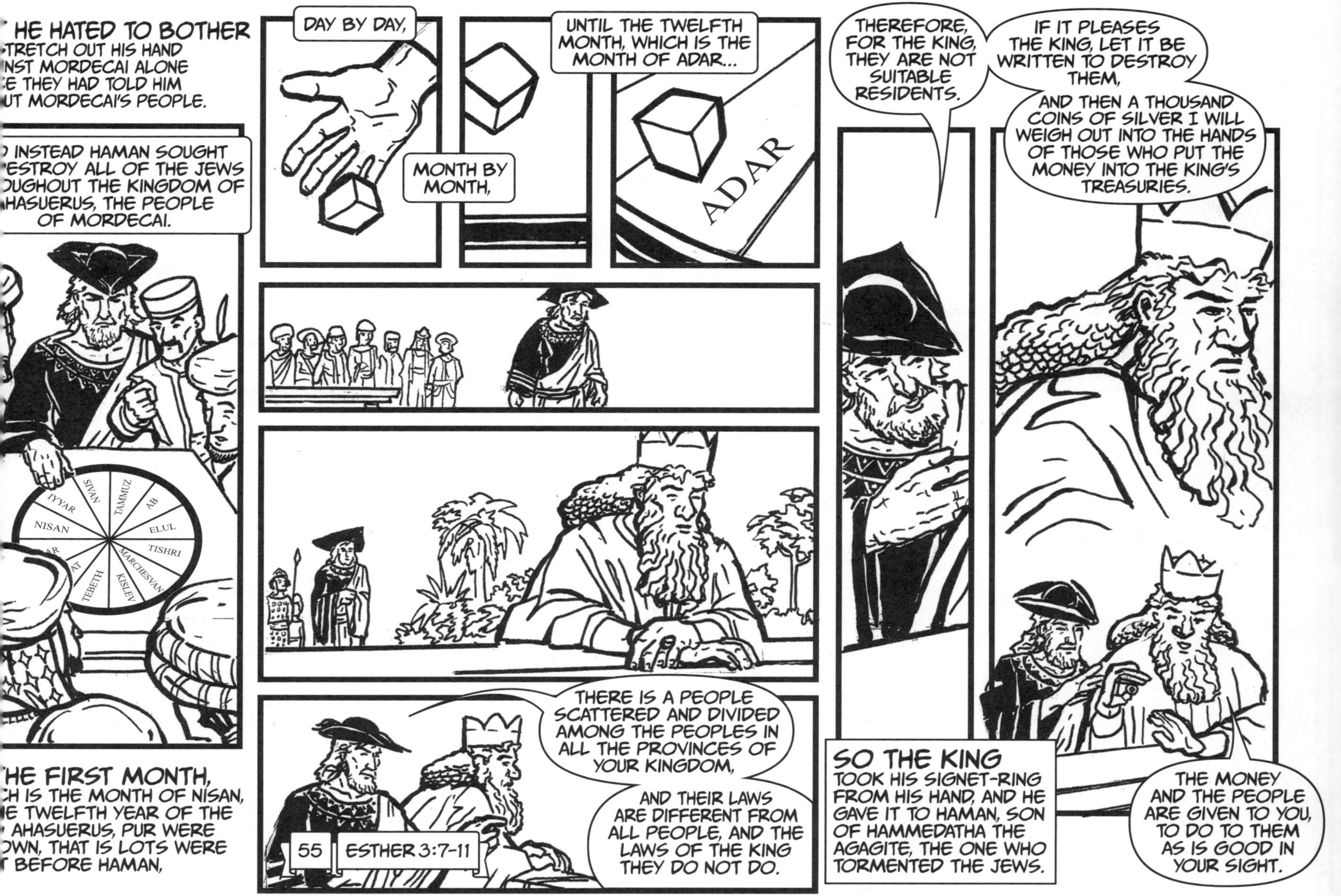

HE HATED TO BOTHER
TRETCH OUT HIS HAND
NST MORDECAI ALONE
E THEY HAD TOLD HIM
UT MORDECAI'S PEOPLE.
INSTEAD HAMAN SOUGHT
ESTROY ALL OF THE JEWS
OUGHOUT THE KINGDOM OF
HASUERUS, THE PEOPLE
OF MORDECAI.
IYYAR
SIVAN
TAMMUZ
AB
NISAN
ELUL
TISHRI
MARCHESVAN
KISLEV
TEBETH
HE FIRST MONTH,
H IS THE MONTH OF NISAN,
E TWELFTH YEAR OF THE
AHASUERUS, PUR WERE
WN, THAT IS LOTS WERE
BEFORE HAMAN,
DAY BY DAY,
MONTH BY MONTH,
UNTIL THE TWELFTH MONTH, WHICH IS THE MONTH OF ADAR...
ADAR
THERE IS A PEOPLE SCATTERED AND DIVIDED AMONG THE PEOPLES IN ALL THE PROVINCES OF YOUR KINGDOM,
AND THEIR LAWS ARE DIFFERENT FROM ALL PEOPLE, AND THE LAWS OF THE KING THEY DO NOT DO.
THEREFORE, FOR THE KING, THEY ARE NOT SUITABLE RESIDENTS.
IF IT PLEASES THE KING, LET IT BE WRITTEN TO DESTROY THEM,
AND THEN A THOUSAND COINS OF SILVER I WILL WEIGH OUT INTO THE HANDS OF THOSE WHO PUT THE MONEY INTO THE KING'S TREASURIES.
SO THE KING TOOK HIS SIGNET-RING FROM HIS HAND, AND HE GAVE IT TO HAMAN, SON OF HAMMEDATHA THE AGAGITE, THE ONE WHO TORMENTED THE JEWS.
THE MONEY AND THE PEOPLE ARE GIVEN TO YOU, TO DO TO THEM AS IS GOOD IN YOUR SIGHT.

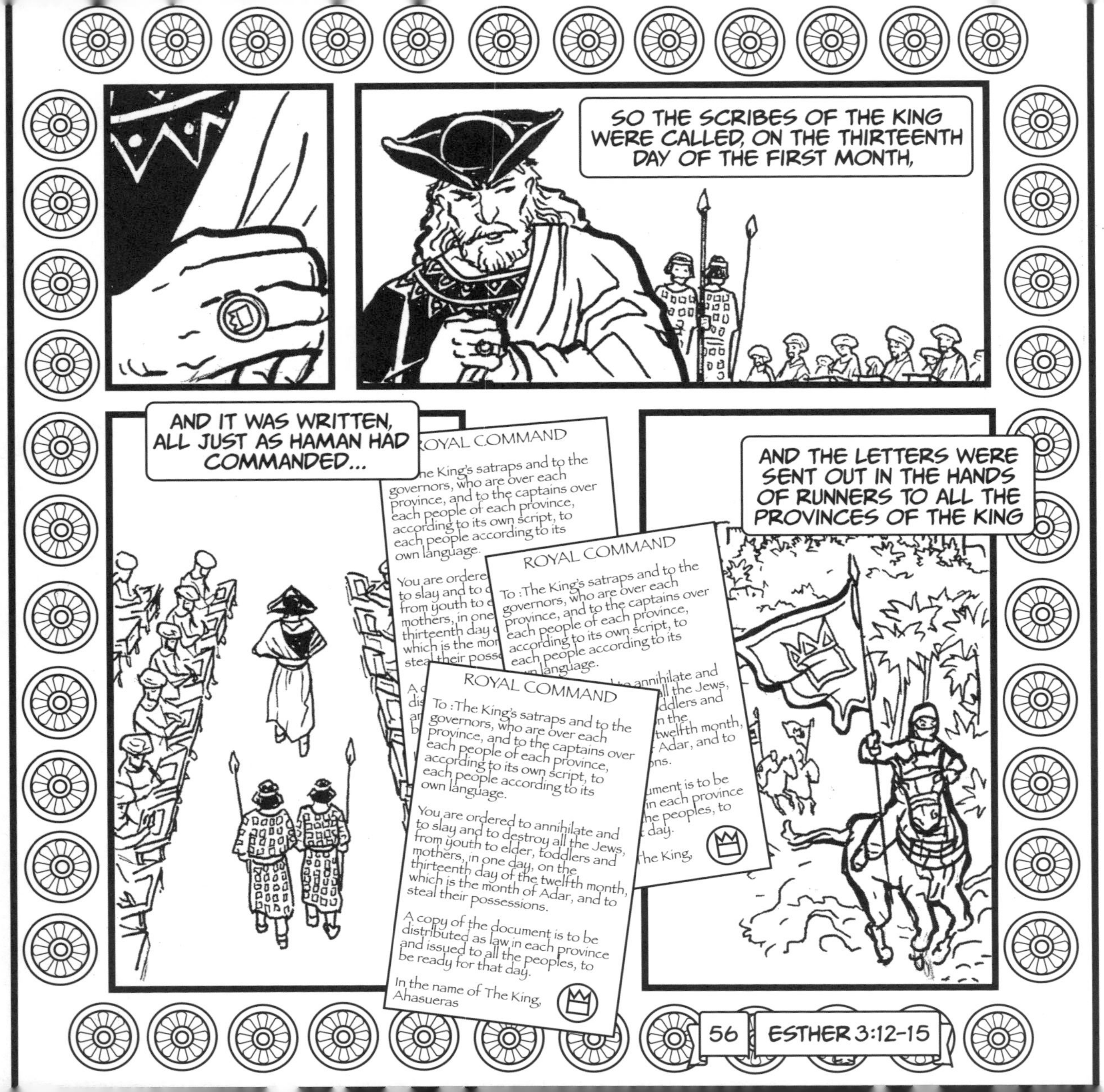

SO THE SCRIBES OF THE KING WERE CALLED, ON THE THIRTEENTH DAY OF THE FIRST MONTH,
AND IT WAS WRITTEN, ALL JUST AS HAMAN HAD COMMANDED...
ROYAL COMMAND
ROYAL COMMAND
To :The King's satraps and to the governors, who are over each province, and to the captains over each people of each province, according to its own script, to each people according to its own language.
ROYAL COMMAND
To :The King's satraps and to the governors, who are over each province, and to the captains over each people of each province, according to its own script, to each people according to its own language.
You are ordered to annihilate and to slay and to destroy all the Jews, from youth to elder, toddlers and mothers, in one day, on the thirteenth day of the twelfth month, which is the month of Adar, and to steal their possessions.
A copy of the document is to be distributed as law in each province and issued to all the peoples, to be ready for that day.
In the name of The King, Ahasueras
AND THE LETTERS WERE SENT OUT IN THE HANDS OF RUNNERS TO ALL THE PROVINCES OF THE KING

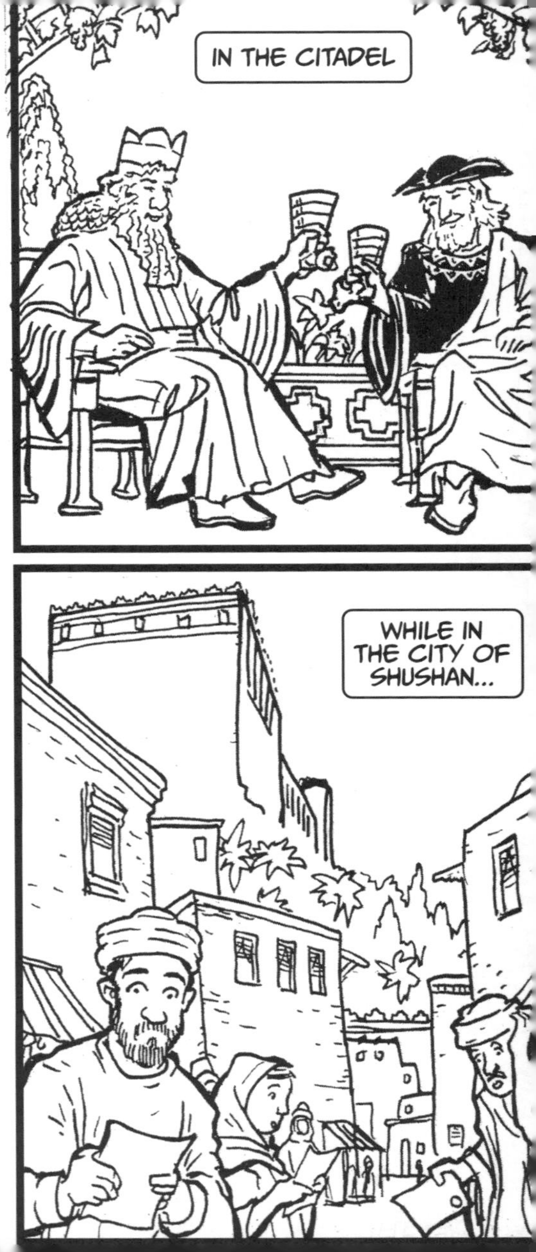

IN THE CITADEL
WHILE IN THE CITY OF SHUSHAN...

CHAPTER 4

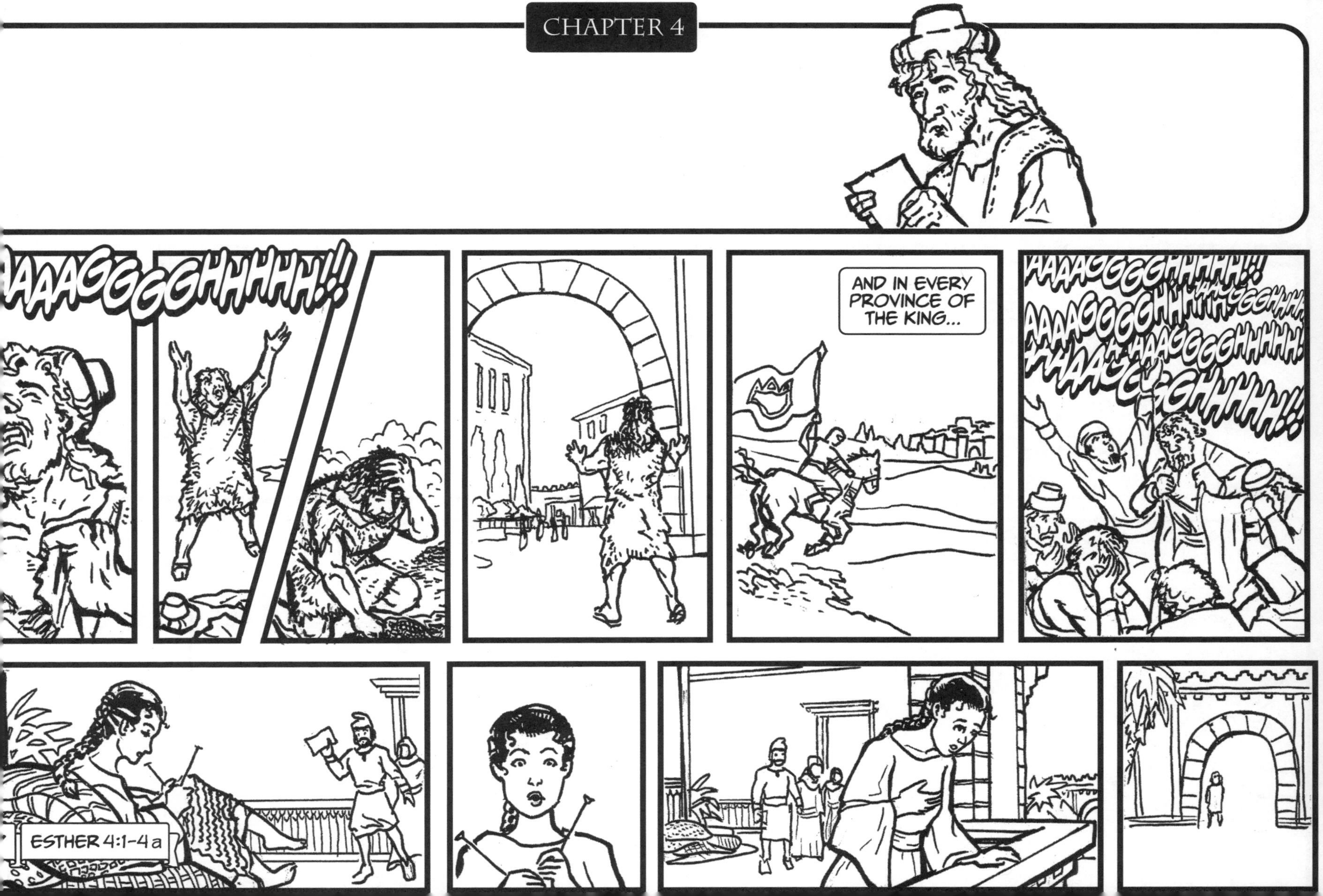

AAAAGGGGHHHHH!!!
AND IN EVERY PROVINCE OF THE KING...
AAAAGGGGHHHHH!!!
AAAAGGGGHHHHH!!!
ESTHER 4:1–4 a

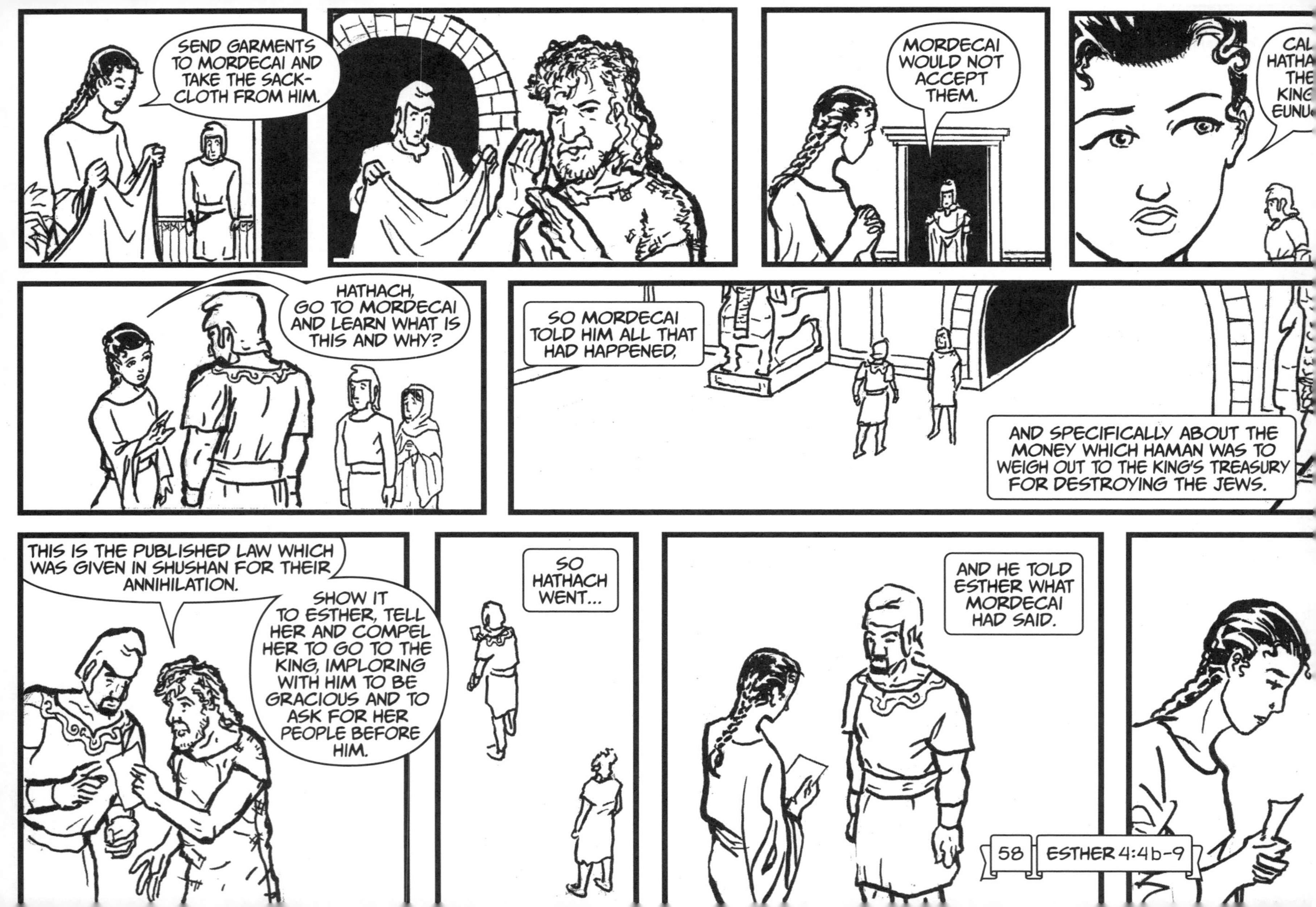

SEND GARMENTS TO MORDECAI AND TAKE THE SACK-CLOTH FROM HIM.
MORDECAI WOULD NOT ACCEPT THEM.
HATHACH, GO TO MORDECAI AND LEARN WHAT IS THIS AND WHY?
SO MORDECAI TOLD HIM ALL THAT HAD HAPPENED,
AND SPECIFICALLY ABOUT THE MONEY WHICH HAMAN WAS TO WEIGH OUT TO THE KING'S TREASURY FOR DESTROYING THE JEWS.
THIS IS THE PUBLISHED LAW WHICH WAS GIVEN IN SHUSHAN FOR THEIR ANNIHILATION.
SHOW IT TO ESTHER, TELL HER AND COMPEL HER TO GO TO THE KING, IMPLORING WITH HIM TO BE GRACIOUS AND TO ASK FOR HER PEOPLE BEFORE HIM.
SO HATHACH WENT...
AND HE TOLD ESTHER WHAT MORDECAI HAD SAID.

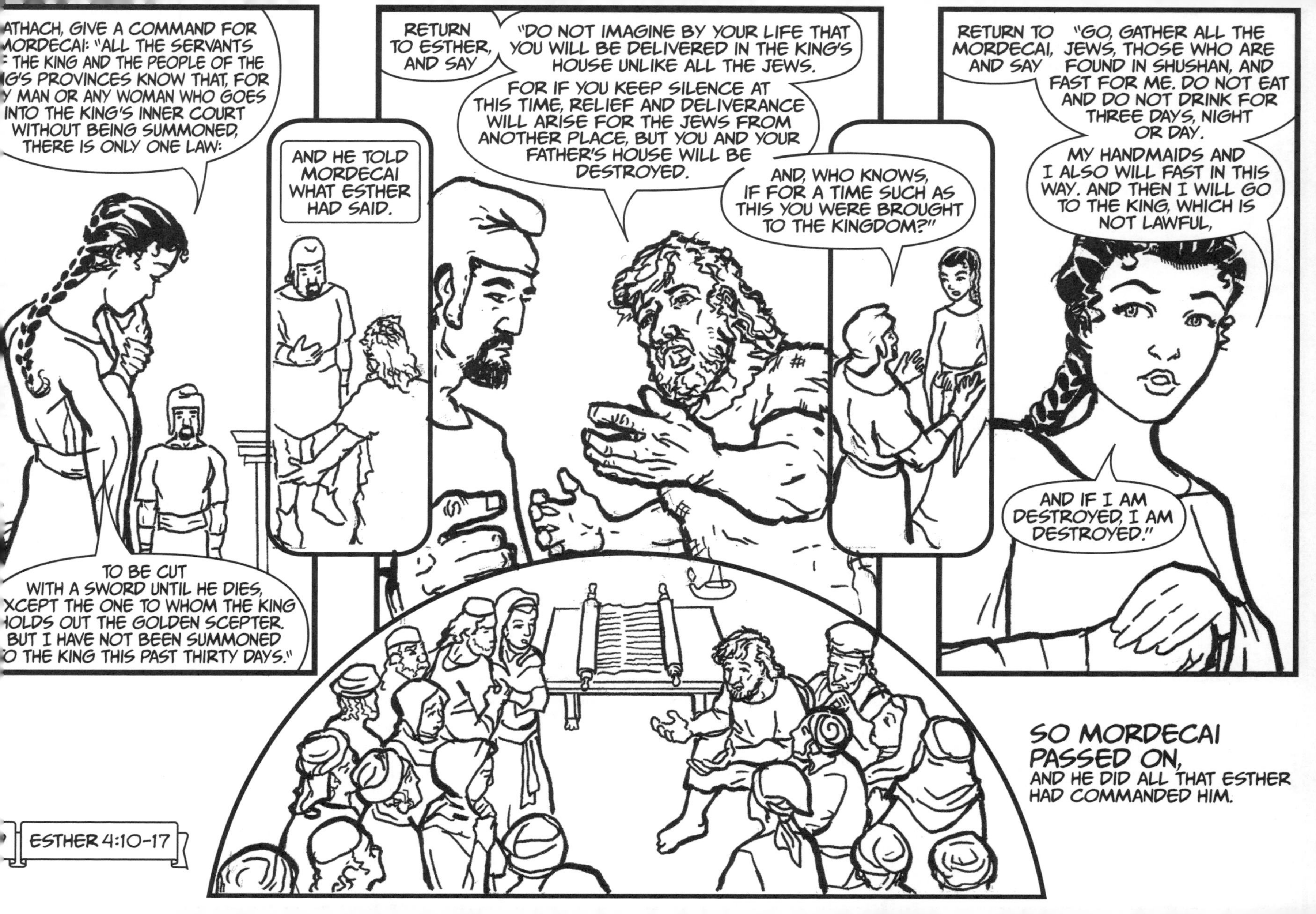

ATHACH, GIVE A COMMAND FOR MORDECAI: "ALL THE SERVANTS OF THE KING AND THE PEOPLE OF THE KING'S PROVINCES KNOW THAT, FOR ANY MAN OR ANY WOMAN WHO GOES INTO THE KING'S INNER COURT WITHOUT BEING SUMMONED, THERE IS ONLY ONE LAW:
TO BE CUT WITH A SWORD UNTIL HE DIES, EXCEPT THE ONE TO WHOM THE KING HOLDS OUT THE GOLDEN SCEPTER. BUT I HAVE NOT BEEN SUMMONED TO THE KING THIS PAST THIRTY DAYS."
AND HE TOLD MORDECAI WHAT ESTHER HAD SAID.
RETURN TO ESTHER, AND SAY
"DO NOT IMAGINE BY YOUR LIFE THAT YOU WILL BE DELIVERED IN THE KING'S HOUSE UNLIKE ALL THE JEWS.
FOR IF YOU KEEP SILENCE AT THIS TIME, RELIEF AND DELIVERANCE WILL ARISE FOR THE JEWS FROM ANOTHER PLACE, BUT YOU AND YOUR FATHER'S HOUSE WILL BE DESTROYED.
AND, WHO KNOWS, IF FOR A TIME SUCH AS THIS YOU WERE BROUGHT TO THE KINGDOM?"
RETURN TO MORDECAI, AND SAY
"GO, GATHER ALL THE JEWS, THOSE WHO ARE FOUND IN SHUSHAN, AND FAST FOR ME. DO NOT EAT AND DO NOT DRINK FOR THREE DAYS, NIGHT OR DAY.
MY HANDMAIDS AND I ALSO WILL FAST IN THIS WAY. AND THEN I WILL GO TO THE KING, WHICH IS NOT LAWFUL,
AND IF I AM DESTROYED, I AM DESTROYED."
SO MORDECAI PASSED ON,
AND HE DID ALL THAT ESTHER HAD COMMANDED HIM.
ESTHER 4:10-17

CHAPTER 5

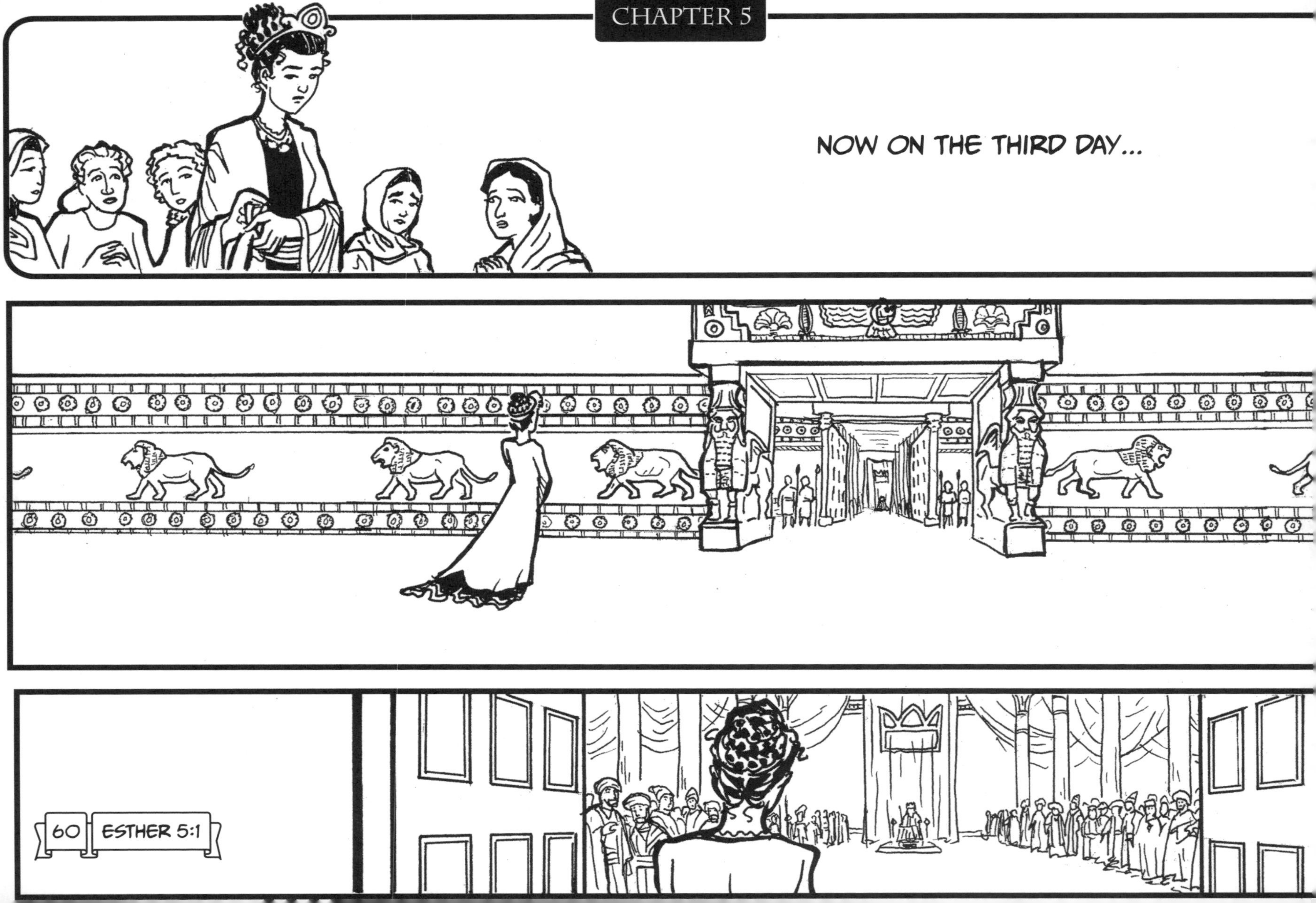
NOW ON THE THIRD DAY...

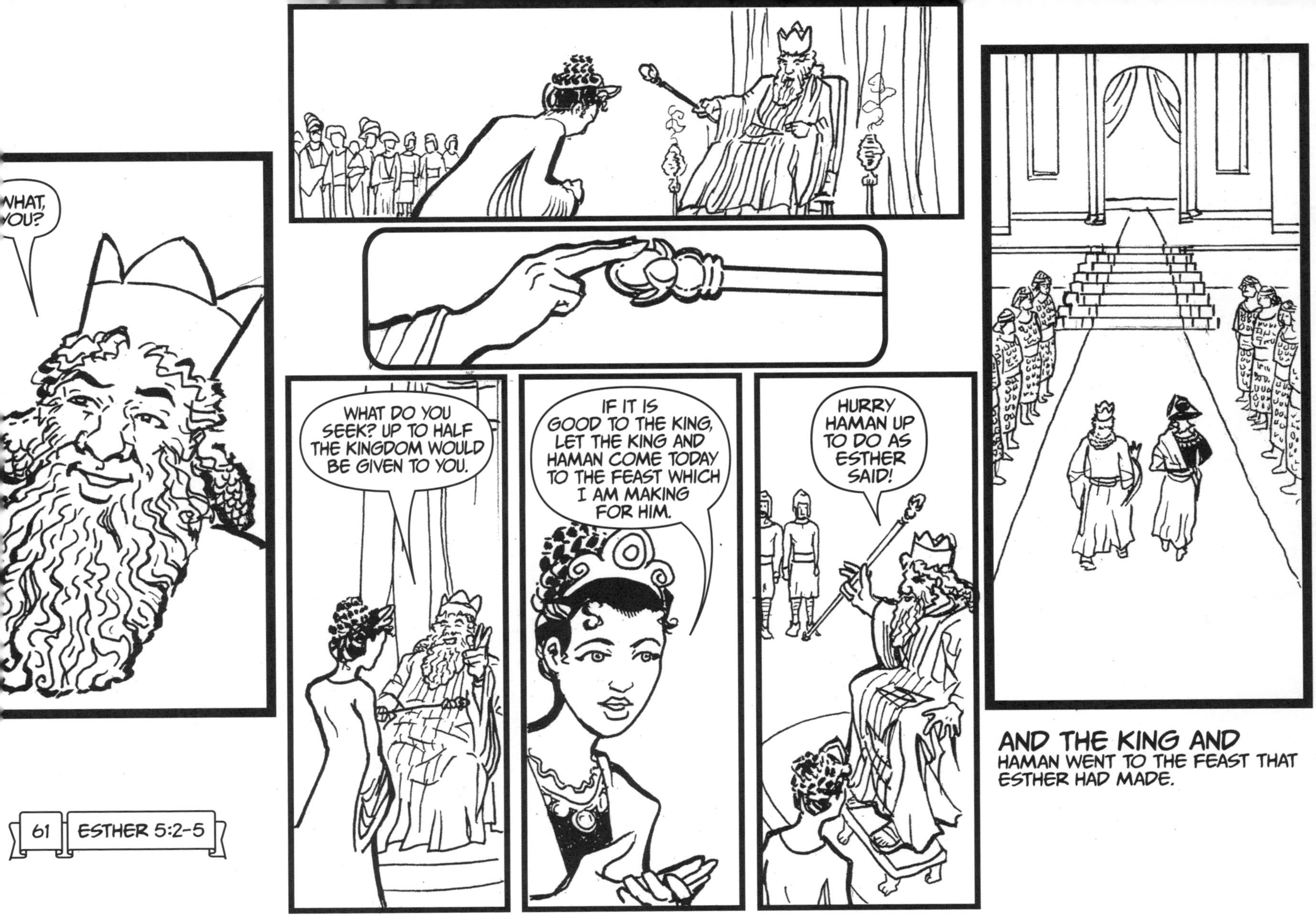
WHAT, YOU?
WHAT DO YOU SEEK? UP TO HALF THE KINGDOM WOULD BE GIVEN TO YOU.
IF IT IS GOOD TO THE KING, LET THE KING AND HAMAN COME TODAY TO THE FEAST WHICH I AM MAKING FOR HIM.
HURRY HAMAN UP TO DO AS ESTHER SAID!
AND THE KING AND HAMAN WENT TO THE FEAST THAT ESTHER HAD MADE.

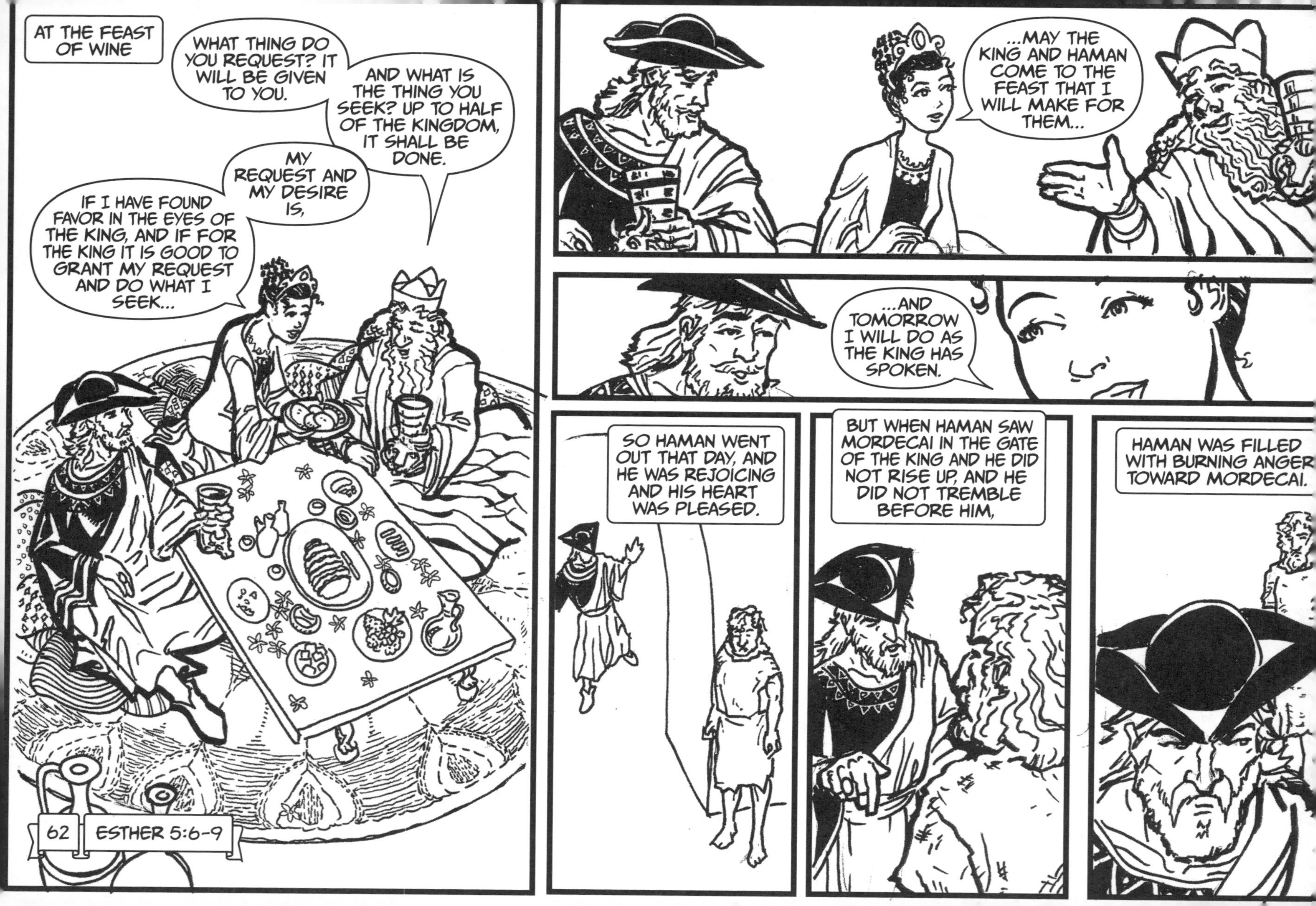
AT THE FEAST OF WINE
WHAT THING DO YOU REQUEST? IT WILL BE GIVEN TO YOU.
AND WHAT IS THE THING YOU SEEK? UP TO HALF OF THE KINGDOM, IT SHALL BE DONE.
MY REQUEST AND MY DESIRE IS,
IF I HAVE FOUND FAVOR IN THE EYES OF THE KING, AND IF FOR THE KING IT IS GOOD TO GRANT MY REQUEST AND DO WHAT I SEEK...
...MAY THE KING AND HAMAN COME TO THE FEAST THAT I WILL MAKE FOR THEM...
...AND TOMORROW I WILL DO AS THE KING HAS SPOKEN.
SO HAMAN WENT OUT THAT DAY, AND HE WAS REJOICING AND HIS HEART WAS PLEASED.
BUT WHEN HAMAN SAW MORDECAI IN THE GATE OF THE KING AND HE DID NOT RISE UP, AND HE DID NOT TREMBLE BEFORE HIM,
HAMAN WAS FILLED WITH BURNING ANGER TOWARD MORDECAI.

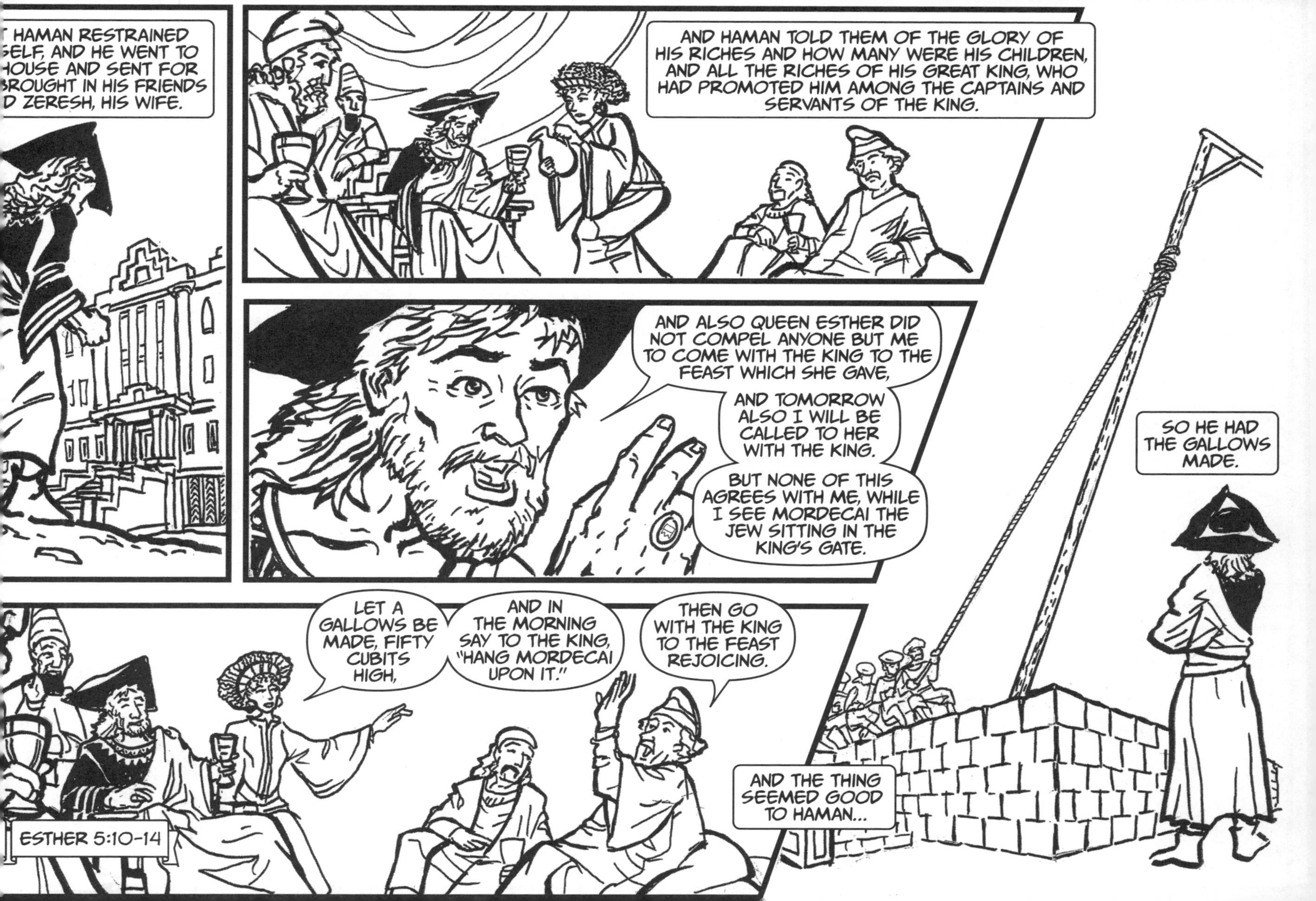

T HAMAN RESTRAINED
SELF, AND HE WENT TO
HOUSE AND SENT FOR
BROUGHT IN HIS FRIENDS
D ZERESH, HIS WIFE.
AND HAMAN TOLD THEM OF THE GLORY OF HIS RICHES AND HOW MANY WERE HIS CHILDREN, AND ALL THE RICHES OF HIS GREAT KING, WHO HAD PROMOTED HIM AMONG THE CAPTAINS AND SERVANTS OF THE KING.
AND ALSO QUEEN ESTHER DID NOT COMPEL ANYONE BUT ME TO COME WITH THE KING TO THE FEAST WHICH SHE GAVE,
AND TOMORROW ALSO I WILL BE CALLED TO HER WITH THE KING.
BUT NONE OF THIS AGREES WITH ME, WHILE I SEE MORDECAI THE JEW SITTING IN THE KING'S GATE.
LET A GALLOWS BE MADE, FIFTY CUBITS HIGH,
AND IN THE MORNING SAY TO THE KING, "HANG MORDECAI UPON IT."
THEN GO WITH THE KING TO THE FEAST REJOICING.
AND THE THING SEEMED GOOD TO HAMAN...
SO HE HAD THE GALLOWS MADE.
ESTHER 5:10-14

CHAPTER 6

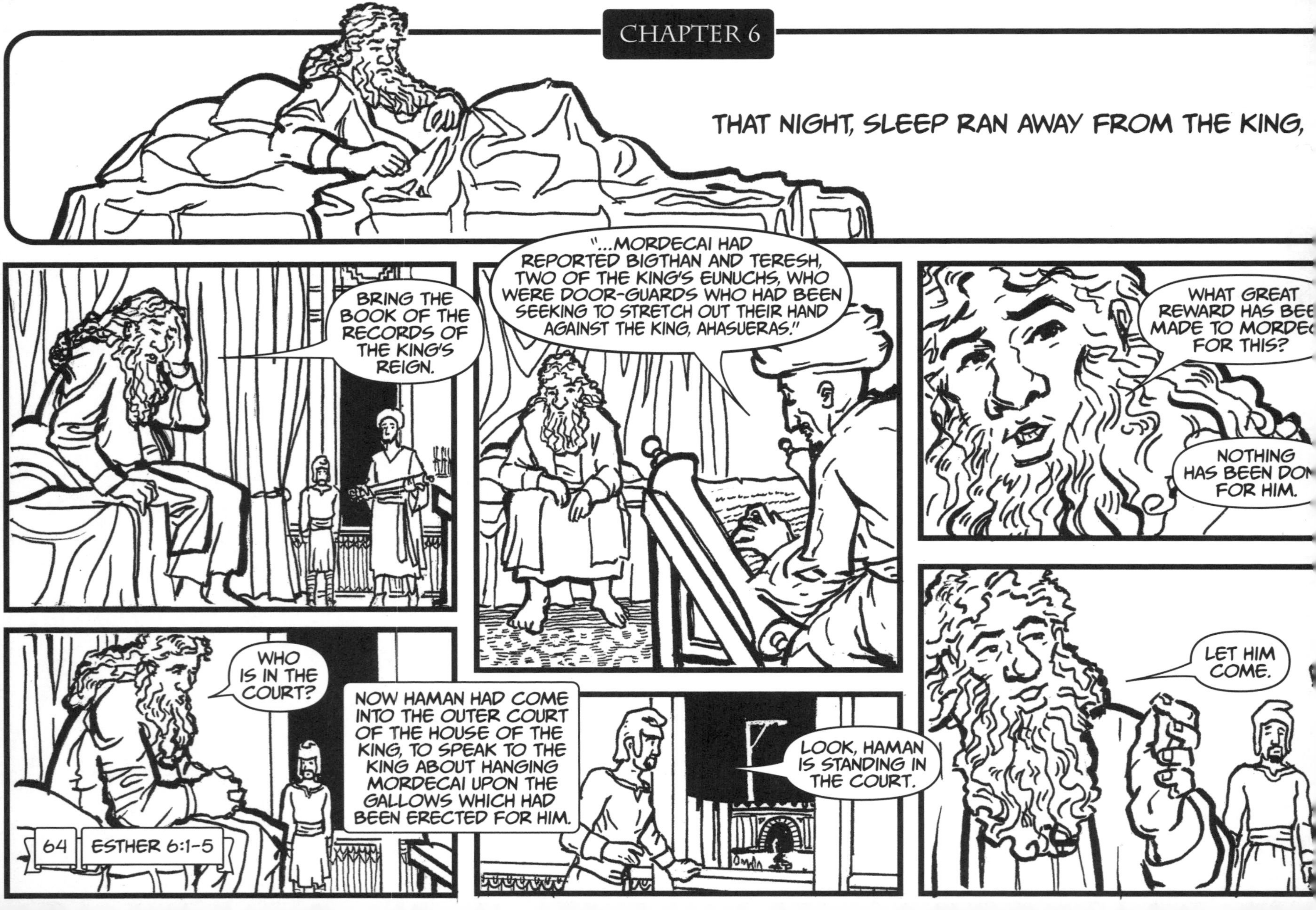
THAT NIGHT, SLEEP RAN AWAY FROM THE KING,
BRING THE BOOK OF THE RECORDS OF THE KING'S REIGN.
"...MORDECAI HAD REPORTED BIGTHAN AND TERESH, TWO OF THE KING'S EUNUCHS, WHO WERE DOOR-GUARDS WHO HAD BEEN SEEKING TO STRETCH OUT THEIR HAND AGAINST THE KING, AHASUERAS."
WHAT GREAT REWARD HAS BEE MADE TO MORDEC FOR THIS?
NOTHING HAS BEEN DON FOR HIM.
WHO IS IN THE COURT?
NOW HAMAN HAD COME INTO THE OUTER COURT OF THE HOUSE OF THE KING, TO SPEAK TO THE KING ABOUT HANGING MORDECAI UPON THE GALLOWS WHICH HAD BEEN ERECTED FOR HIM.
LOOK, HAMAN IS STANDING IN THE COURT.
LET HIM COME.

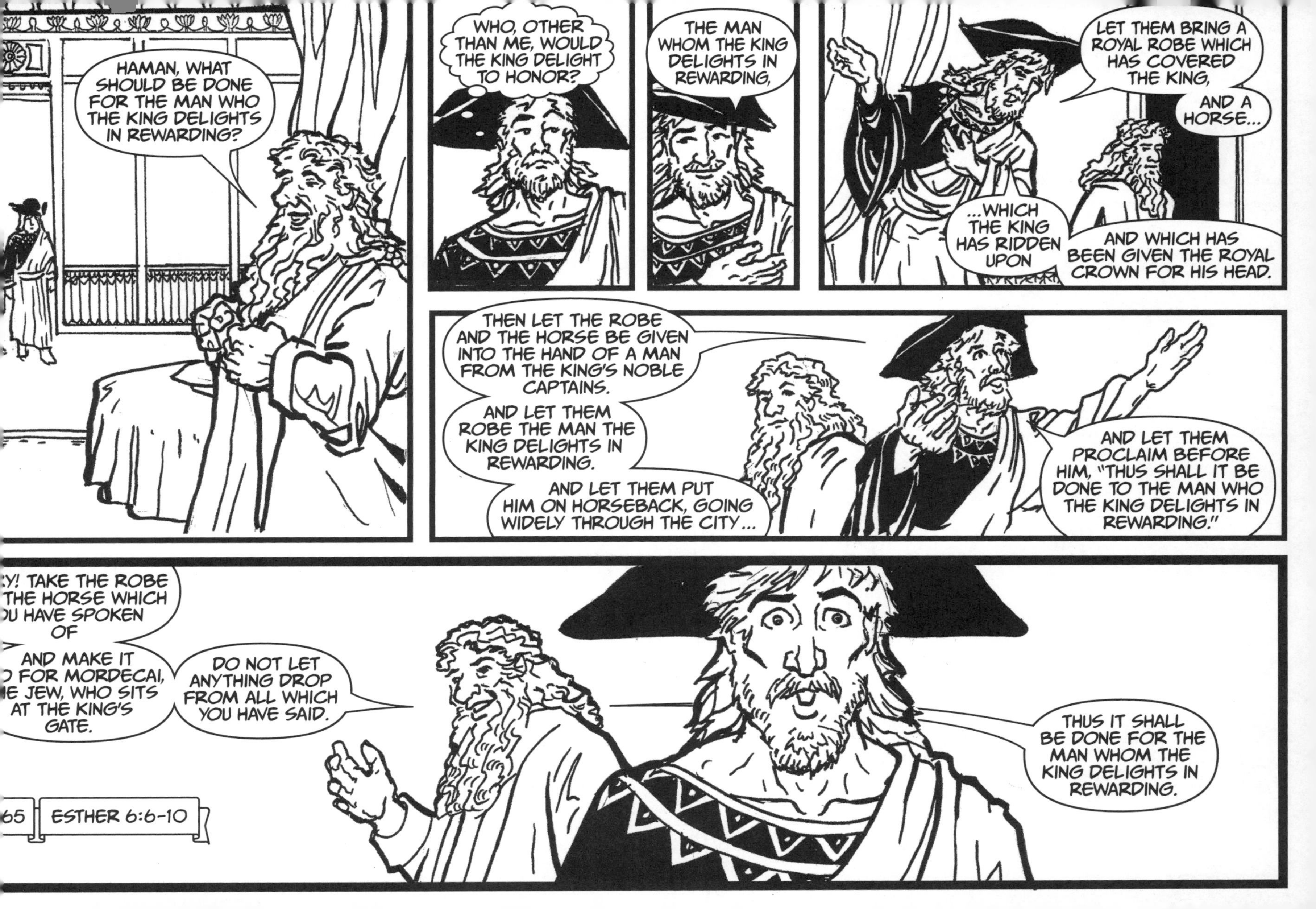
HAMAN, WHAT SHOULD BE DONE FOR THE MAN WHO THE KING DELIGHTS IN REWARDING?
WHO, OTHER THAN ME, WOULD THE KING DELIGHT TO HONOR?
THE MAN WHOM THE KING DELIGHTS IN REWARDING,
LET THEM BRING A ROYAL ROBE WHICH HAS COVERED THE KING,
AND A HORSE...
...WHICH THE KING HAS RIDDEN UPON
AND WHICH HAS BEEN GIVEN THE ROYAL CROWN FOR HIS HEAD.
THEN LET THE ROBE AND THE HORSE BE GIVEN INTO THE HAND OF A MAN FROM THE KING'S NOBLE CAPTAINS.
AND LET THEM ROBE THE MAN THE KING DELIGHTS IN REWARDING.
AND LET THEM PUT HIM ON HORSEBACK, GOING WIDELY THROUGH THE CITY...
AND LET THEM PROCLAIM BEFORE HIM, "THUS SHALL IT BE DONE TO THE MAN WHO THE KING DELIGHTS IN REWARDING."
TAKE THE ROBE THE HORSE WHICH HAVE SPOKEN OF
AND MAKE IT FOR MORDECAI, JEW, WHO SITS AT THE KING'S GATE.
DO NOT LET ANYTHING DROP FROM ALL WHICH YOU HAVE SAID.
THUS IT SHALL BE DONE FOR THE MAN WHOM THE KING DELIGHTS IN REWARDING.

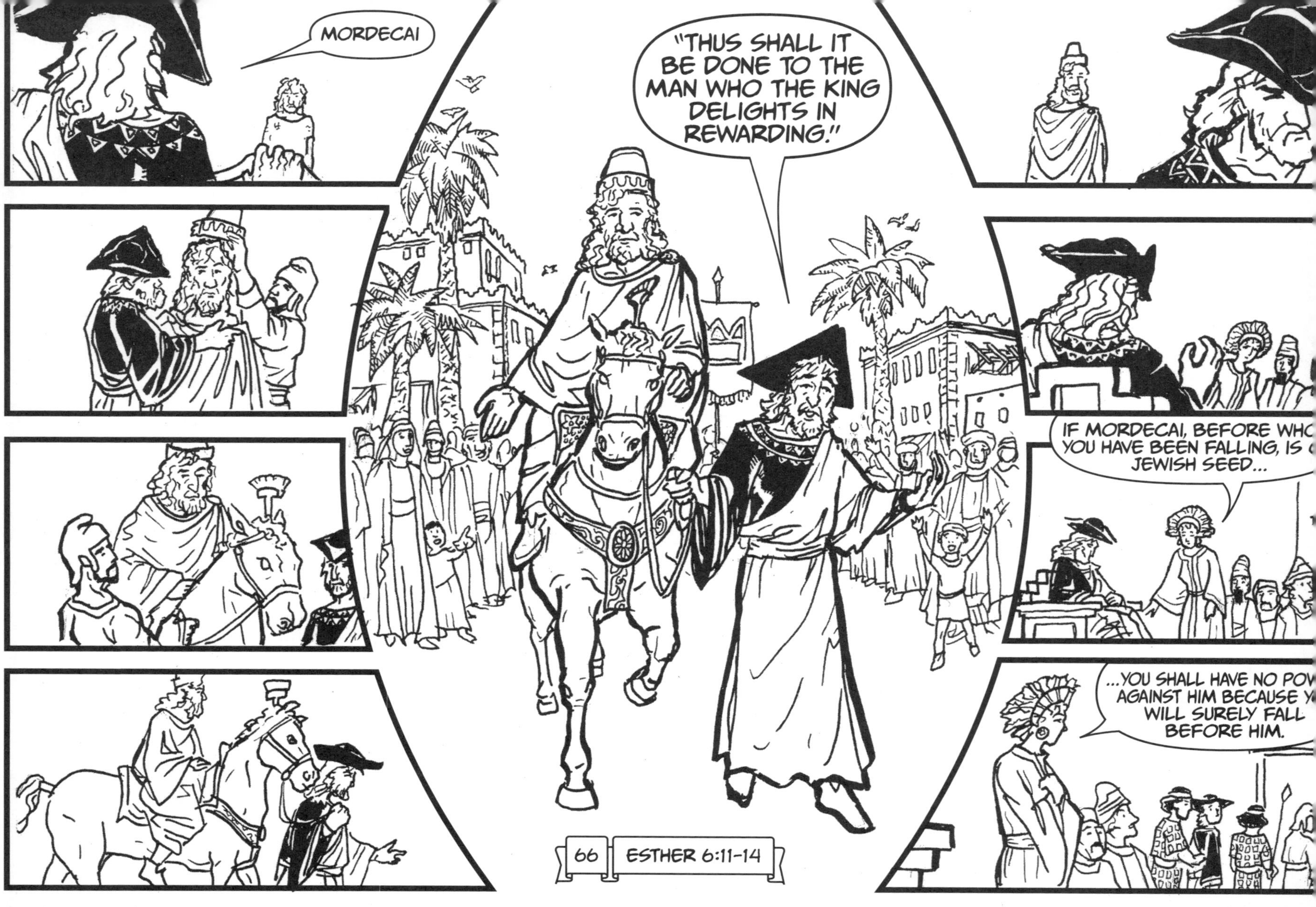
MORDECAI
"THUS SHALL IT BE DONE TO THE MAN WHO THE KING DELIGHTS IN REWARDING."
IF MORDECAI, BEFORE WHO YOU HAVE BEEN FALLING, IS JEWISH SEED...
...YOU SHALL HAVE NO POW AGAINST HIM BECAUSE Y WILL SURELY FALL BEFORE HIM.

CHAPTER 7

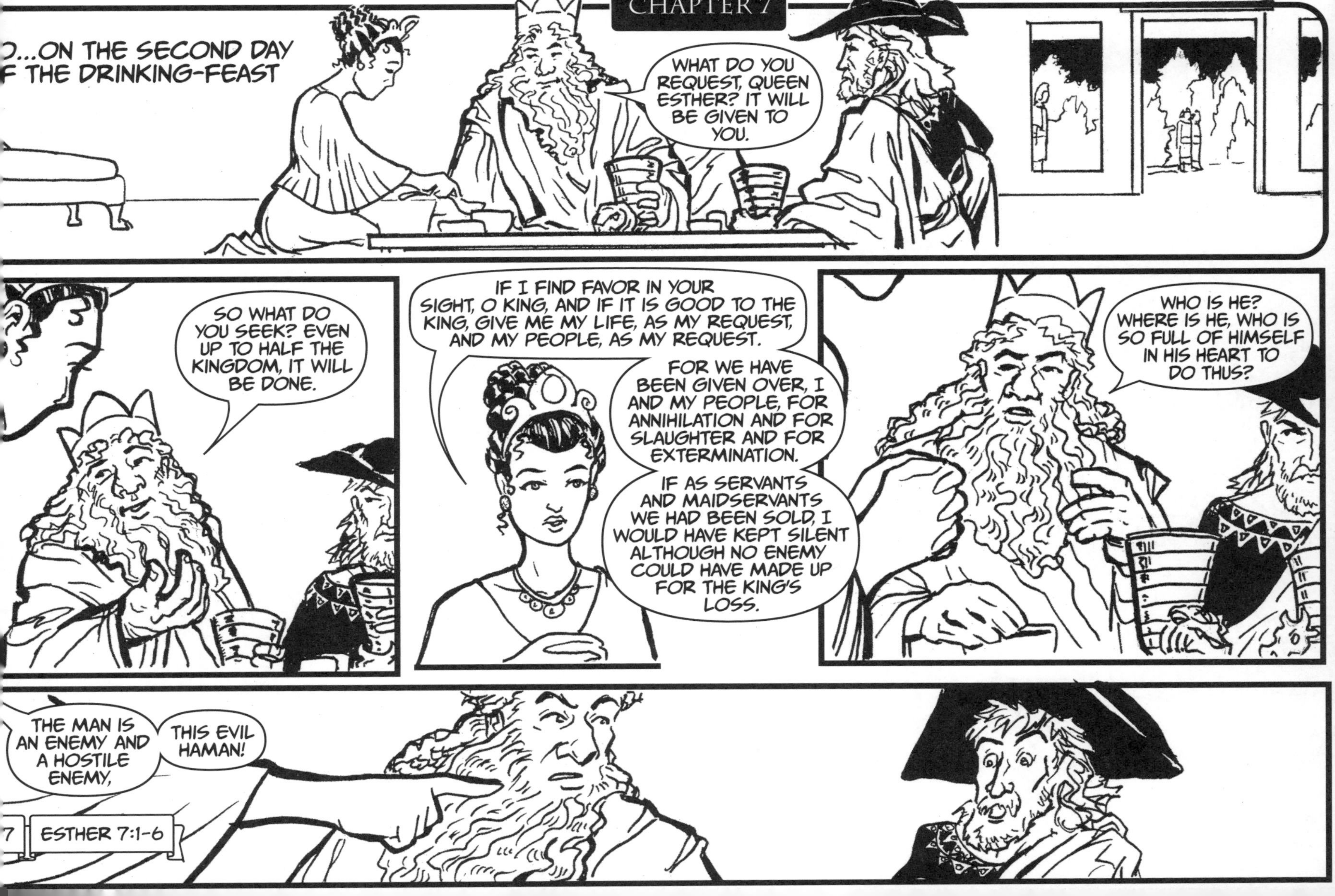

O...ON THE SECOND DAY
F THE DRINKING-FEAST
WHAT DO YOU REQUEST, QUEEN ESTHER? IT WILL BE GIVEN TO YOU.
SO WHAT DO YOU SEEK? EVEN UP TO HALF THE KINGDOM, IT WILL BE DONE.
IF I FIND FAVOR IN YOUR SIGHT, O KING, AND IF IT IS GOOD TO THE KING, GIVE ME MY LIFE, AS MY REQUEST, AND MY PEOPLE, AS MY REQUEST.
FOR WE HAVE BEEN GIVEN OVER, I AND MY PEOPLE, FOR ANNIHILATION AND FOR SLAUGHTER AND FOR EXTERMINATION.
IF AS SERVANTS AND MAIDSERVANTS WE HAD BEEN SOLD, I WOULD HAVE KEPT SILENT ALTHOUGH NO ENEMY COULD HAVE MADE UP FOR THE KING'S LOSS.
WHO IS HE? WHERE IS HE, WHO IS SO FULL OF HIMSELF IN HIS HEART TO DO THUS?
THE MAN IS AN ENEMY AND A HOSTILE ENEMY,
THIS EVIL HAMAN!
7
ESTHER 7:1-6

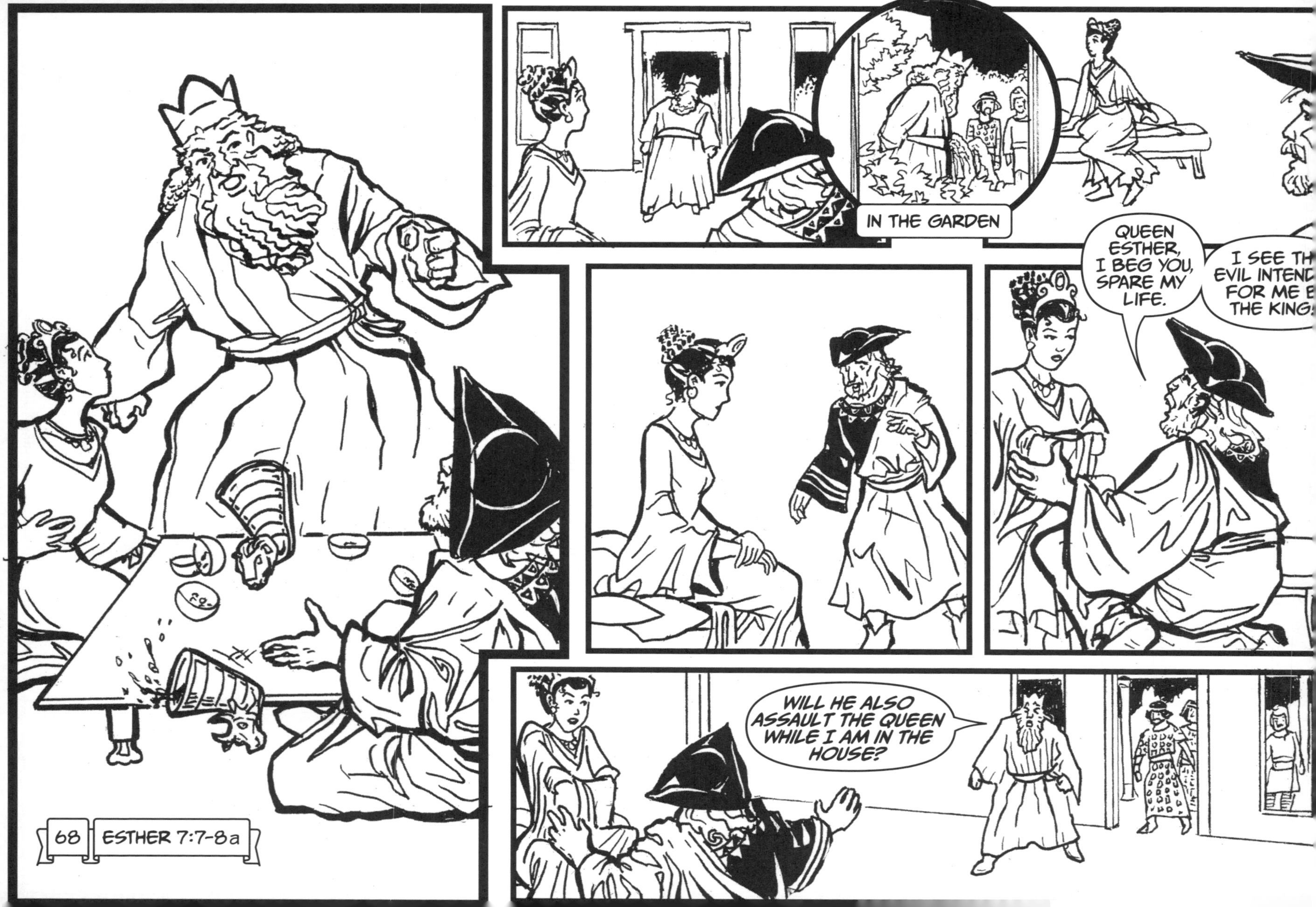
IN THE GARDEN
QUEEN ESTHER, I BEG YOU, SPARE MY LIFE.
WILL HE ALSO ASSAULT THE QUEEN WHILE I AM IN THE HOUSE?

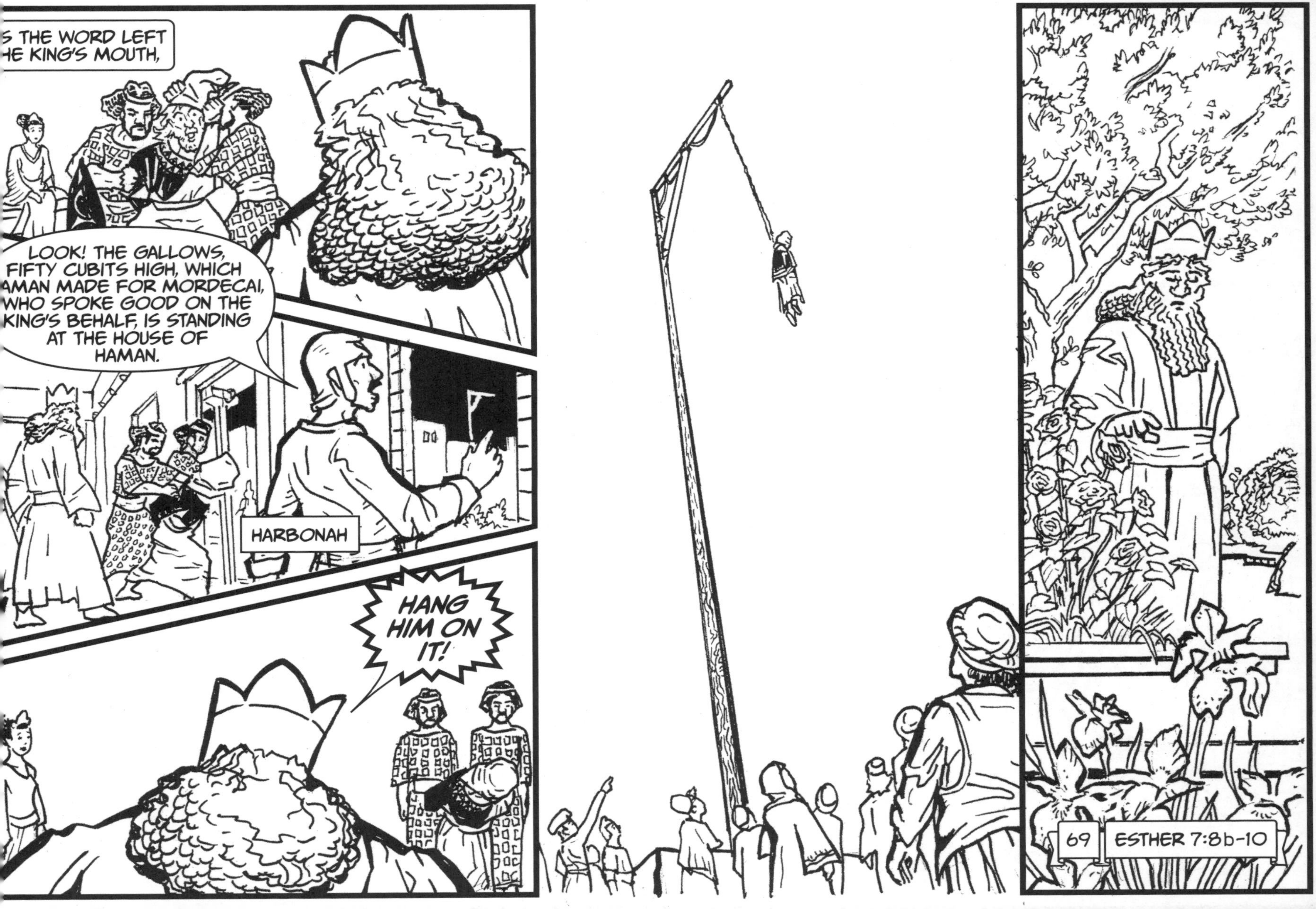
S THE WORD LEFT
HE KING'S MOUTH,
LOOK! THE GALLOWS, FIFTY CUBITS HIGH, WHICH AMAN MADE FOR MORDECAI, WHO SPOKE GOOD ON THE KING'S BEHALF, IS STANDING AT THE HOUSE OF HAMAN.
HARBONAH
HANG HIM ON IT!

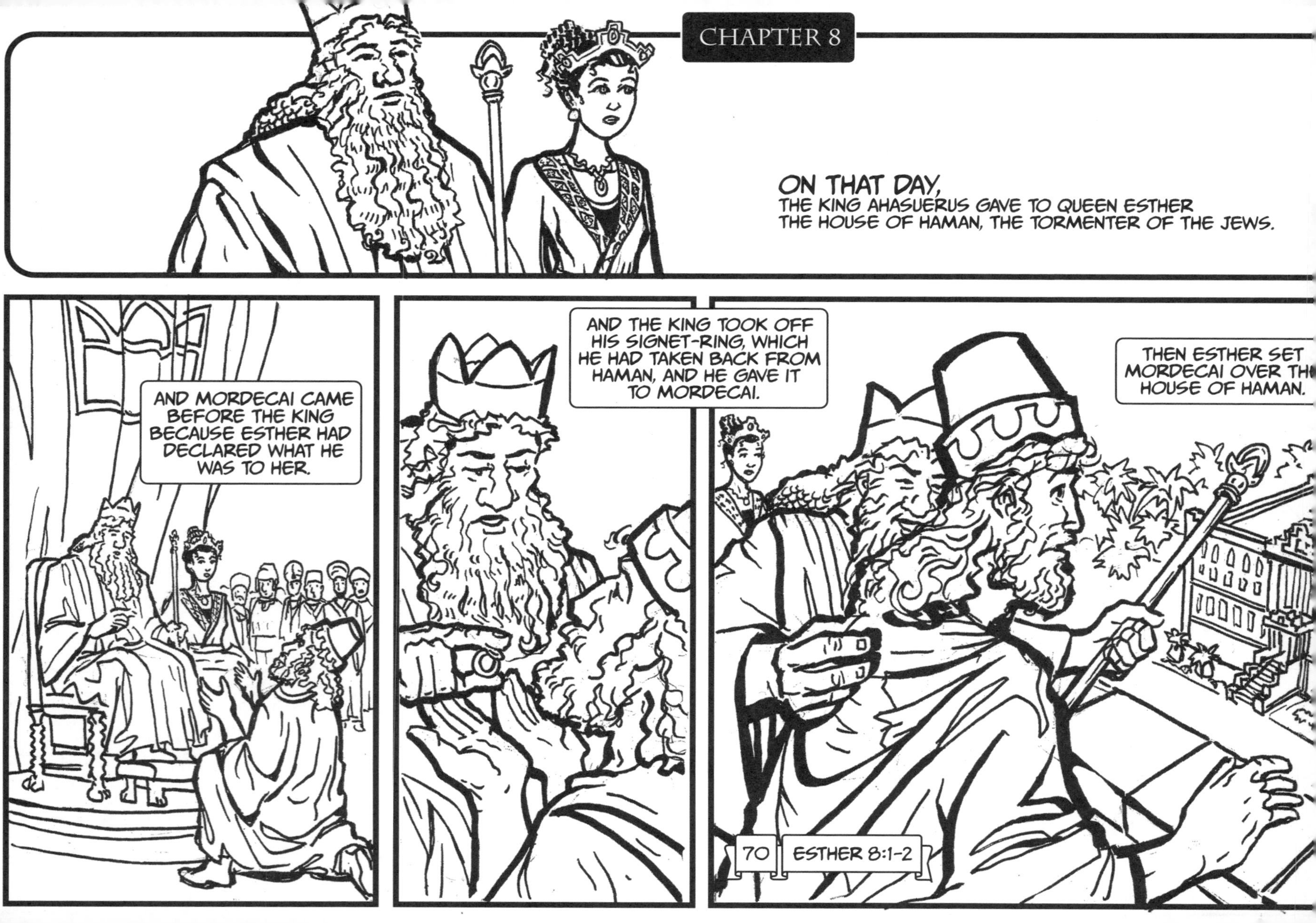
CHAPTER 8
ON THAT DAY,
THE KING AHASUERUS GAVE TO QUEEN ESTHER THE HOUSE OF HAMAN, THE TORMENTER OF THE JEWS.
AND MORDECAI CAME BEFORE THE KING BECAUSE ESTHER HAD DECLARED WHAT HE WAS TO HER.
AND THE KING TOOK OFF HIS SIGNET-RING, WHICH HE HAD TAKEN BACK FROM HAMAN, AND HE GAVE IT TO MORDECAI.
THEN ESTHER SET MORDECAI OVER TH HOUSE OF HAMAN.
70
ESTHER 8:1-2

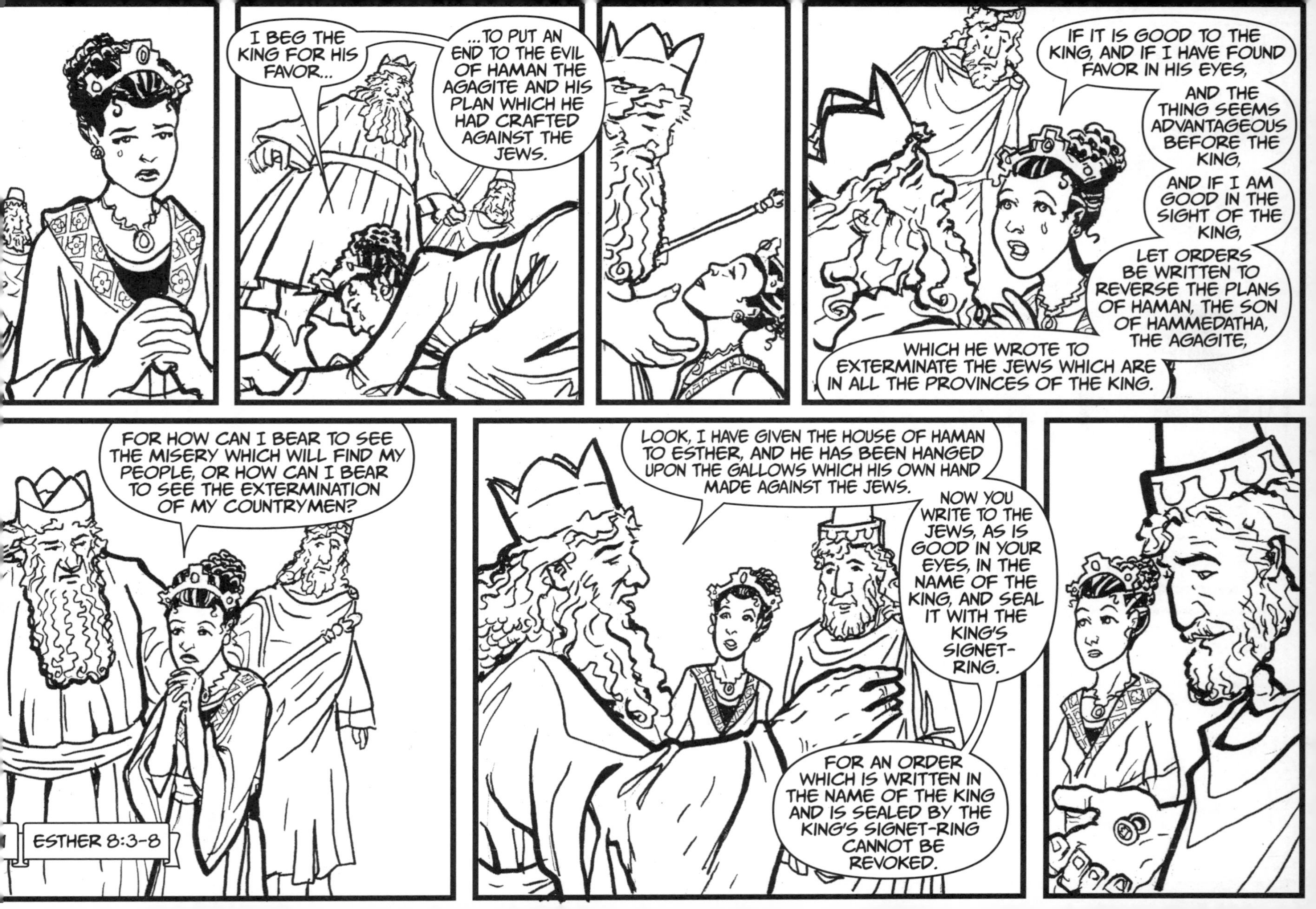
I BEG THE KING FOR HIS FAVOR...
...TO PUT AN END TO THE EVIL OF HAMAN THE AGAGITE AND HIS PLAN WHICH HE HAD CRAFTED AGAINST THE JEWS.
IF IT IS GOOD TO THE KING, AND IF I HAVE FOUND FAVOR IN HIS EYES,
AND THE THING SEEMS ADVANTAGEOUS BEFORE THE KING,
AND IF I AM GOOD IN THE SIGHT OF THE KING,
LET ORDERS BE WRITTEN TO REVERSE THE PLANS OF HAMAN, THE SON OF HAMMEDATHA, THE AGAGITE,
WHICH HE WROTE TO EXTERMINATE THE JEWS WHICH ARE IN ALL THE PROVINCES OF THE KING.
FOR HOW CAN I BEAR TO SEE THE MISERY WHICH WILL FIND MY PEOPLE, OR HOW CAN I BEAR TO SEE THE EXTERMINATION OF MY COUNTRYMEN?
ESTHER 8:3-8
LOOK, I HAVE GIVEN THE HOUSE OF HAMAN TO ESTHER, AND HE HAS BEEN HANGED UPON THE GALLOWS WHICH HIS OWN HAND MADE AGAINST THE JEWS.
NOW YOU WRITE TO THE JEWS, AS IS GOOD IN YOUR EYES, IN THE NAME OF THE KING, AND SEAL IT WITH THE KING'S SIGNET-RING.
FOR AN ORDER WHICH IS WRITTEN IN THE NAME OF THE KING AND IS SEALED BY THE KING'S SIGNET-RING CANNOT BE REVOKED.

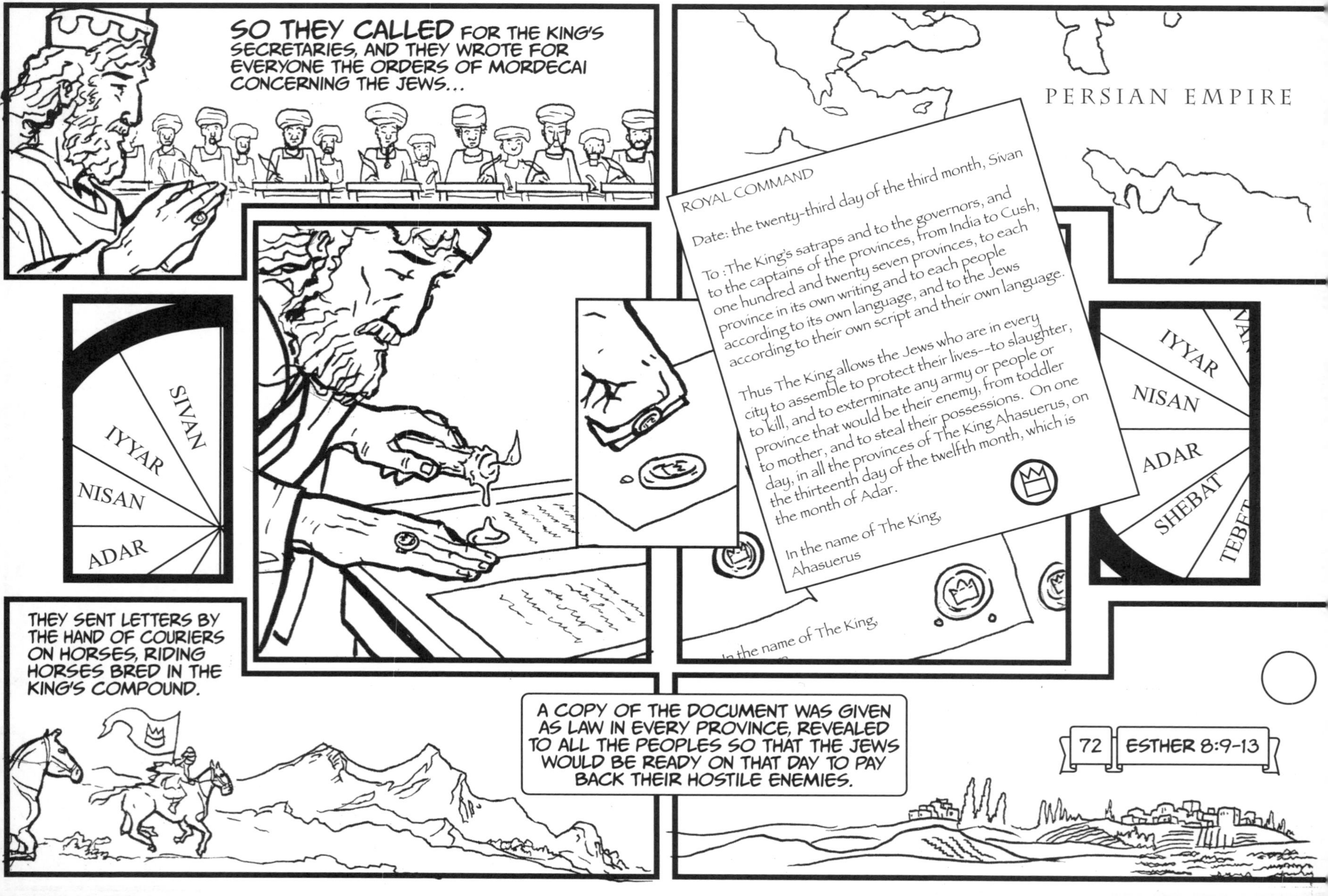

SO THEY CALLED FOR THE KING'S SECRETARIES, AND THEY WROTE FOR EVERYONE THE ORDERS OF MORDECAI CONCERNING THE JEWS...
PERSIAN EMPIRE
ROYAL COMMAND
Date: the twenty-third day of the third month, Sivan
To :The King's satraps and to the governors, and to the captains of the provinces, from India to Cush, one hundred and twenty seven provinces, to each province in its own writing and to each people according to its own language, and to the Jews according to their own script and their own language.
Thus The King allows the Jews who are in every city to assemble to protect their lives--to slaughter, to kill, and to exterminate any army or people or province that would be their enemy, from toddler to mother, and to steal their possessions. On one day, in all the provinces of The King Ahasuerus, on the thirteenth day of the twelfth month, which is the month of Adar.
In the name of The King,
Ahasuerus
SIVAN
IYYAR
NISAN
ADAR
IYYAR
NISAN
ADAR
SHEBAT
TEBET
In the name of The King,
THEY SENT LETTERS BY THE HAND OF COURIERS ON HORSES, RIDING HORSES BRED IN THE KING'S COMPOUND.
A COPY OF THE DOCUMENT WAS GIVEN AS LAW IN EVERY PROVINCE, REVEALED TO ALL THE PEOPLES SO THAT THE JEWS WOULD BE READY ON THAT DAY TO PAY BACK THEIR HOSTILE ENEMIES.
72
ESTHER 8:9-13

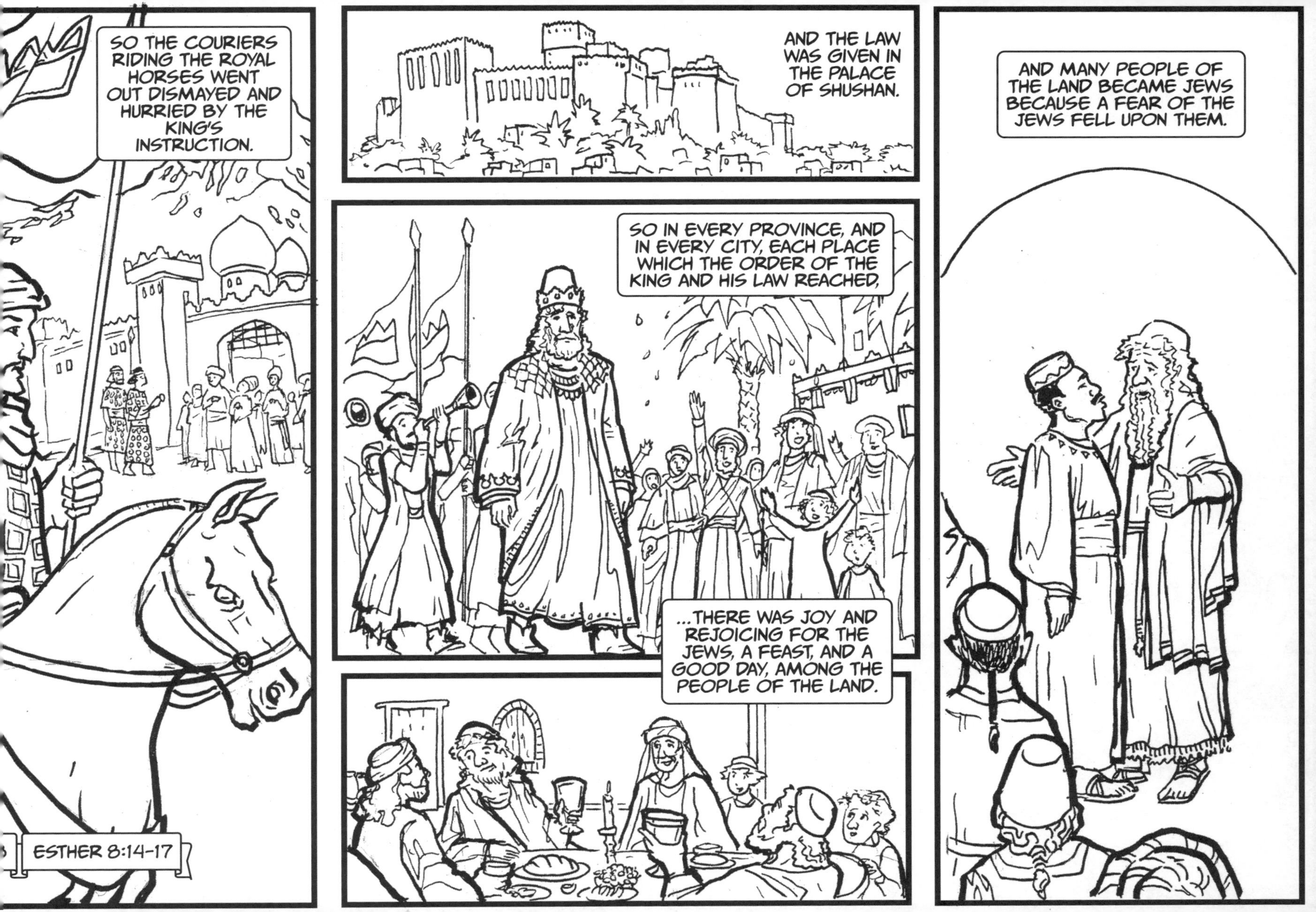

SO THE COURIERS RIDING THE ROYAL HORSES WENT OUT DISMAYED AND HURRIED BY THE KING'S INSTRUCTION.
ESTHER 8:14-17
AND THE LAW WAS GIVEN IN THE PALACE OF SHUSHAN.
SO IN EVERY PROVINCE, AND IN EVERY CITY, EACH PLACE WHICH THE ORDER OF THE KING AND HIS LAW REACHED,
...THERE WAS JOY AND REJOICING FOR THE JEWS, A FEAST, AND A GOOD DAY, AMONG THE PEOPLE OF THE LAND.
AND MANY PEOPLE OF THE LAND BECAME JEWS BECAUSE A FEAR OF THE JEWS FELL UPON THEM.

CHAPTER 9

IN THE TWELFTH MONTH, WHICH WAS THE MONTH OF ADAR, ON THE THIRTEENTH DAY OF IT, WHEN THE KING'S ORDER AND LAW WAS MADE TO BE APPLIED AND DONE,

...ON THE DAY WHICH THE ENEMIES OF THE JEWS WERE CONSIDERING THEIR POWER OVER THEM,

74 | ESTHER 9:1-3

THOUGH IT WAS REVERSED AND THE JEWS MASTERED THEM THAT HATED THEM,

THE JEWS ASSEMBLED THEMSELVES IN ALL THEIR CITIES, IN ALL THE PROVINCES OF THE KING AHASUERUS, TO STRETCH OUT A HAND AGAINST THOSE WHO SOUGHT EVIL FOR THEM.

AND NO MAN COULD STAND BEFORE THEM BECAUSE FEAR OF THEM FELL UPON ALL THE PEOPLES.

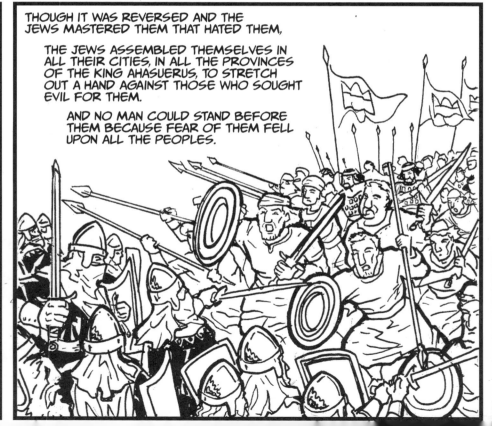

AND ALL THE CAPTAINS O[F] THE PROVINCES, THE SATRA[PS] THE GOVERNORS AND THO[SE] DOING THE KING'S WORK WE[RE] ASSISTING THE JEWS BECAU[SE] A FEAR OF MORDECAI FE[LL] UPON THEM.

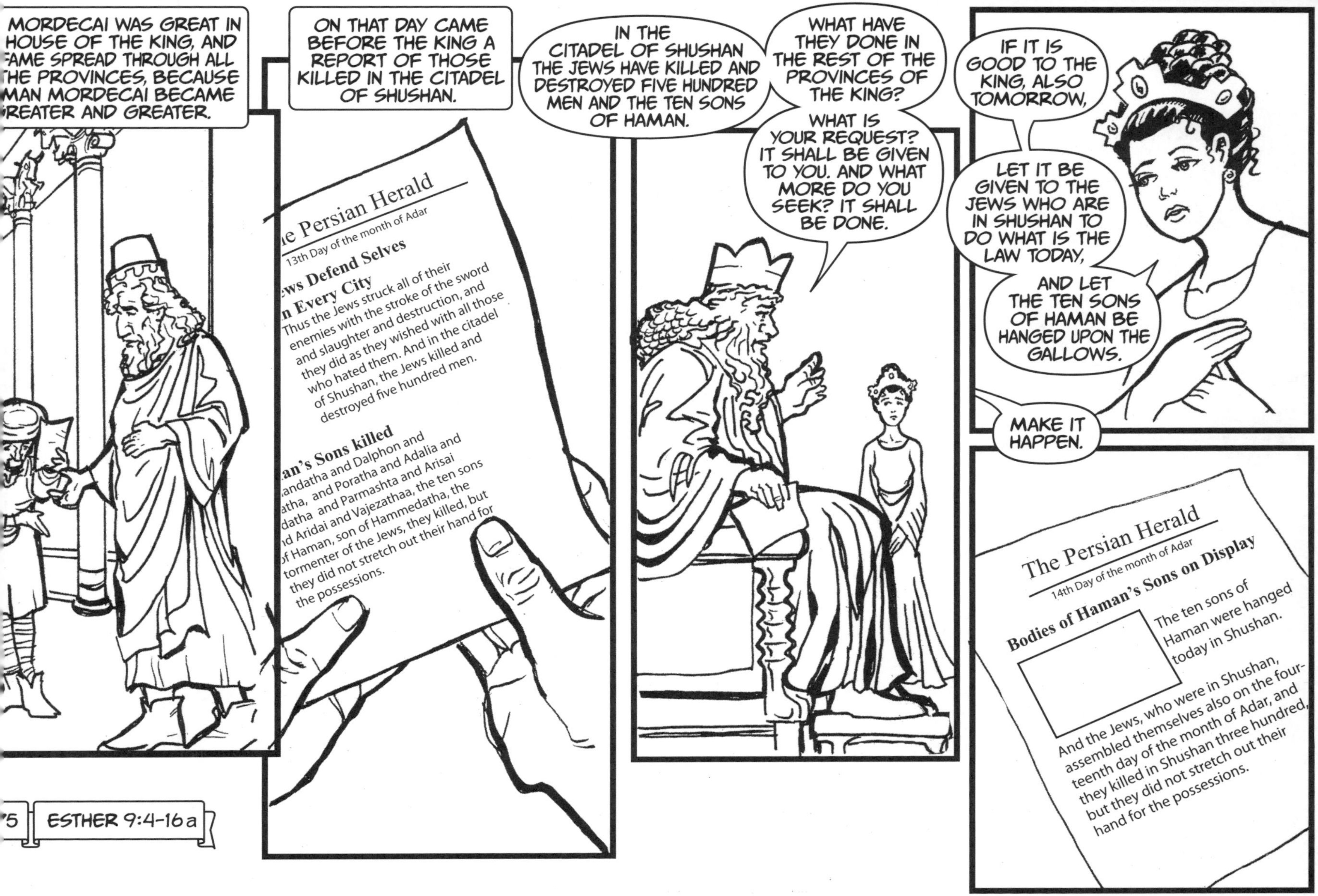
MORDECAI WAS GREAT IN HOUSE OF THE KING, AND FAME SPREAD THROUGH ALL THE PROVINCES, BECAUSE MAN MORDECAI BECAME GREATER AND GREATER.
ON THAT DAY CAME BEFORE THE KING A REPORT OF THOSE KILLED IN THE CITADEL OF SHUSHAN.
he Persian Herald
13th Day of the month of Adar
ews Defend Selves
n Every City
Thus the Jews struck all of their enemies with the stroke of the sword and slaughter and destruction, and they did as they wished with all those who hated them. And in the citadel of Shushan, the Jews killed and destroyed five hundred men.
an's Sons killed
andatha and Dalphon and atha, and Poratha and Adalia and datha and Parmashta and Arisai d Aridai and Vajezathaa, the ten sons f Haman, son of Hammedatha, the tormenter of the Jews, they killed, but they did not stretch out their hand for the possessions.
IN THE CITADEL OF SHUSHAN THE JEWS HAVE KILLED AND DESTROYED FIVE HUNDRED MEN AND THE TEN SONS OF HAMAN.
WHAT HAVE THEY DONE IN THE REST OF THE PROVINCES OF THE KING?
WHAT IS YOUR REQUEST? IT SHALL BE GIVEN TO YOU. AND WHAT MORE DO YOU SEEK? IT SHALL BE DONE.
IF IT IS GOOD TO THE KING, ALSO TOMORROW,
LET IT BE GIVEN TO THE JEWS WHO ARE IN SHUSHAN TO DO WHAT IS THE LAW TODAY,
AND LET THE TEN SONS OF HAMAN BE HANGED UPON THE GALLOWS.
MAKE IT HAPPEN.
The Persian Herald
14th Day of the month of Adar
Bodies of Haman's Sons on Display
The ten sons of Haman were hanged today in Shushan.
And the Jews, who were in Shushan, assembled themselves also on the fourteenth day of the month of Adar, and they killed in Shushan three hundred, but they did not stretch out their hand for the possessions.

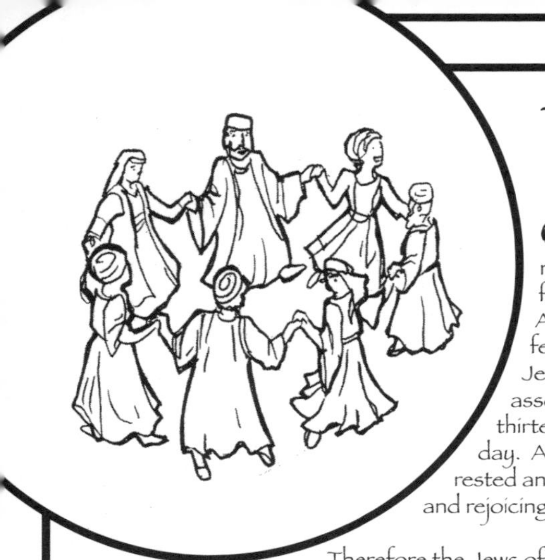

THE FEAST OF PURIM

On the thirteenth day of the month of Adar and on the fourteenth, they rested. And they made it a day of feasting and rejoicing. So the Jews who were in Shushan assembled themselves on the thirteenth day and the fourteenth day. And on the fifteenth day, they rested and made it a day of feasting and rejoicing.

Therefore the Jews of the villages, who were dwellers in the country towns, celebrated the fourteenth day of the month of Adar and feasted, a good day, a day of sending gifts of food from the hands of each man.

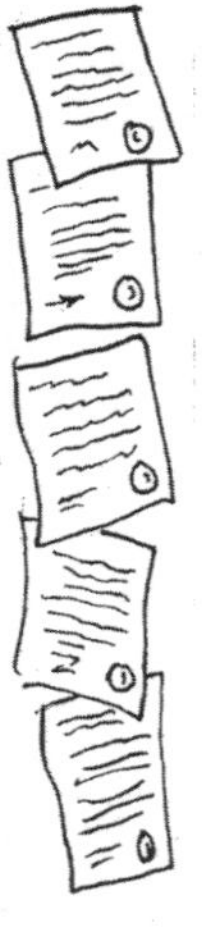

Then Mordecai recorded these things, and he sent letters to all the Jews who were in all the provinces of the King Ahasuerus, near and far, to establish among them an event on the fourteenth day of the month of Adar and on the fifteenth day of it, every year, as on these days of rest from their enemies, for the Jews, in the month which was turned for them from grief to joy and from mourning to a good day, to make for themselves days of feasting and joy and of men outreaching hands to give gifts of food and gifts to the poor.

So the Jews accepted what they had begun to do and what Mordecai had written to them, because Haman, son of Hammedatha the Agagite, tormenter of all the Jews, had planned for the Jews to destroy them and had caused the Pur to be thrown, which was the lot to confuse them and destroy them.

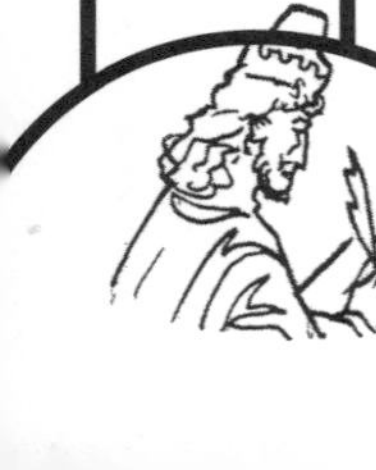

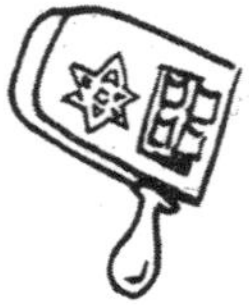

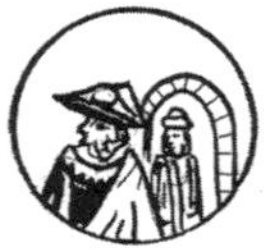

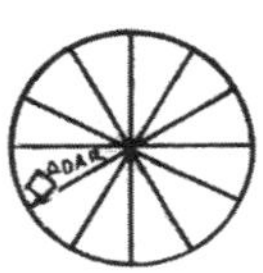

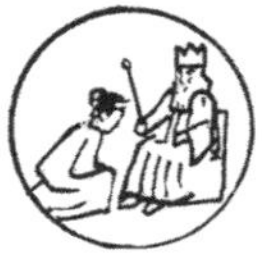

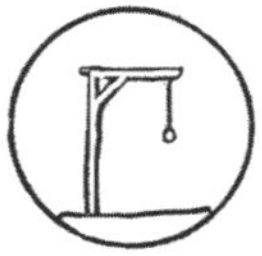

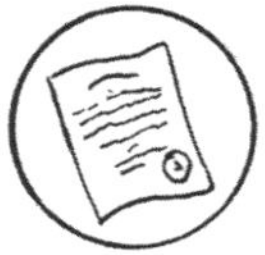

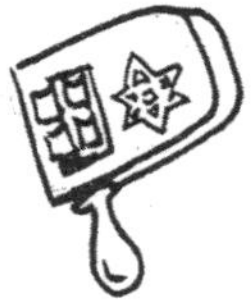

פּוּרִים

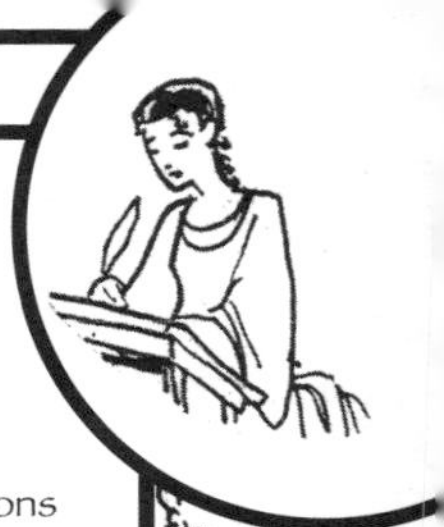

But when Esther came before the King, he wrote that Haman's evil plan which he had thought up against the Jews should be turned against his own head and that he and his sons should be hanged upon the gallows.

So they called these days Purim for the name of the Pur, for all the words of this royal letter and what they had seen concerning this and what had touched them.

The Jews established and accepted for themselves and their descendents and for all who would join them not to miss making, yearly, these days, as were written and as were appointed for every year.

And these days were remembered and kept in every generation, in every family, in every province, and every city. And these days of Purim will not be overlooked among the Jews, and the memory of them will never end for their descendents.

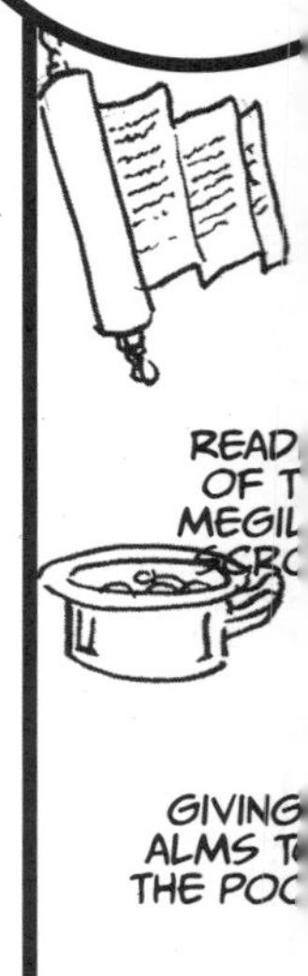

READ
OF T
MEGIL
SCRO
GIVING
ALMS T
THE POO

And Queen Esther, the daughter of Abihail, and Mordecai, the Jew, wrote with all power, to confirm this second royal letter about Purim. And he sent letters to all the Jews, to the 127 provinces of the kingdom of Ahasuerus, words of peace and truth, to establish these days of Purim, at their appointed time, which Mordecai the Jew and Esther the queen had established for them, and as they had established for themselves and their descendents the story of fasting and their outcry.

So the decree of Esther confirmed these things of Purim, and in the book it was recorded.

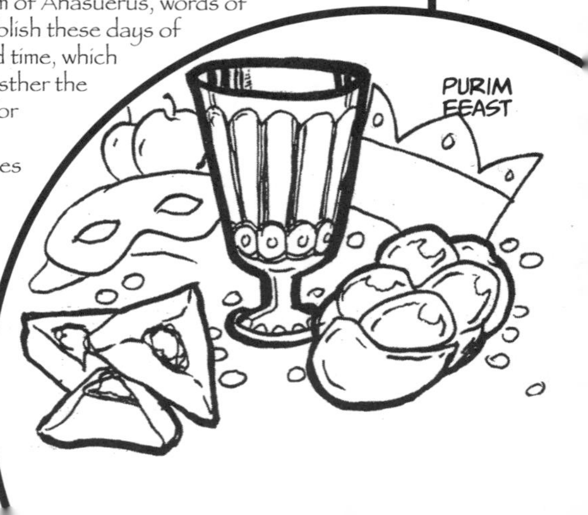

PURIM
FEAST

CHAPTER 10

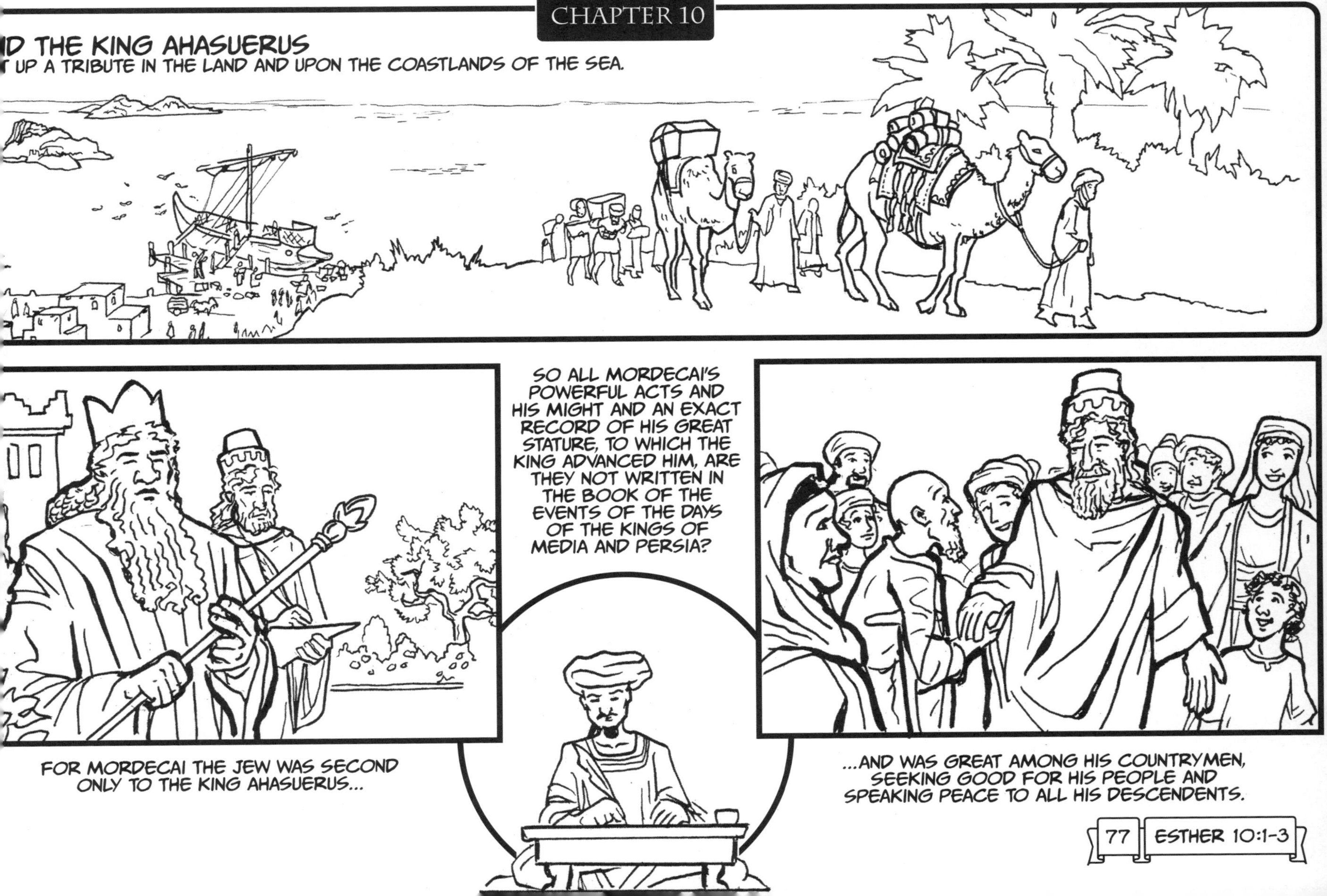

D THE KING AHASUERUS
T UP A TRIBUTE IN THE LAND AND UPON THE COASTLANDS OF THE SEA.
FOR MORDECAI THE JEW WAS SECOND ONLY TO THE KING AHASUERUS...
SO ALL MORDECAI'S POWERFUL ACTS AND HIS MIGHT AND AN EXACT RECORD OF HIS GREAT STATURE, TO WHICH THE KING ADVANCED HIM, ARE THEY NOT WRITTEN IN THE BOOK OF THE EVENTS OF THE DAYS OF THE KINGS OF MEDIA AND PERSIA?
...AND WAS GREAT AMONG HIS COUNTRYMEN, SEEKING GOOD FOR HIS PEOPLE AND SPEAKING PEACE TO ALL HIS DESCENDENTS.

AMOS

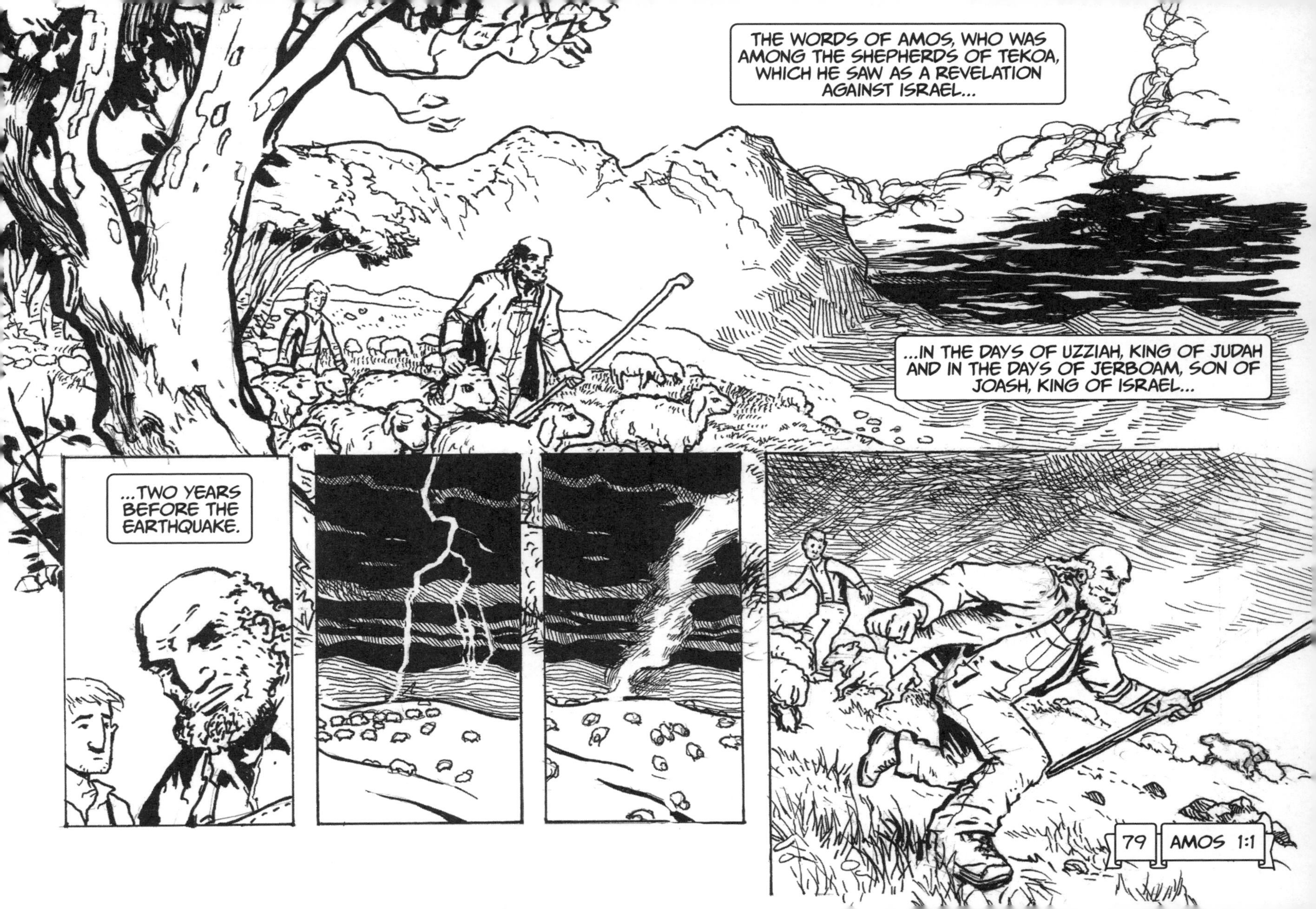
THE WORDS OF AMOS, WHO WAS AMONG THE SHEPHERDS OF TEKOA, WHICH HE SAW AS A REVELATION AGAINST ISRAEL...
...IN THE DAYS OF UZZIAH, KING OF JUDAH AND IN THE DAYS OF JERBOAM, SON OF JOASH, KING OF ISRAEL...
...TWO YEARS BEFORE THE EARTHQUAKE.

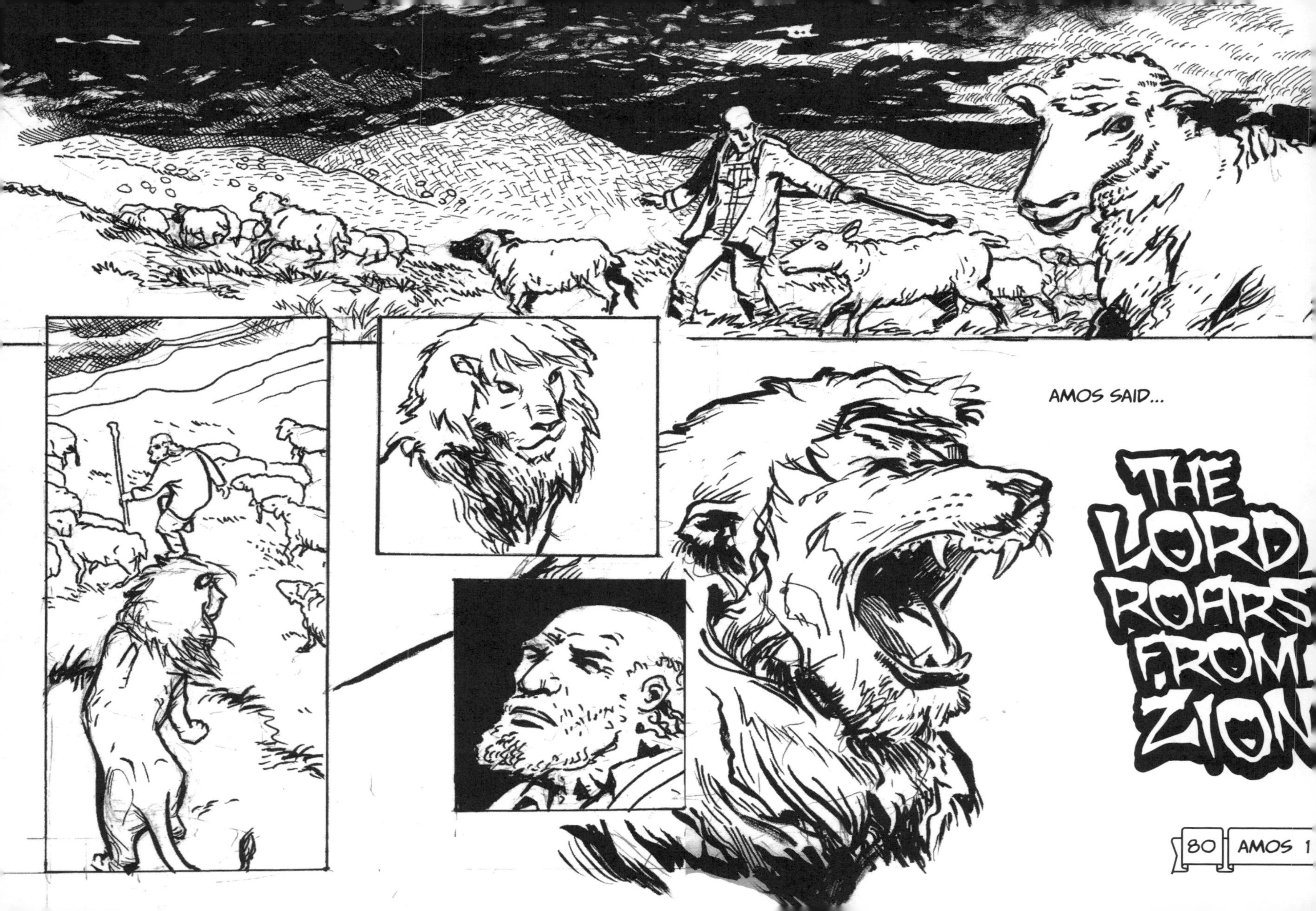
AMOS SAID...
THE LORD ROARS FROM ZION

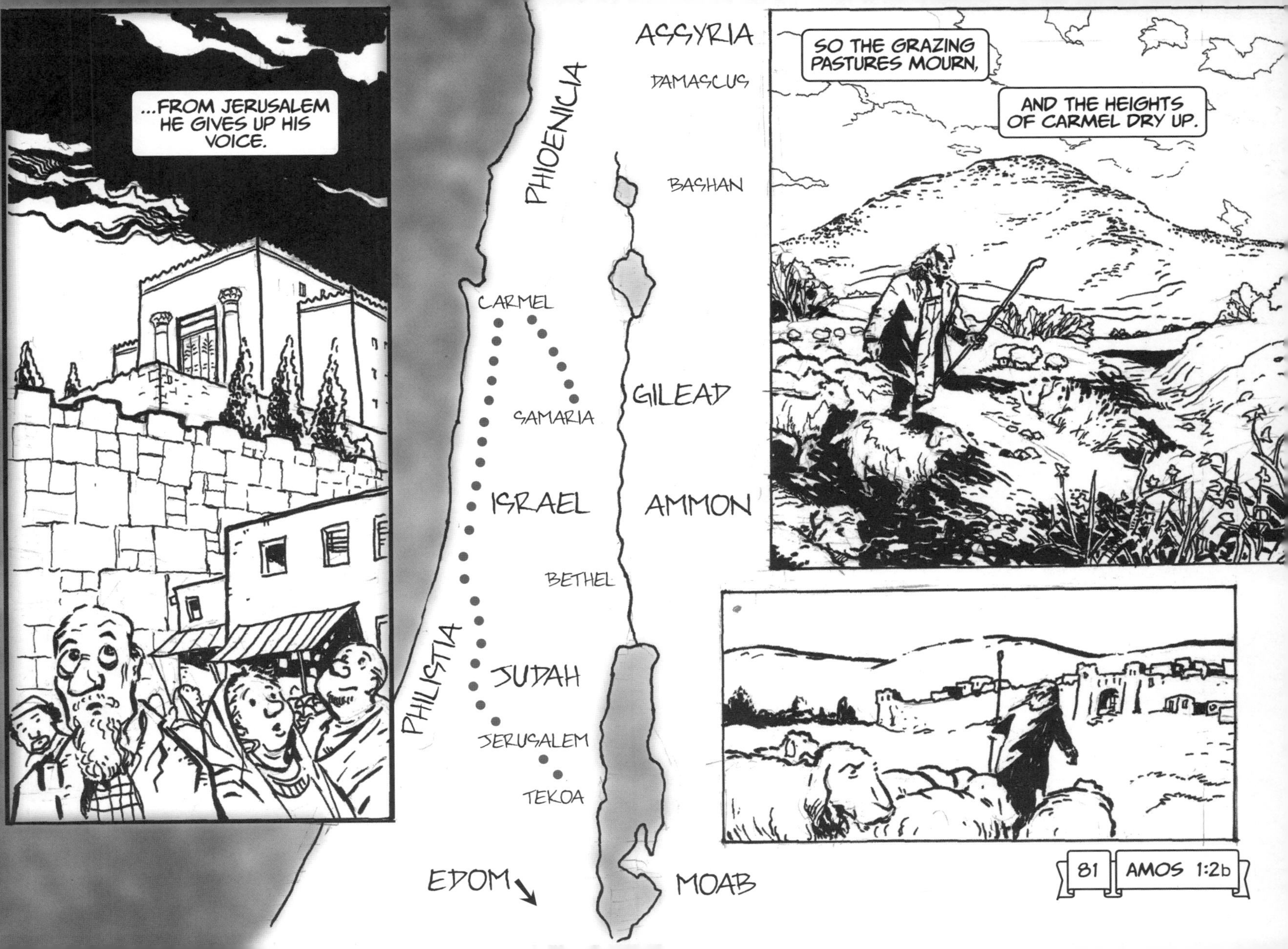

...FROM JERUSALEM HE GIVES UP HIS VOICE.
ASSYRIA
DAMASCUS
PHOENICIA
BASHAN
CARMEL
SAMARIA
GILEAD
ISRAEL
AMMON
BETHEL
PHILISTIA
JUDAH
JERUSALEM
TEKOA
EDOM
MOAB
SO THE GRAZING PASTURES MOURN,
AND THE HEIGHTS OF CARMEL DRY UP.

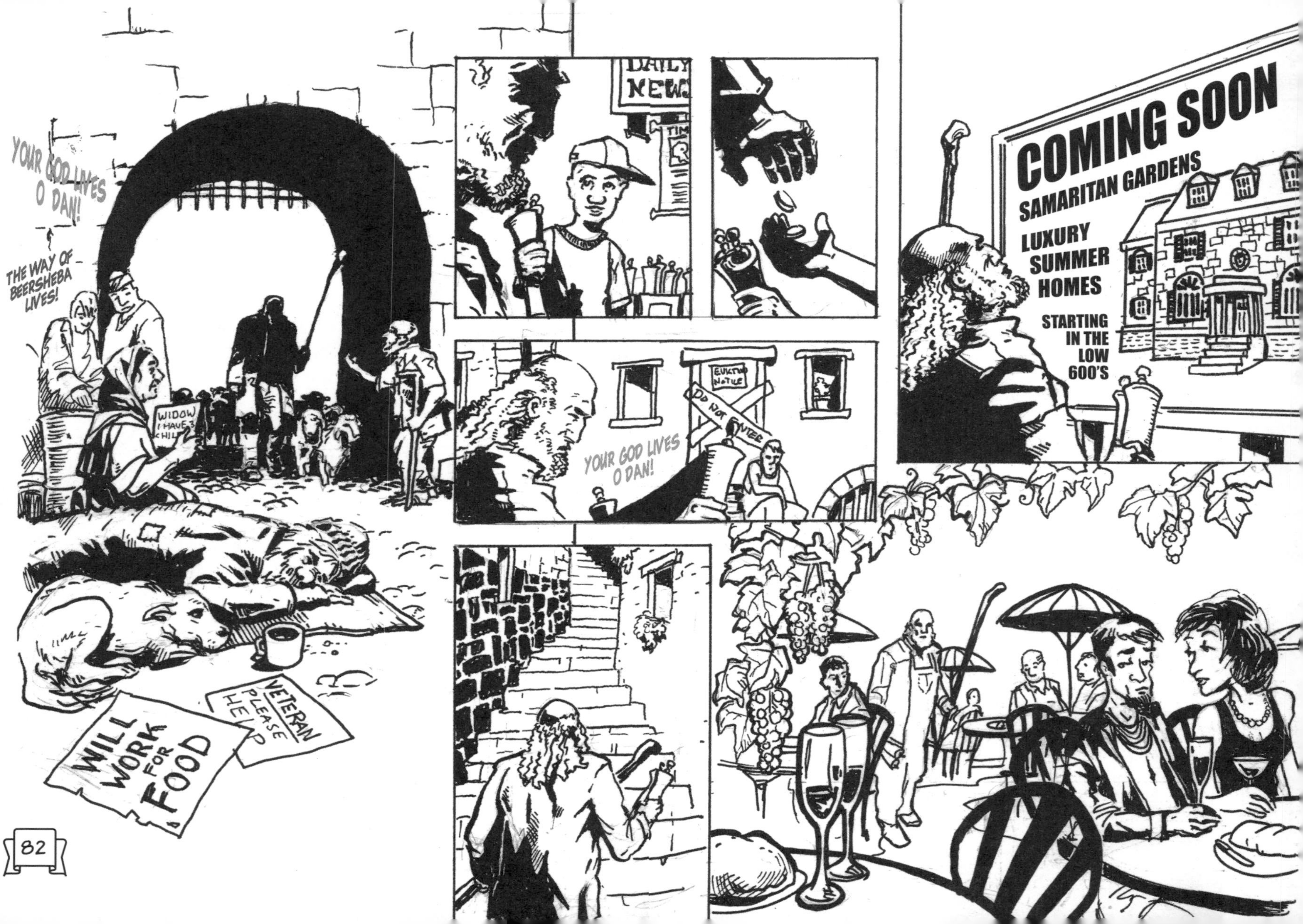
YOUR GOD LIVES O DAN!
THE WAY OF BEERSHEBA LIVES!
WIDOW I HAVE 3 CHIL
WILL WORK FOR FOOD
VETERAN PLEASE HELP
DAILY NEWS
EVICTION NOTICE
DO NOT ENTER
YOUR GOD LIVES O DAN!
COMING SOON
SAMARITAN GARDENS
LUXURY SUMMER HOMES
STARTING IN THE LOW 600'S

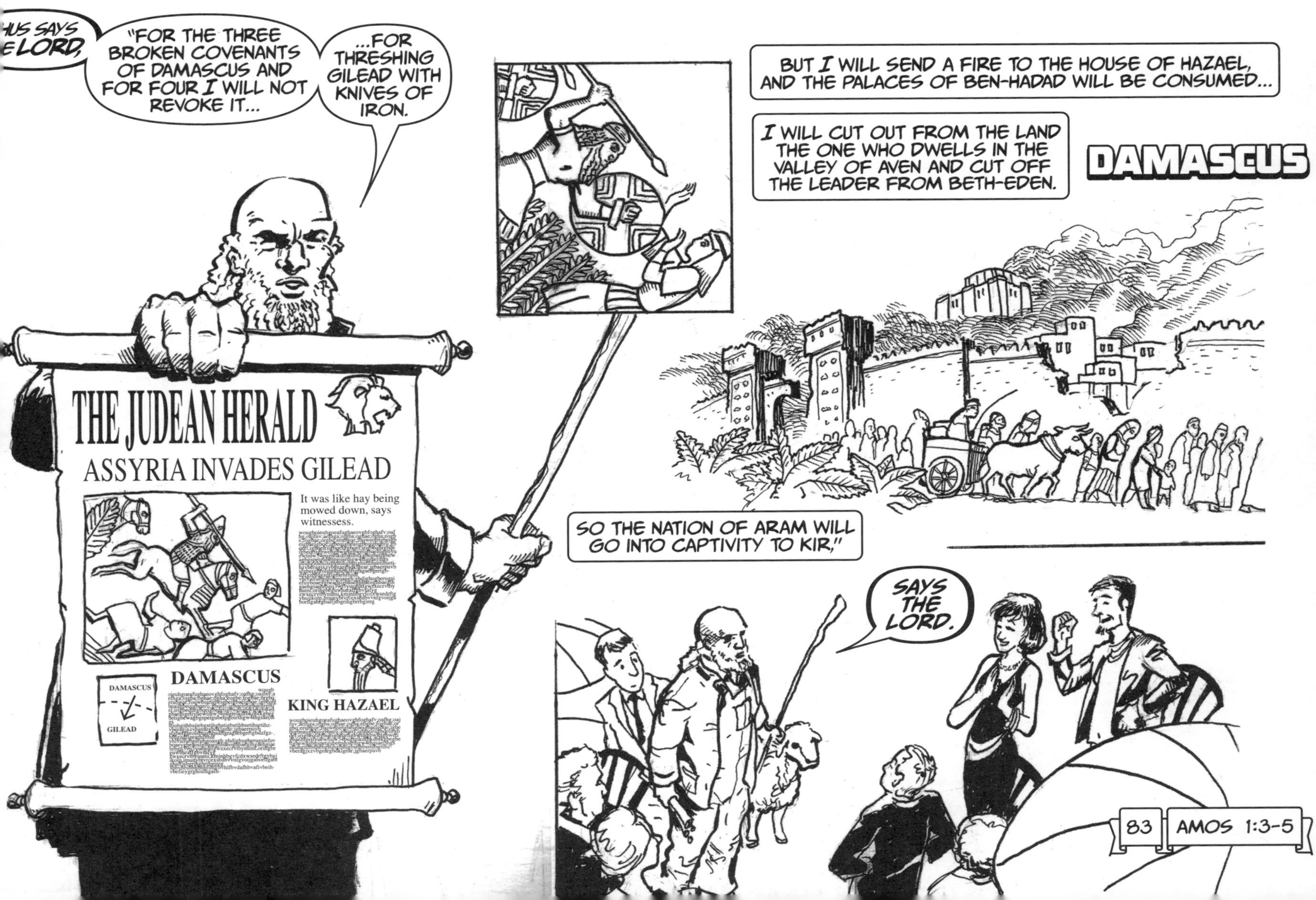
HUS SAYS E LORD,
"FOR THE THREE BROKEN COVENANTS OF DAMASCUS AND FOR FOUR I WILL NOT REVOKE IT...
...FOR THRESHING GILEAD WITH KNIVES OF IRON.
THE JUDEAN HERALD
ASSYRIA INVADES GILEAD
It was like hay being mowed down, says witnessess.
DAMASCUS
GILEAD
DAMASCUS
KING HAZAEL
BUT I WILL SEND A FIRE TO THE HOUSE OF HAZAEL, AND THE PALACES OF BEN-HADAD WILL BE CONSUMED...
I WILL CUT OUT FROM THE LAND THE ONE WHO DWELLS IN THE VALLEY OF AVEN AND CUT OFF THE LEADER FROM BETH-EDEN.
DAMASCUS
SO THE NATION OF ARAM WILL GO INTO CAPTIVITY TO KIR,"
SAYS THE LORD.

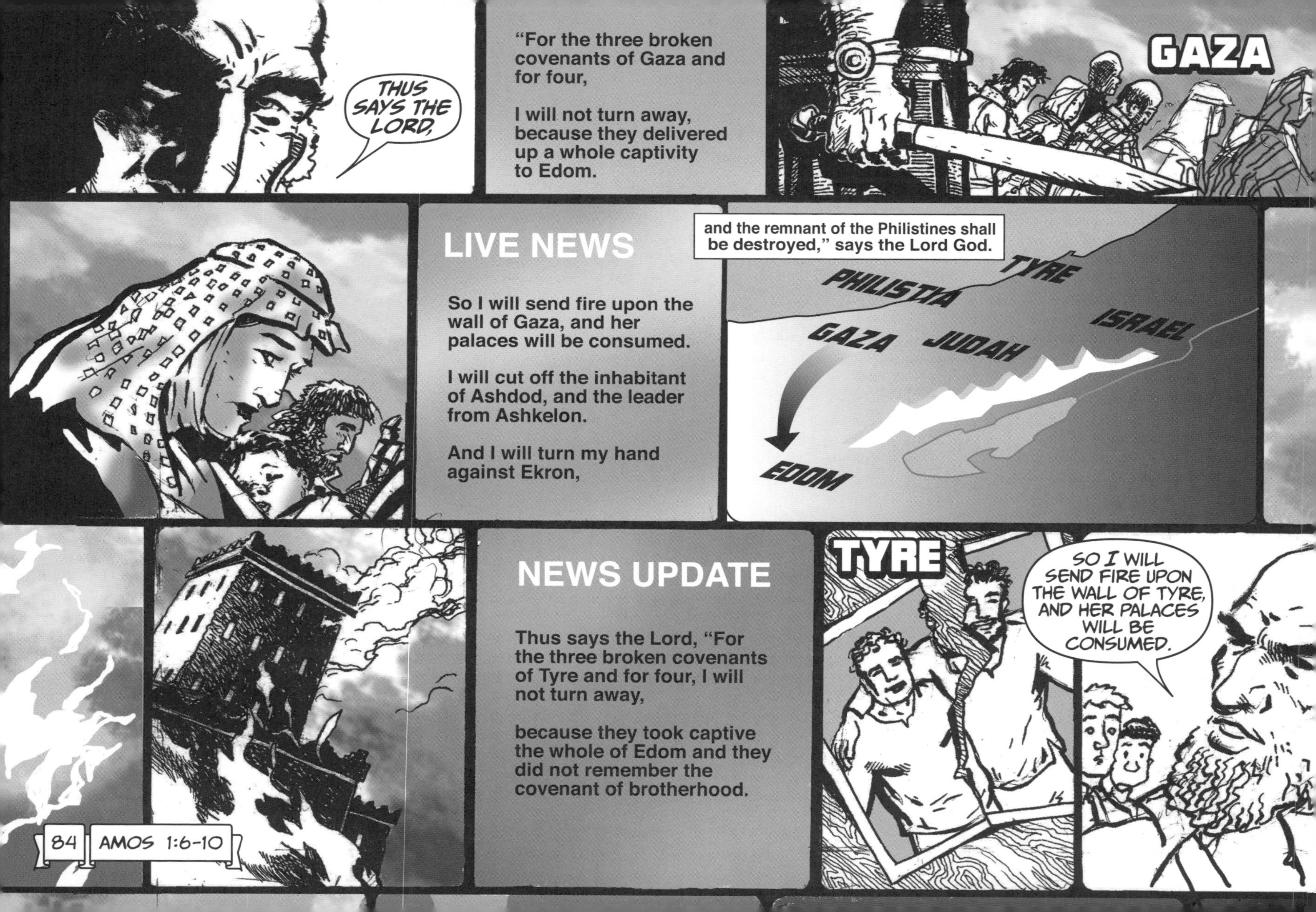

THUS SAYS THE LORD,
"For the three broken covenants of Gaza and for four,
I will not turn away, because they delivered up a whole captivity to Edom.
GAZA
LIVE NEWS
So I will send fire upon the wall of Gaza, and her palaces will be consumed.
I will cut off the inhabitant of Ashdod, and the leader from Ashkelon.
And I will turn my hand against Ekron,
and the remnant of the Philistines shall be destroyed," says the Lord God.
TYRE
PHILISTIA
ISRAEL
GAZA
JUDAH
EDOM
NEWS UPDATE
Thus says the Lord, "For the three broken covenants of Tyre and for four, I will not turn away,
because they took captive the whole of Edom and they did not remember the covenant of brotherhood.
TYRE
SO I WILL SEND FIRE UPON THE WALL OF TYRE, AND HER PALACES WILL BE CONSUMED.

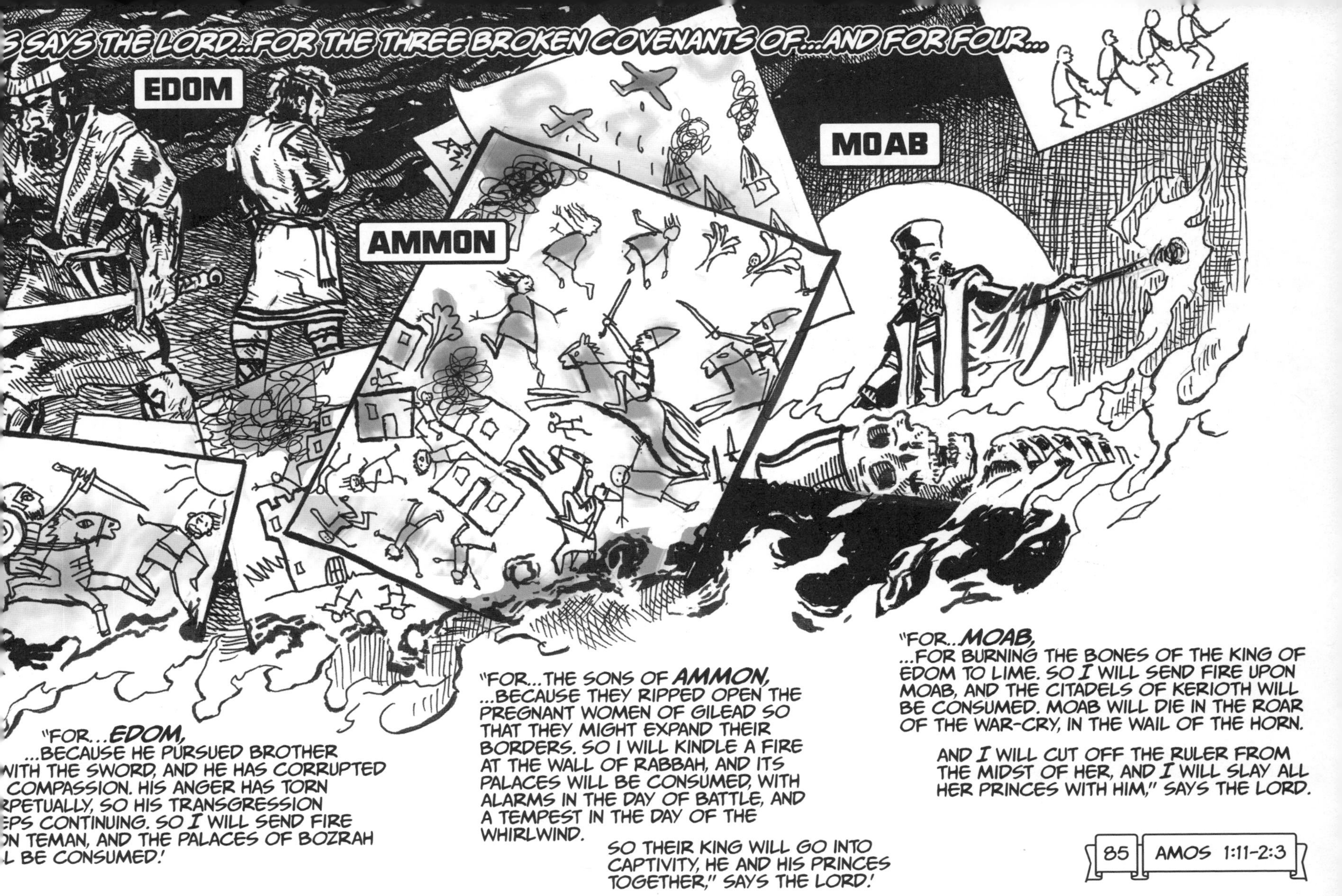
S SAYS THE LORD...FOR THE THREE BROKEN COVENANTS OF...AND FOR FOUR...
EDOM
AMMON
MOAB
"FOR...EDOM,
...BECAUSE HE PURSUED BROTHER
WITH THE SWORD, AND HE HAS CORRUPTED
COMPASSION. HIS ANGER HAS TORN
RPETUALLY, SO HIS TRANSGRESSION
EPS CONTINUING. SO I WILL SEND FIRE
N TEMAN, AND THE PALACES OF BOZRAH
L BE CONSUMED.'
"FOR...THE SONS OF AMMON,
...BECAUSE THEY RIPPED OPEN THE PREGNANT WOMEN OF GILEAD SO THAT THEY MIGHT EXPAND THEIR BORDERS. SO I WILL KINDLE A FIRE AT THE WALL OF RABBAH, AND ITS PALACES WILL BE CONSUMED, WITH ALARMS IN THE DAY OF BATTLE, AND A TEMPEST IN THE DAY OF THE WHIRLWIND.
SO THEIR KING WILL GO INTO CAPTIVITY, HE AND HIS PRINCES TOGETHER," SAYS THE LORD.'
"FOR...MOAB,
...FOR BURNING THE BONES OF THE KING OF EDOM TO LIME. SO I WILL SEND FIRE UPON MOAB, AND THE CITADELS OF KERIOTH WILL BE CONSUMED. MOAB WILL DIE IN THE ROAR OF THE WAR-CRY, IN THE WAIL OF THE HORN.
AND I WILL CUT OFF THE RULER FROM THE MIDST OF HER, AND I WILL SLAY ALL HER PRINCES WITH HIM," SAYS THE LORD.

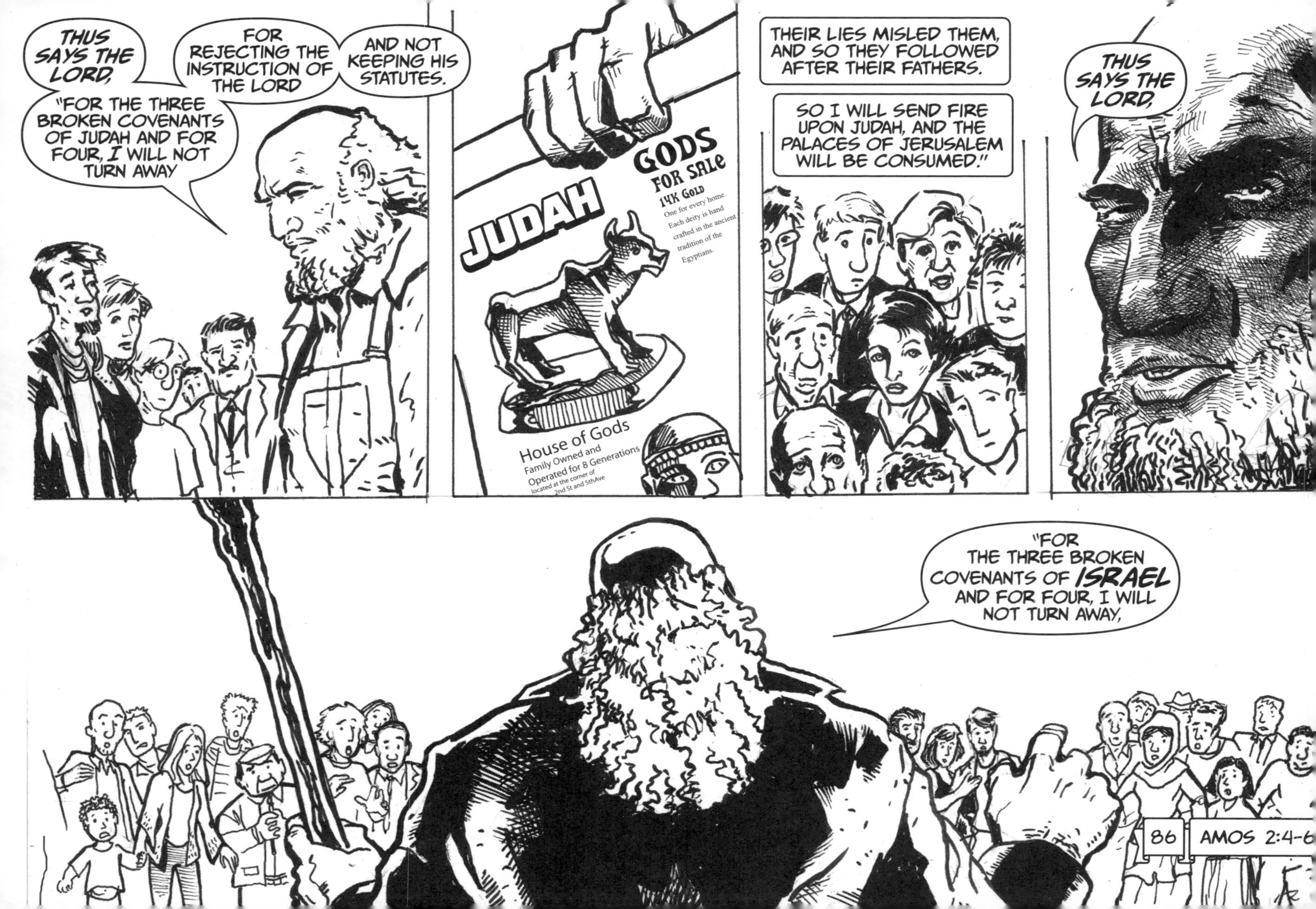
THUS SAYS THE LORD,
FOR REJECTING THE INSTRUCTION OF THE LORD
AND NOT KEEPING HIS STATUTES.
"FOR THE THREE BROKEN COVENANTS OF JUDAH AND FOR FOUR, I WILL NOT TURN AWAY
JUDAH
GODS FOR SALE
14K GOLD
One for every home. Each deity is hand crafted in the ancient tradition of the Egyptians.
House of Gods
Family Owned and Operated for 8 Generations
located at the corner of 2nd St and 5thAve
THEIR LIES MISLED THEM, AND SO THEY FOLLOWED AFTER THEIR FATHERS.
SO I WILL SEND FIRE UPON JUDAH, AND THE PALACES OF JERUSALEM WILL BE CONSUMED."
THUS SAYS THE LORD,
"FOR THE THREE BROKEN COVENANTS OF ISRAEL AND FOR FOUR, I WILL NOT TURN AWAY,
86
AMOS 2:4-6

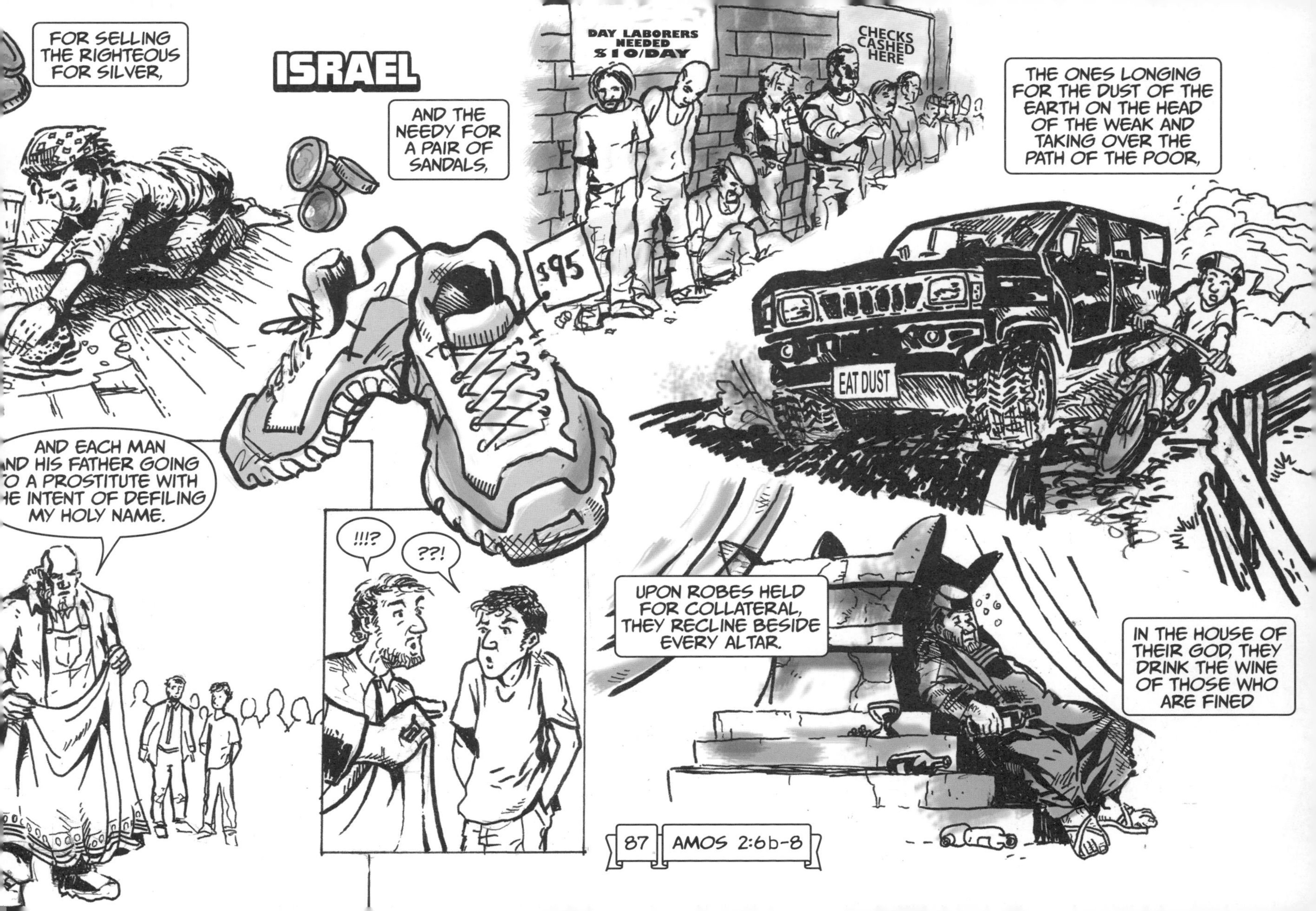
ISRAEL
FOR SELLING THE RIGHTEOUS FOR SILVER,
AND THE NEEDY FOR A PAIR OF SANDALS,
$95
DAY LABORERS NEEDED $10/DAY
CHECKS CASHED HERE
THE ONES LONGING FOR THE DUST OF THE EARTH ON THE HEAD OF THE WEAK AND TAKING OVER THE PATH OF THE POOR,
EAT DUST
AND EACH MAN AND HIS FATHER GOING TO A PROSTITUTE WITH THE INTENT OF DEFILING MY HOLY NAME.
!!!?
??!
UPON ROBES HELD FOR COLLATERAL, THEY RECLINE BESIDE EVERY ALTAR.
IN THE HOUSE OF THEIR GOD, THEY DRINK THE WINE OF THOSE WHO ARE FINED

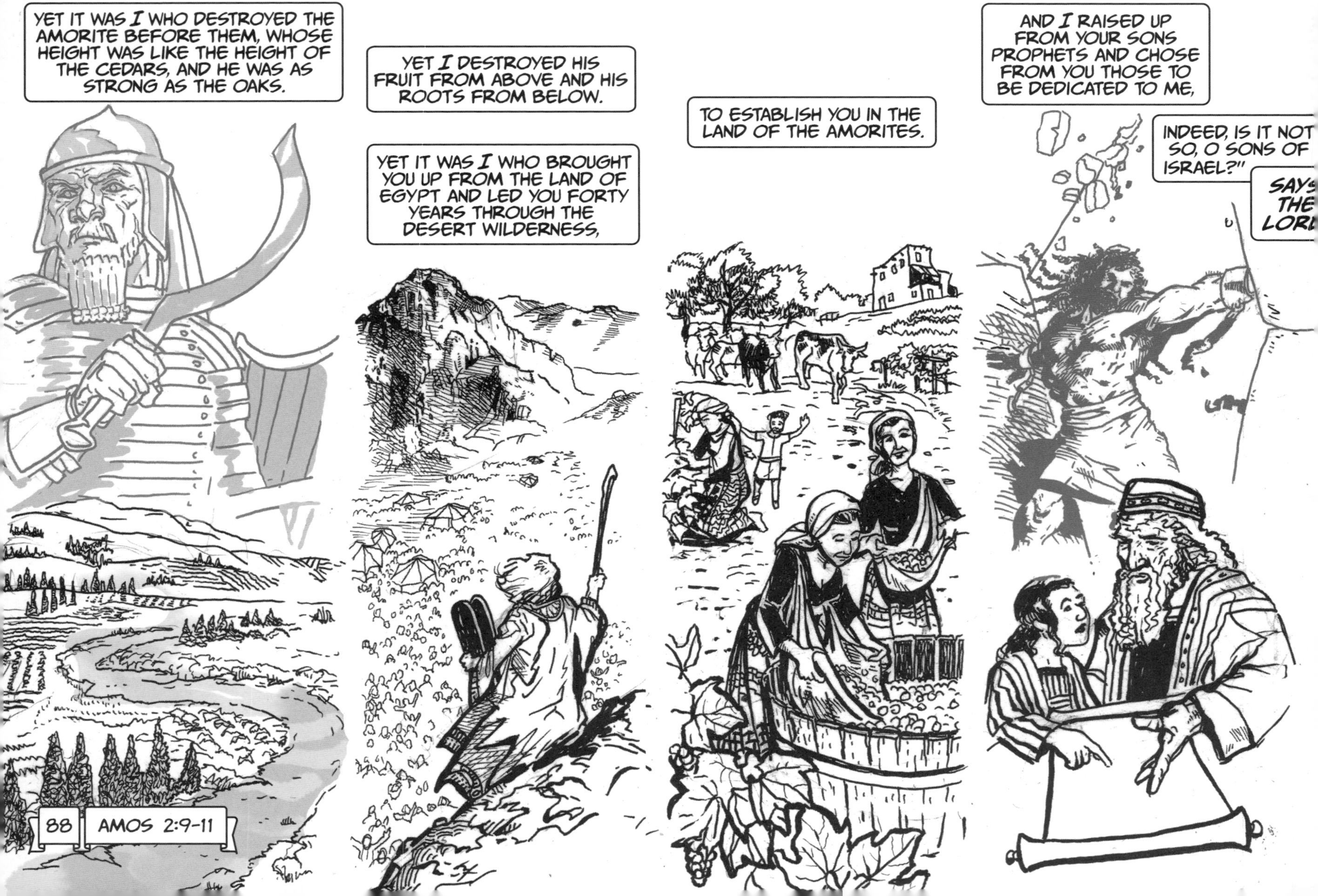
YET IT WAS I WHO DESTROYED THE AMORITE BEFORE THEM, WHOSE HEIGHT WAS LIKE THE HEIGHT OF THE CEDARS, AND HE WAS AS STRONG AS THE OAKS.
YET I DESTROYED HIS FRUIT FROM ABOVE AND HIS ROOTS FROM BELOW.
YET IT WAS I WHO BROUGHT YOU UP FROM THE LAND OF EGYPT AND LED YOU FORTY YEARS THROUGH THE DESERT WILDERNESS,
TO ESTABLISH YOU IN THE LAND OF THE AMORITES.
AND I RAISED UP FROM YOUR SONS PROPHETS AND CHOSE FROM YOU THOSE TO BE DEDICATED TO ME,
INDEED, IS IT NOT SO, O SONS OF ISRAEL?"
SAY THE LOR

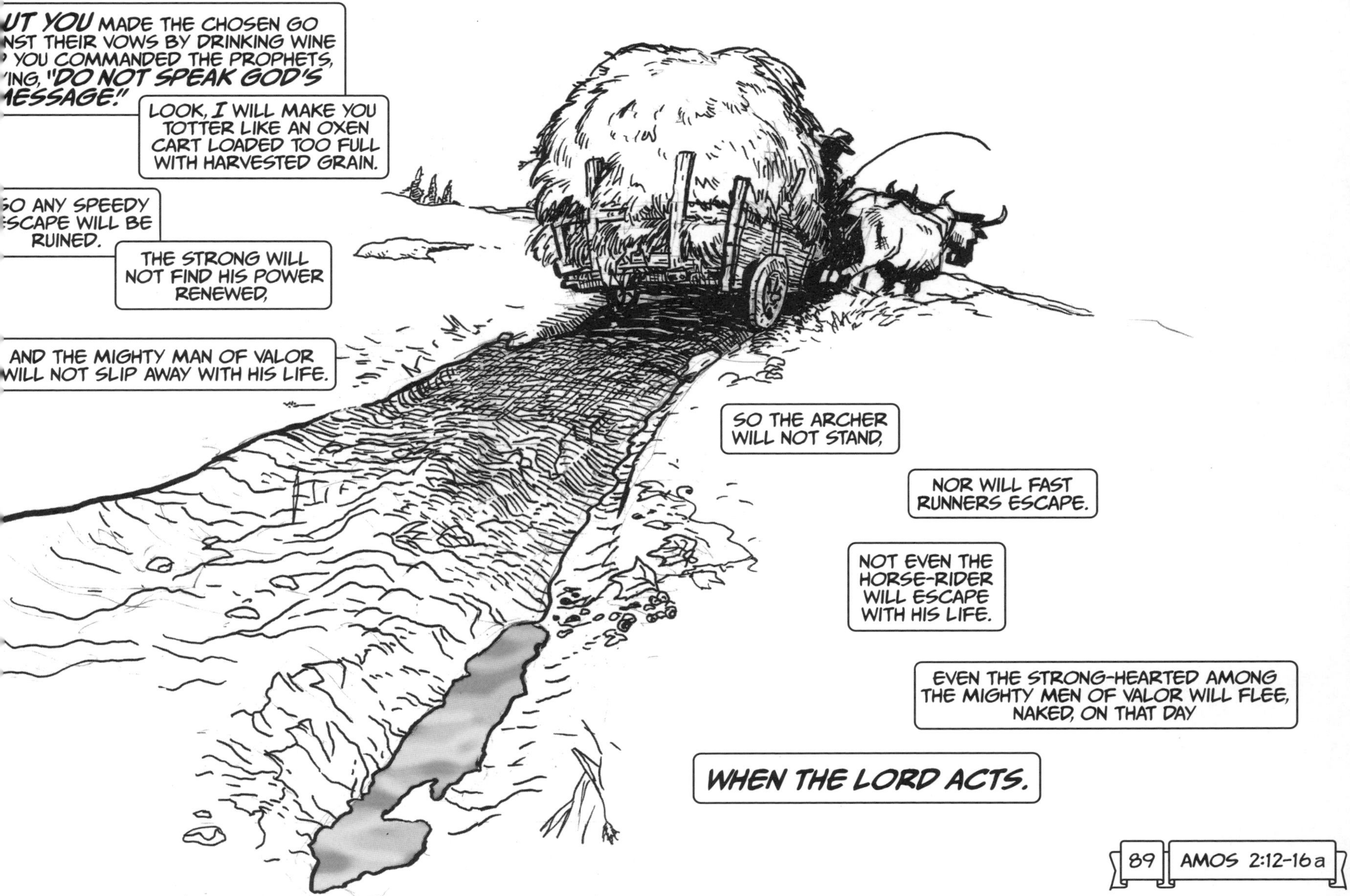
UT YOU MADE THE CHOSEN GO
NST THEIR VOWS BY DRINKING WINE
YOU COMMANDED THE PROPHETS,
ING, "DO NOT SPEAK GOD'S
MESSAGE!"
LOOK, I WILL MAKE YOU TOTTER LIKE AN OXEN CART LOADED TOO FULL WITH HARVESTED GRAIN.
O ANY SPEEDY SCAPE WILL BE RUINED.
THE STRONG WILL NOT FIND HIS POWER RENEWED,
AND THE MIGHTY MAN OF VALOR WILL NOT SLIP AWAY WITH HIS LIFE.
SO THE ARCHER WILL NOT STAND,
NOR WILL FAST RUNNERS ESCAPE.
NOT EVEN THE HORSE-RIDER WILL ESCAPE WITH HIS LIFE.
EVEN THE STRONG-HEARTED AMONG THE MIGHTY MEN OF VALOR WILL FLEE, NAKED, ON THAT DAY
WHEN THE LORD ACTS.

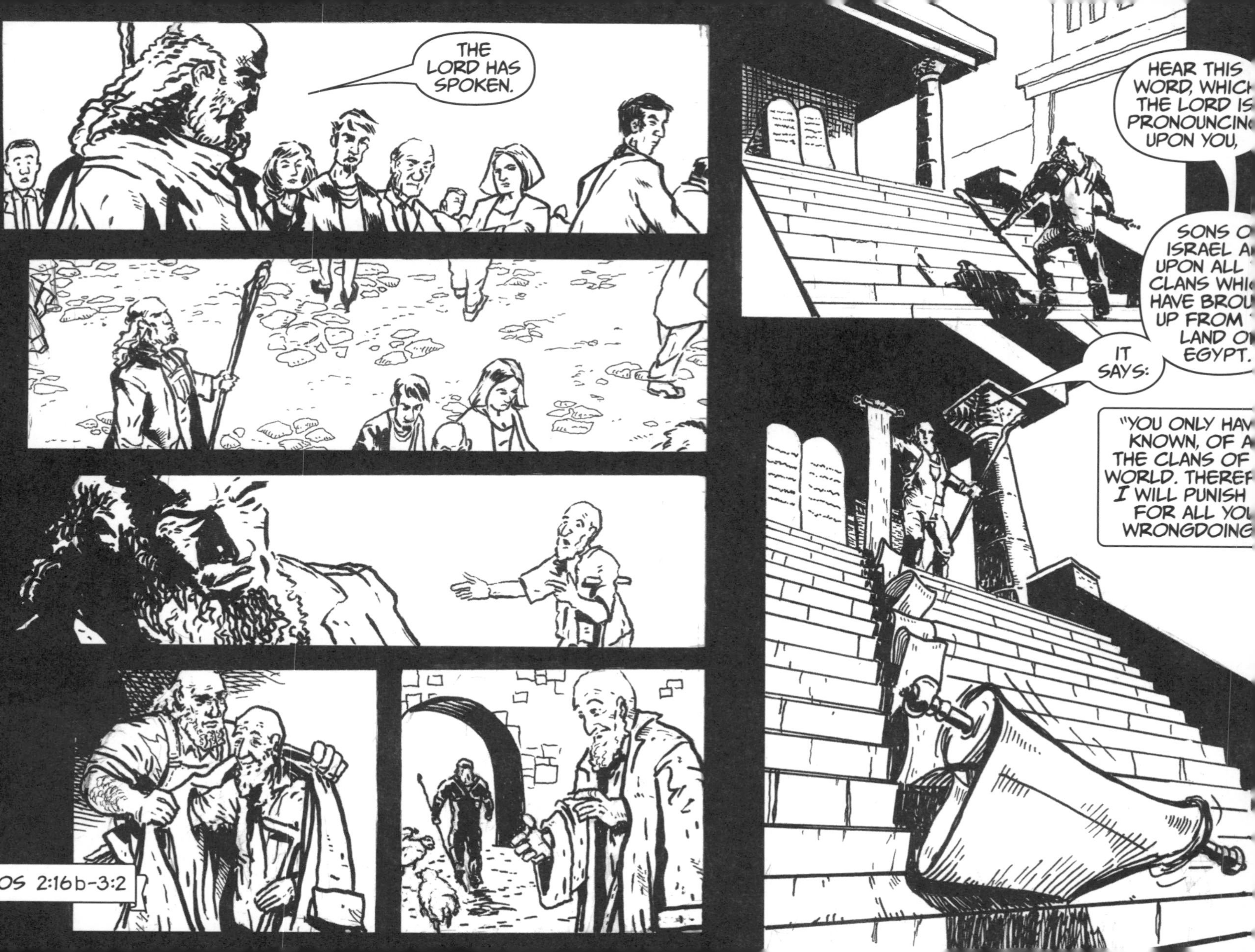

THE LORD HAS SPOKEN.
HEAR THIS WORD, WHIC THE LORD IS PRONOUNCIN UPON YOU,
SONS O ISRAEL A UPON ALL CLANS WHI HAVE BROU UP FROM LAND O EGYPT.
IT SAYS:
"YOU ONLY HAV KNOWN, OF A THE CLANS OF WORLD. THEREF I WILL PUNISH FOR ALL YO WRONGDOING

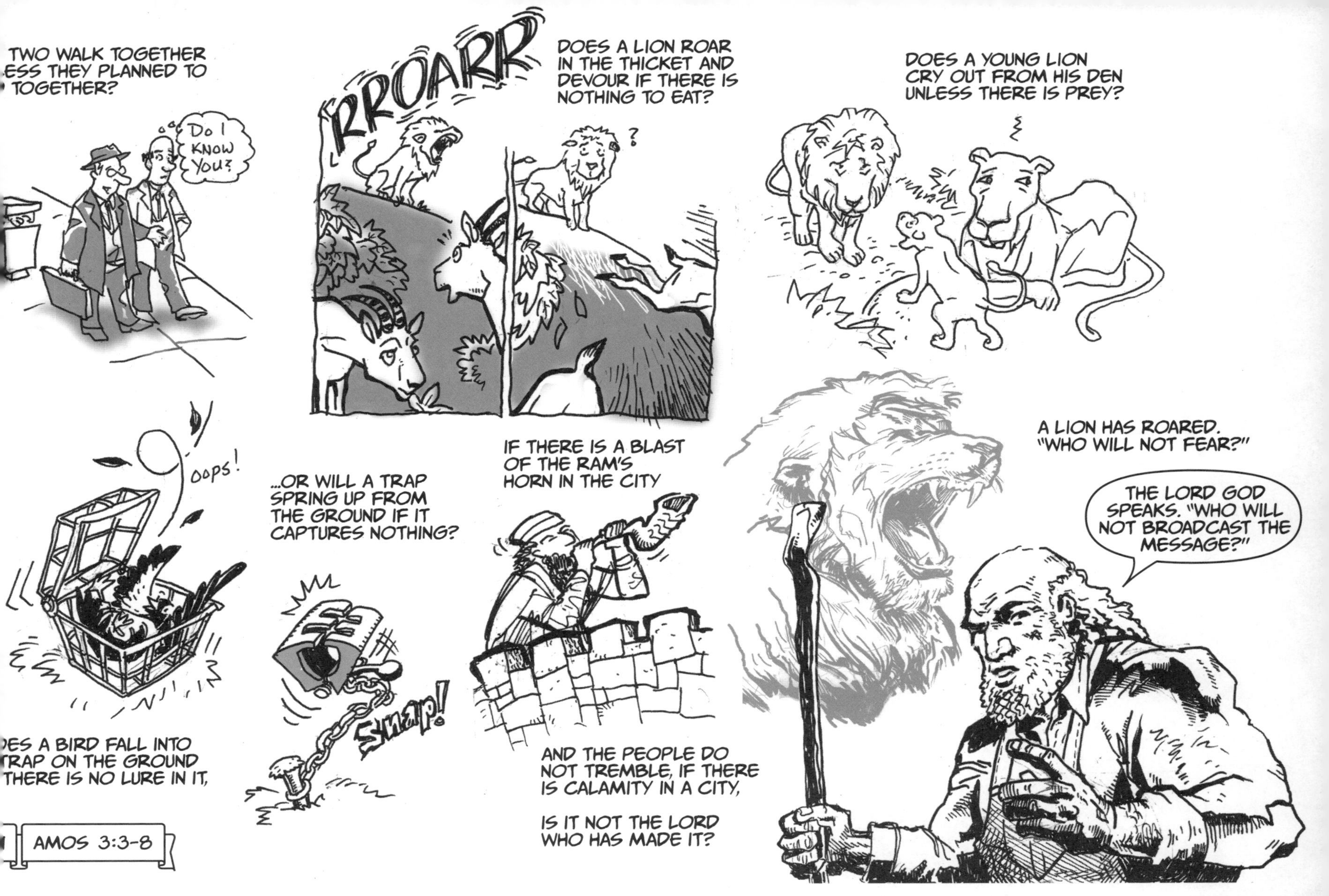
TWO WALK TOGETHER
ESS THEY PLANNED TO
TOGETHER?
Do I KNOW YOU?
RROARR
DOES A LION ROAR IN THE THICKET AND DEVOUR IF THERE IS NOTHING TO EAT?
?
DOES A YOUNG LION CRY OUT FROM HIS DEN UNLESS THERE IS PREY?
OOPS!
ES A BIRD FALL INTO
TRAP ON THE GROUND
THERE IS NO LURE IN IT,
...OR WILL A TRAP SPRING UP FROM THE GROUND IF IT CAPTURES NOTHING?
SNAP!
IF THERE IS A BLAST OF THE RAM'S HORN IN THE CITY
AND THE PEOPLE DO NOT TREMBLE, IF THERE IS CALAMITY IN A CITY,
IS IT NOT THE LORD WHO HAS MADE IT?
A LION HAS ROARED. "WHO WILL NOT FEAR?"
THE LORD GOD SPEAKS. "WHO WILL NOT BROADCAST THE MESSAGE?"
AMOS 3:3-8

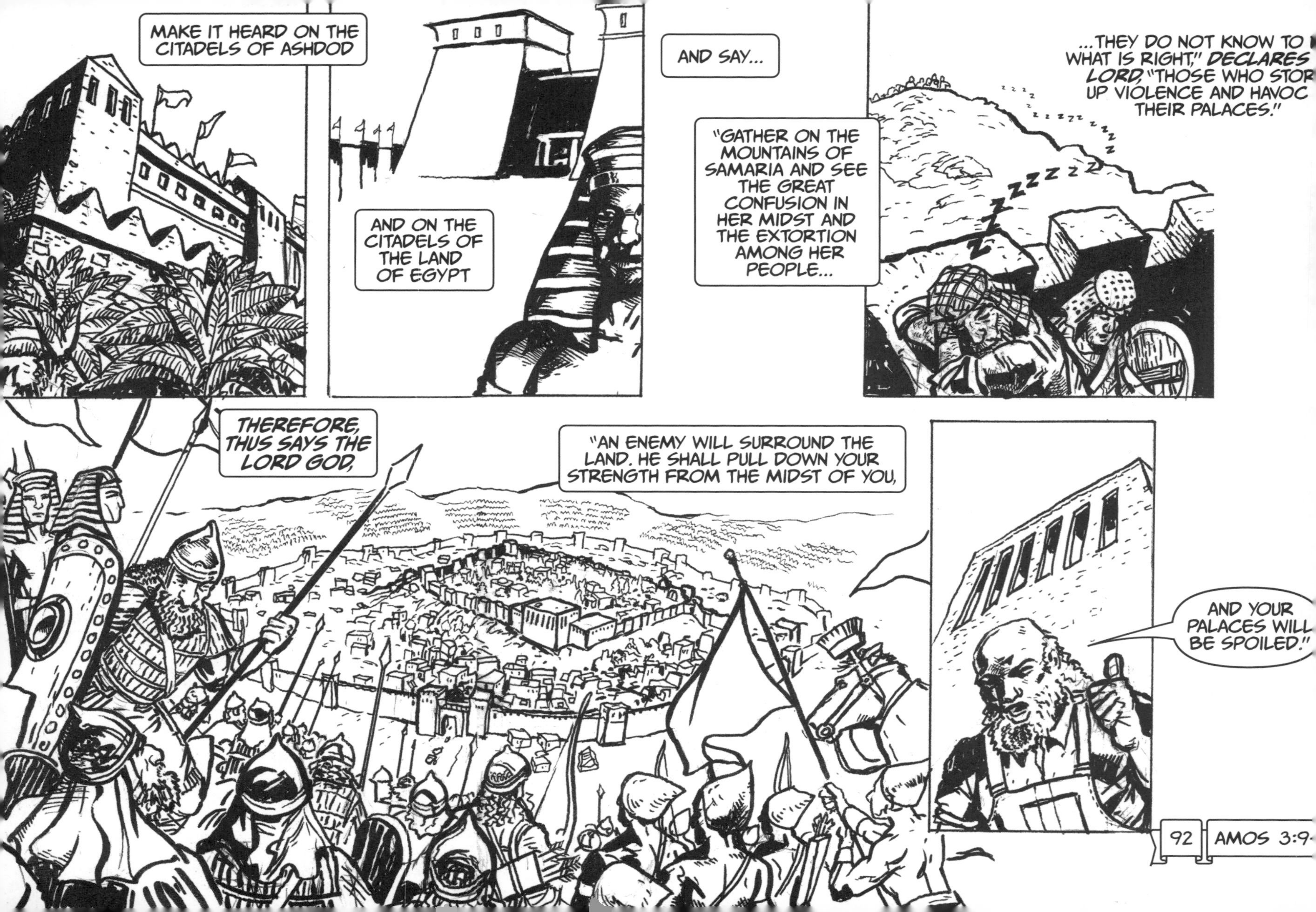
MAKE IT HEARD ON THE CITADELS OF ASHDOD
AND ON THE CITADELS OF THE LAND OF EGYPT
AND SAY...
"GATHER ON THE MOUNTAINS OF SAMARIA AND SEE THE GREAT CONFUSION IN HER MIDST AND THE EXTORTION AMONG HER PEOPLE...
...THEY DO NOT KNOW TO WHAT IS RIGHT," DECLARES LORD, "THOSE WHO STOR UP VIOLENCE AND HAVOC THEIR PALACES."
THEREFORE, THUS SAYS THE LORD GOD,
"AN ENEMY WILL SURROUND THE LAND. HE SHALL PULL DOWN YOUR STRENGTH FROM THE MIDST OF YOU,
AND YOUR PALACES WILL BE SPOILED."

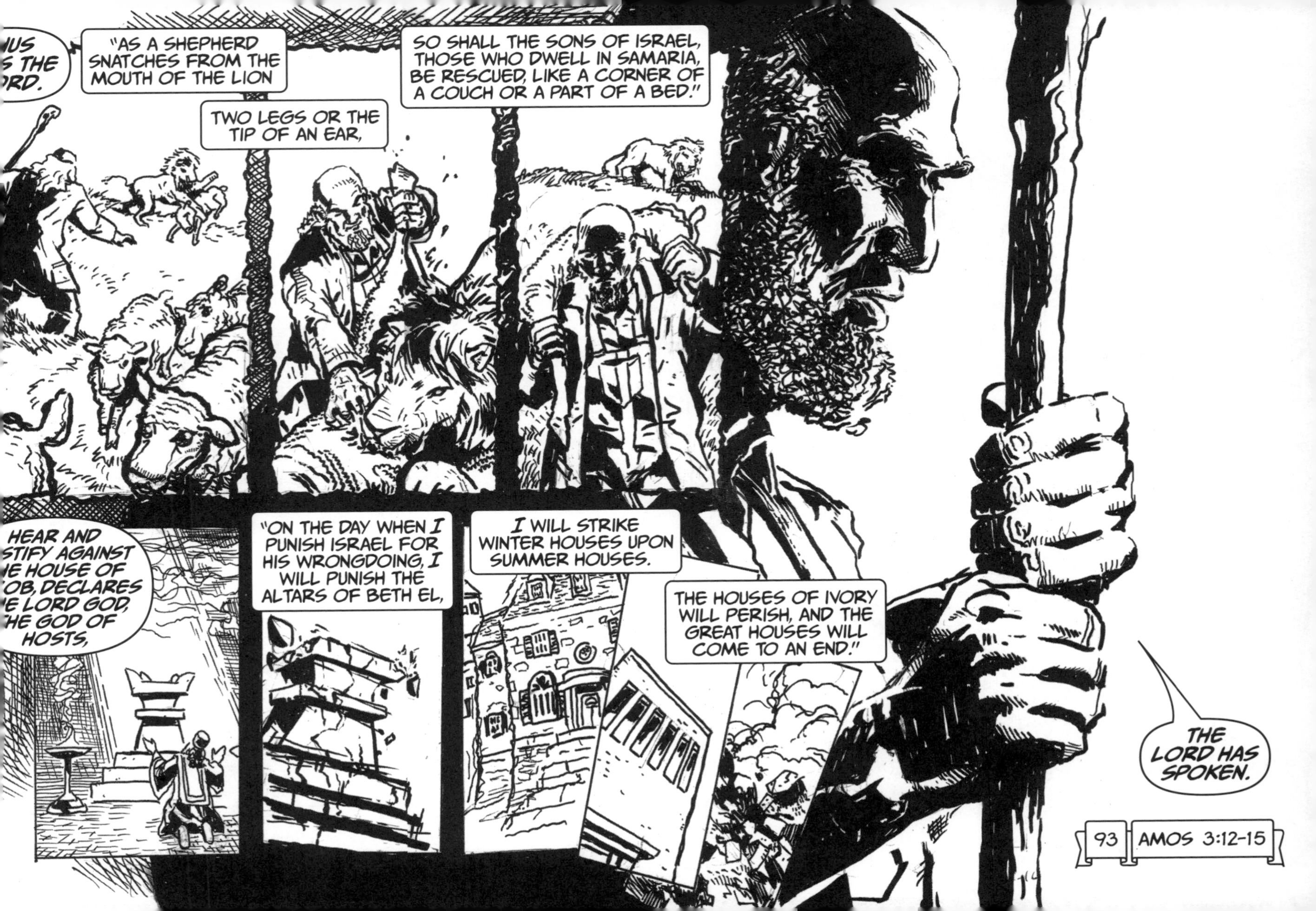

US
S THE
RD.
"AS A SHEPHERD SNATCHES FROM THE MOUTH OF THE LION
TWO LEGS OR THE TIP OF AN EAR,
SO SHALL THE SONS OF ISRAEL, THOSE WHO DWELL IN SAMARIA, BE RESCUED, LIKE A CORNER OF A COUCH OR A PART OF A BED."
HEAR AND STIFY AGAINST E HOUSE OF OB, DECLARES E LORD GOD, HE GOD OF HOSTS,
"ON THE DAY WHEN *I* PUNISH ISRAEL FOR HIS WRONGDOING, *I* WILL PUNISH THE ALTARS OF BETH EL,
I WILL STRIKE WINTER HOUSES UPON SUMMER HOUSES.
THE HOUSES OF IVORY WILL PERISH, AND THE GREAT HOUSES WILL COME TO AN END."
THE LORD HAS SPOKEN.

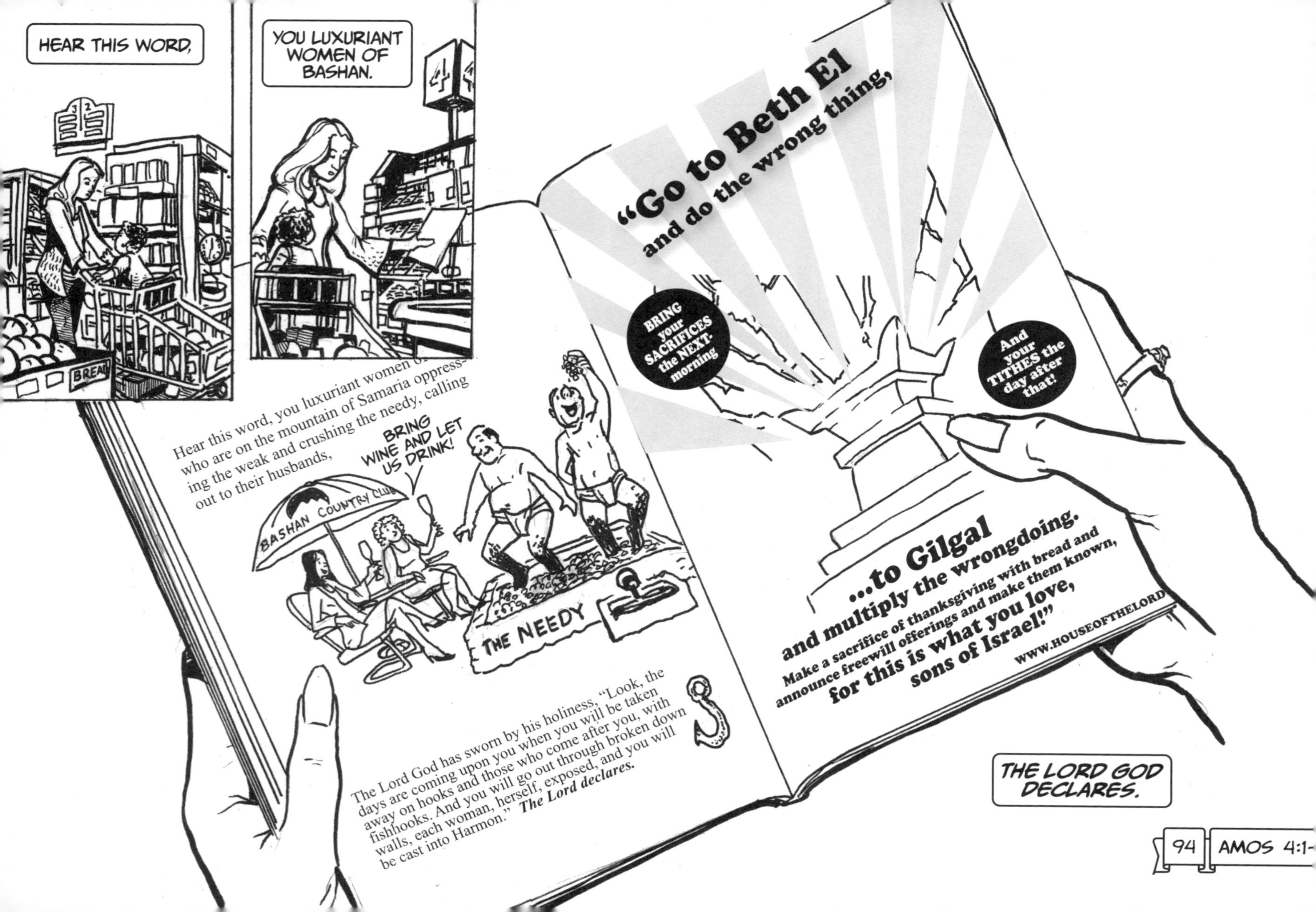

HEAR THIS WORD,
YOU LUXURIANT WOMEN OF BASHAN.
BREAD
Hear this word, you luxuriant women of Bashan who are on the mountain of Samaria oppressing the weak and crushing the needy, calling out to their husbands,
BRING WINE AND LET US DRINK!
BASHAN COUNTRY CLUB
THE NEEDY
The Lord God has sworn by his holiness, "Look, the days are coming upon you when you will be taken away on hooks and those who come after you, with fishhooks. And you will go out through broken down walls, each woman, herself, exposed, and you will be cast into Harmon." *The Lord declares.*
"Go to Beth El
and do the wrong thing,
BRING your SACRIFICES the NEXT-morning
And your TITHES the day after that!
...to Gilgal
and multiply the wrongdoing.
Make a sacrifice of thanksgiving with bread and announce freewill offerings and make them known,
for this is what you love, sons of Israel!"
WWW.HOUSEOFTHELORD
THE LORD GOD DECLARES.

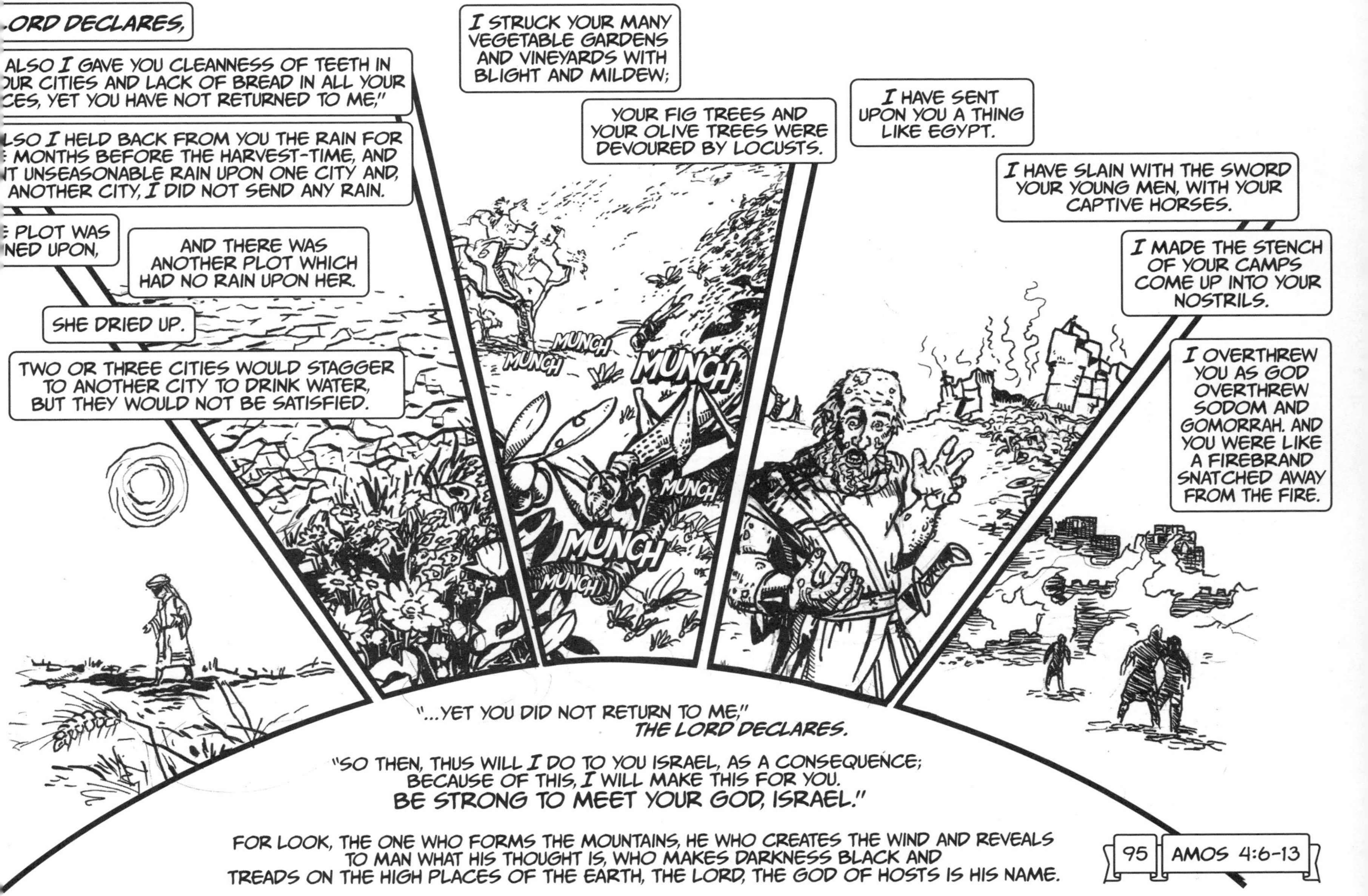

ORD DECLARES,
ALSO I GAVE YOU CLEANNESS OF TEETH IN OUR CITIES AND LACK OF BREAD IN ALL YOUR CES, YET YOU HAVE NOT RETURNED TO ME,"
LSO I HELD BACK FROM YOU THE RAIN FOR MONTHS BEFORE THE HARVEST-TIME, AND IT UNSEASONABLE RAIN UPON ONE CITY AND, ANOTHER CITY, I DID NOT SEND ANY RAIN.
PLOT WAS NED UPON,
AND THERE WAS ANOTHER PLOT WHICH HAD NO RAIN UPON HER.
SHE DRIED UP.
TWO OR THREE CITIES WOULD STAGGER TO ANOTHER CITY TO DRINK WATER, BUT THEY WOULD NOT BE SATISFIED.
I STRUCK YOUR MANY VEGETABLE GARDENS AND VINEYARDS WITH BLIGHT AND MILDEW;
YOUR FIG TREES AND YOUR OLIVE TREES WERE DEVOURED BY LOCUSTS.
MUNCH
MUNCH
MUNCH
MUNCH
MUNCH
MUNCH
I HAVE SENT UPON YOU A THING LIKE EGYPT.
I HAVE SLAIN WITH THE SWORD YOUR YOUNG MEN, WITH YOUR CAPTIVE HORSES.
I MADE THE STENCH OF YOUR CAMPS COME UP INTO YOUR NOSTRILS.
I OVERTHREW YOU AS GOD OVERTHREW SODOM AND GOMORRAH. AND YOU WERE LIKE A FIREBRAND SNATCHED AWAY FROM THE FIRE.
"...YET YOU DID NOT RETURN TO ME," THE LORD DECLARES.
"SO THEN, THUS WILL I DO TO YOU ISRAEL, AS A CONSEQUENCE; BECAUSE OF THIS, I WILL MAKE THIS FOR YOU.
BE STRONG TO MEET YOUR GOD, ISRAEL."
FOR LOOK, THE ONE WHO FORMS THE MOUNTAINS, HE WHO CREATES THE WIND AND REVEALS TO MAN WHAT HIS THOUGHT IS, WHO MAKES DARKNESS BLACK AND TREADS ON THE HIGH PLACES OF THE EARTH, THE LORD, THE GOD OF HOSTS IS HIS NAME.

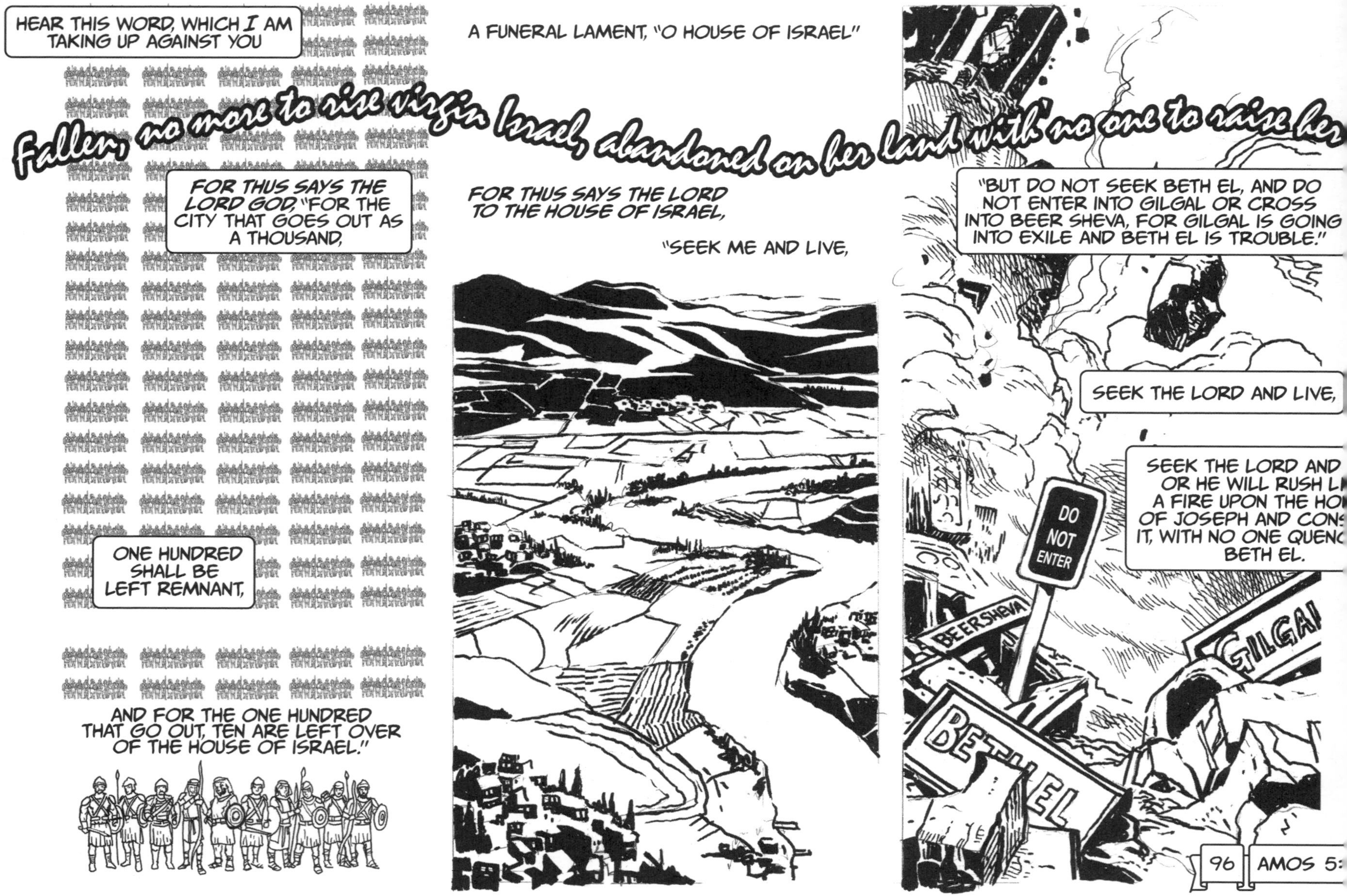
HEAR THIS WORD, WHICH I AM TAKING UP AGAINST YOU
A FUNERAL LAMENT, "O HOUSE OF ISRAEL"
Fallen, no more to rise virgin Israel, abandoned on her land with no one to raise her
FOR THUS SAYS THE LORD GOD, "FOR THE CITY THAT GOES OUT AS A THOUSAND,
ONE HUNDRED SHALL BE LEFT REMNANT,
AND FOR THE ONE HUNDRED THAT GO OUT, TEN ARE LEFT OVER OF THE HOUSE OF ISRAEL."
FOR THUS SAYS THE LORD TO THE HOUSE OF ISRAEL,
"SEEK ME AND LIVE,
"BUT DO NOT SEEK BETH EL, AND DO NOT ENTER INTO GILGAL OR CROSS INTO BEER SHEVA, FOR GILGAL IS GOING INTO EXILE AND BETH EL IS TROUBLE."
SEEK THE LORD AND LIVE,
SEEK THE LORD AND
OR HE WILL RUSH L
A FIRE UPON THE HO
OF JOSEPH AND CONS
IT, WITH NO ONE QUENC
BETH EL.
DO NOT ENTER
BEERSHEVA
GILGA
BETHEL

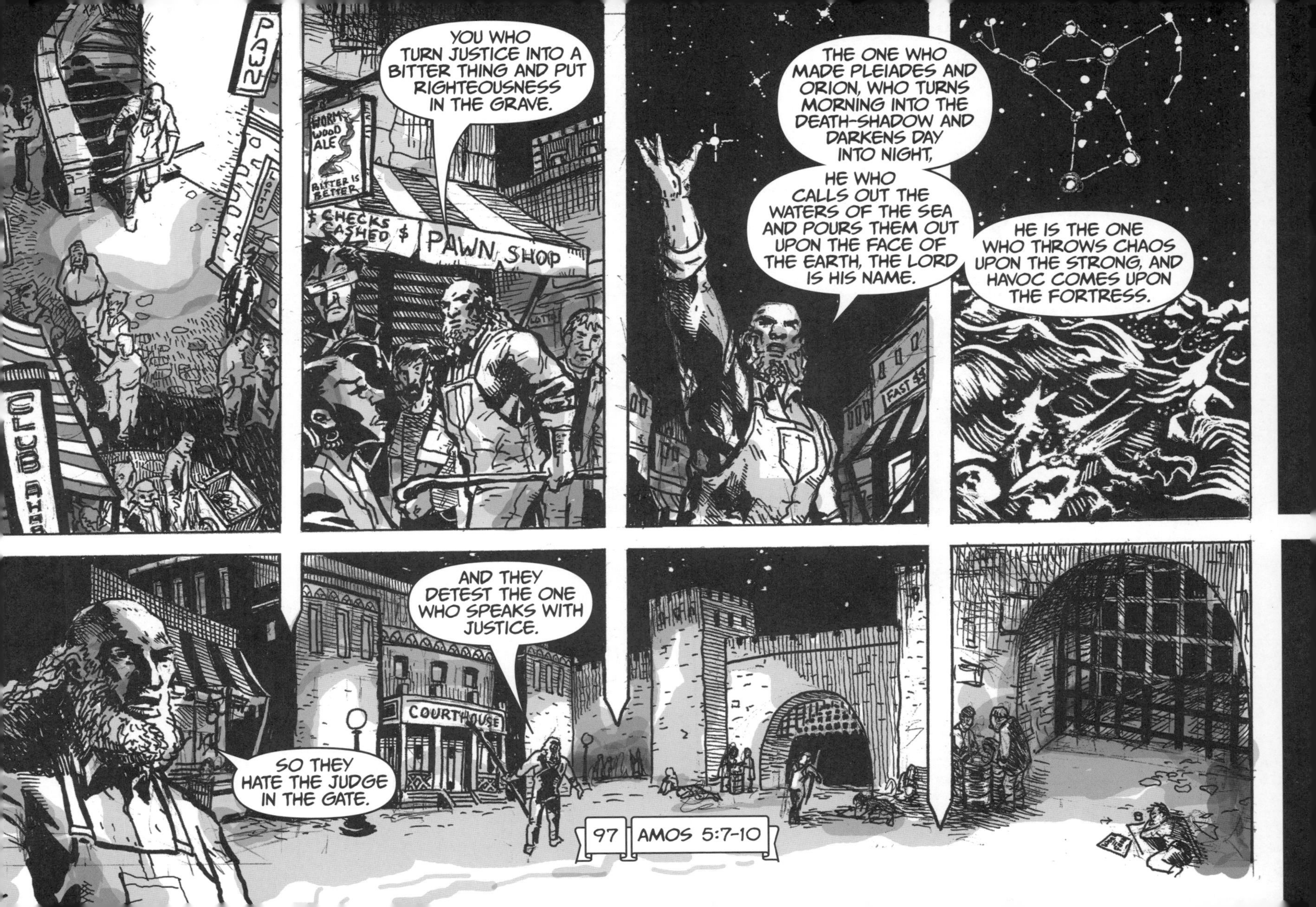
PAWN
LOTTO
WORM WOOD ALE
BITTER IS BETTER
$ CHECKS CASHED $
PAWN SHOP
YOU WHO TURN JUSTICE INTO A BITTER THING AND PUT RIGHTEOUSNESS IN THE GRAVE.
THE ONE WHO MADE PLEIADES AND ORION, WHO TURNS MORNING INTO THE DEATH-SHADOW AND DARKENS DAY INTO NIGHT,
HE WHO CALLS OUT THE WATERS OF THE SEA AND POURS THEM OUT UPON THE FACE OF THE EARTH, THE LORD IS HIS NAME.
FAST $$
HE IS THE ONE WHO THROWS CHAOS UPON THE STRONG, AND HAVOC COMES UPON THE FORTRESS.
COURTHOUSE
AND THEY DETEST THE ONE WHO SPEAKS WITH JUSTICE.
SO THEY HATE THE JUDGE IN THE GATE.

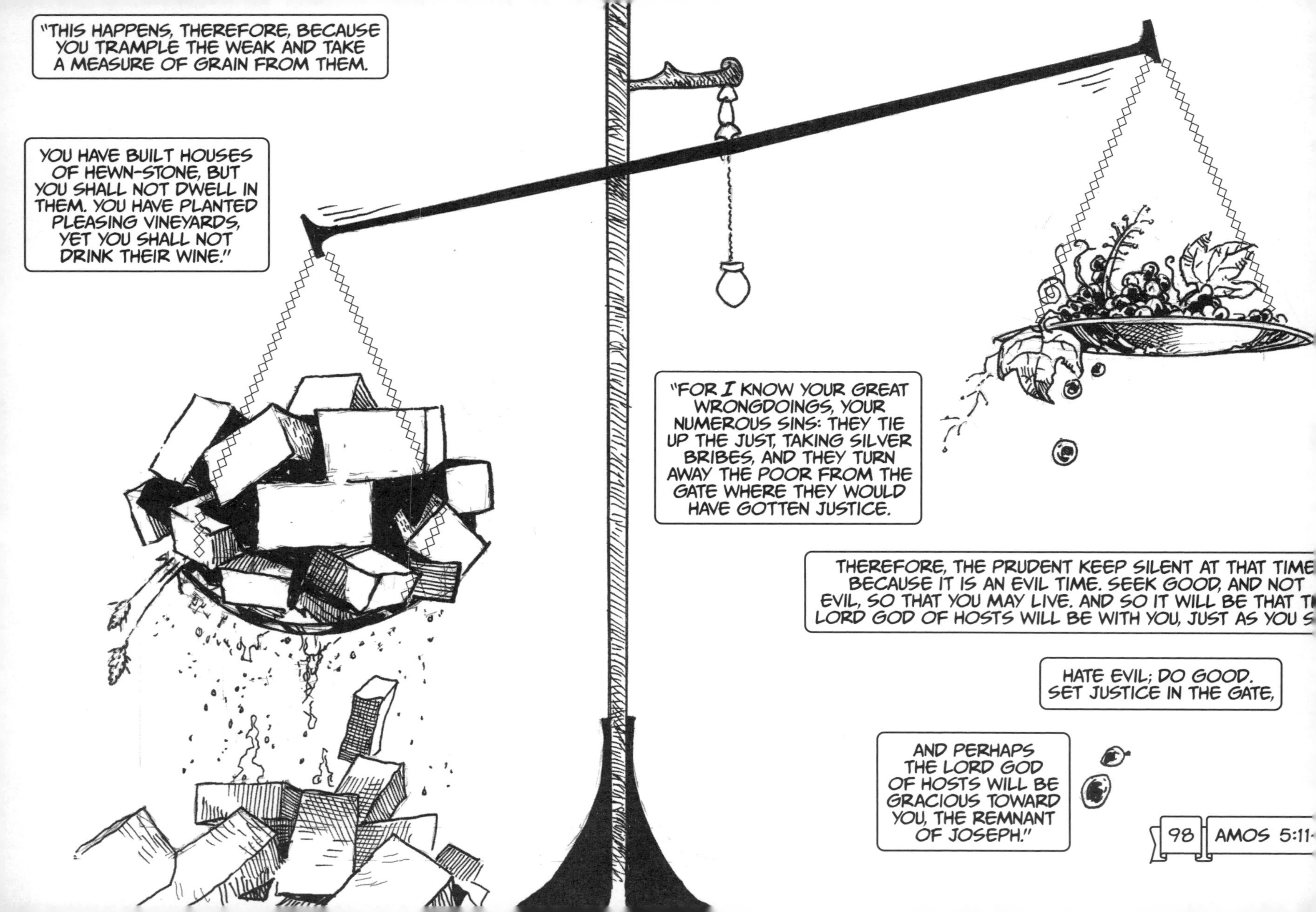
"THIS HAPPENS, THEREFORE, BECAUSE YOU TRAMPLE THE WEAK AND TAKE A MEASURE OF GRAIN FROM THEM.
YOU HAVE BUILT HOUSES OF HEWN-STONE, BUT YOU SHALL NOT DWELL IN THEM. YOU HAVE PLANTED PLEASING VINEYARDS, YET YOU SHALL NOT DRINK THEIR WINE."
"FOR *I* KNOW YOUR GREAT WRONGDOINGS, YOUR NUMEROUS SINS: THEY TIE UP THE JUST, TAKING SILVER BRIBES, AND THEY TURN AWAY THE POOR FROM THE GATE WHERE THEY WOULD HAVE GOTTEN JUSTICE.
THEREFORE, THE PRUDENT KEEP SILENT AT THAT TIME BECAUSE IT IS AN EVIL TIME. SEEK GOOD, AND NOT EVIL, SO THAT YOU MAY LIVE. AND SO IT WILL BE THAT T LORD GOD OF HOSTS WILL BE WITH YOU, JUST AS YOU S
HATE EVIL; DO GOOD. SET JUSTICE IN THE GATE,
AND PERHAPS THE LORD GOD OF HOSTS WILL BE GRACIOUS TOWARD YOU, THE REMNANT OF JOSEPH."

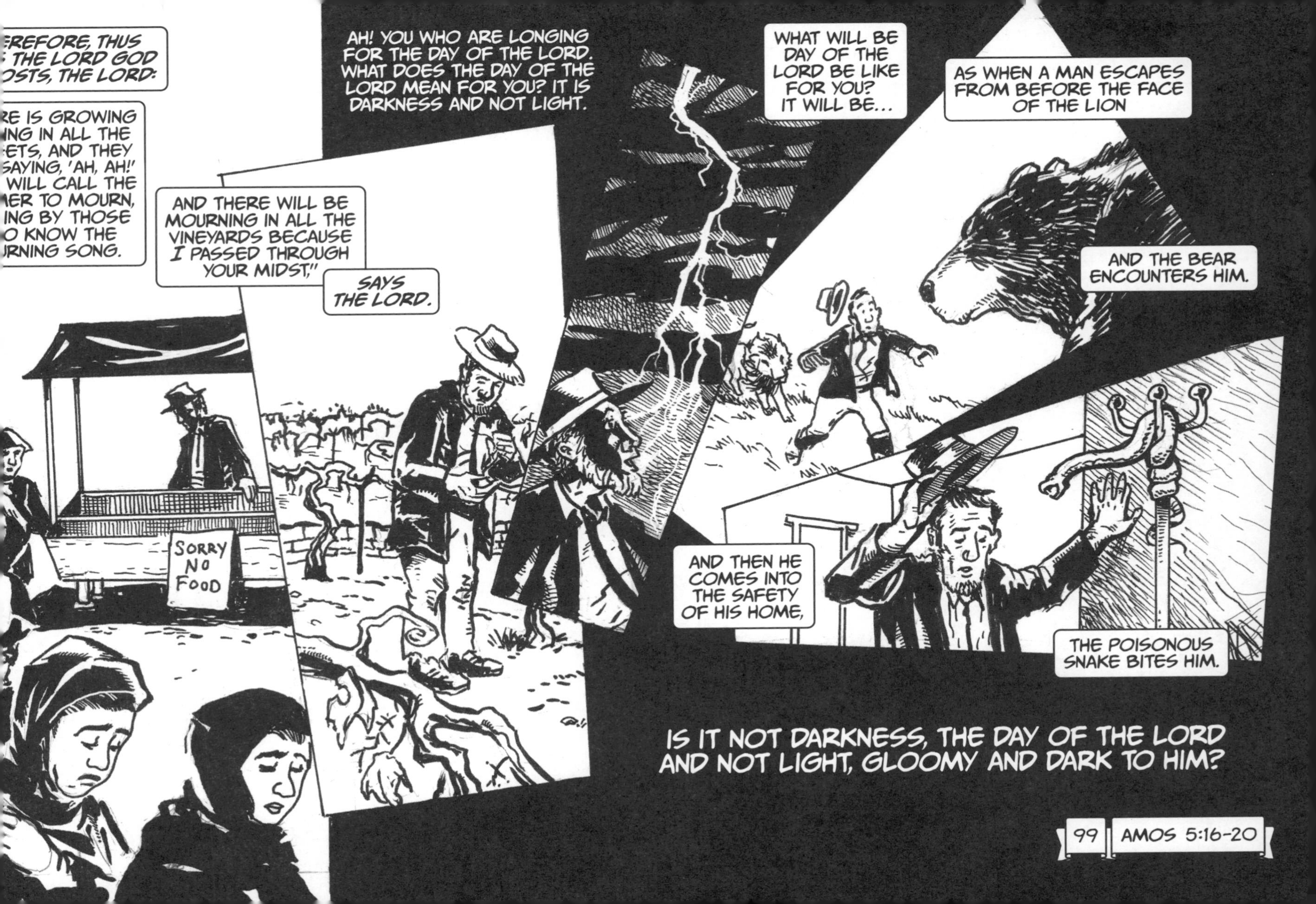

EREFORE, THUS
THE LORD GOD
OSTS, THE LORD:
RE IS GROWING
ING IN ALL THE
ETS, AND THEY
SAYING, 'AH, AH!'
WILL CALL THE
IER TO MOURN,
ING BY THOSE
O KNOW THE
RNING SONG.
SORRY NO FOOD
AND THERE WILL BE MOURNING IN ALL THE VINEYARDS BECAUSE I PASSED THROUGH YOUR MIDST,"
SAYS THE LORD.
AH! YOU WHO ARE LONGING FOR THE DAY OF THE LORD. WHAT DOES THE DAY OF THE LORD MEAN FOR YOU? IT IS DARKNESS AND NOT LIGHT.
WHAT WILL BE DAY OF THE LORD BE LIKE FOR YOU? IT WILL BE...
AS WHEN A MAN ESCAPES FROM BEFORE THE FACE OF THE LION
AND THE BEAR ENCOUNTERS HIM.
AND THEN HE COMES INTO THE SAFETY OF HIS HOME,
THE POISONOUS SNAKE BITES HIM.
IS IT NOT DARKNESS, THE DAY OF THE LORD AND NOT LIGHT, GLOOMY AND DARK TO HIM?

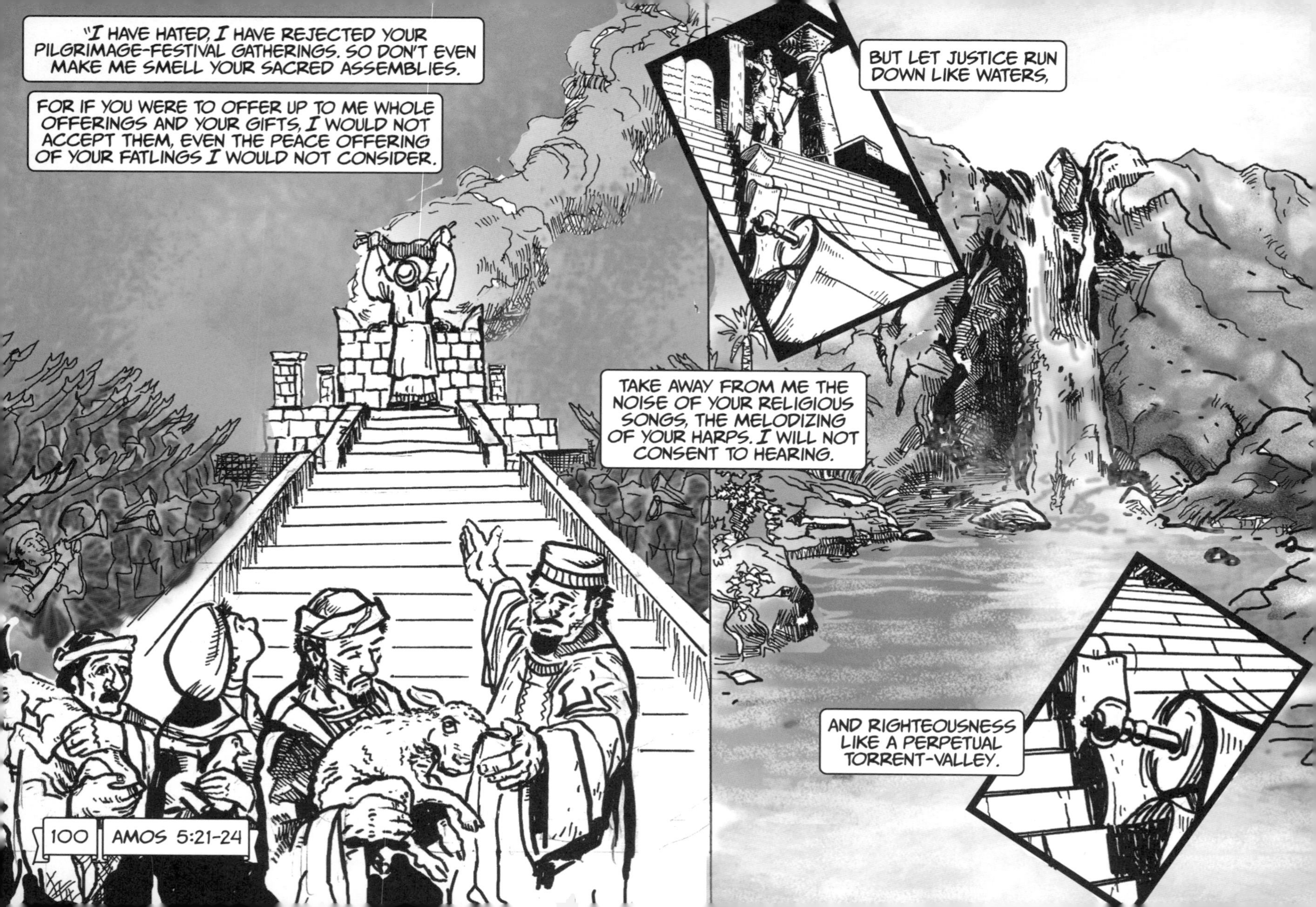
"I HAVE HATED, I HAVE REJECTED YOUR PILGRIMAGE-FESTIVAL GATHERINGS. SO DON'T EVEN MAKE ME SMELL YOUR SACRED ASSEMBLIES.
FOR IF YOU WERE TO OFFER UP TO ME WHOLE OFFERINGS AND YOUR GIFTS, I WOULD NOT ACCEPT THEM, EVEN THE PEACE OFFERING OF YOUR FATLINGS I WOULD NOT CONSIDER.
TAKE AWAY FROM ME THE NOISE OF YOUR RELIGIOUS SONGS, THE MELODIZING OF YOUR HARPS. I WILL NOT CONSENT TO HEARING.
BUT LET JUSTICE RUN DOWN LIKE WATERS,
AND RIGHTEOUSNESS LIKE A PERPETUAL TORRENT-VALLEY.
100
AMOS 5:21-24

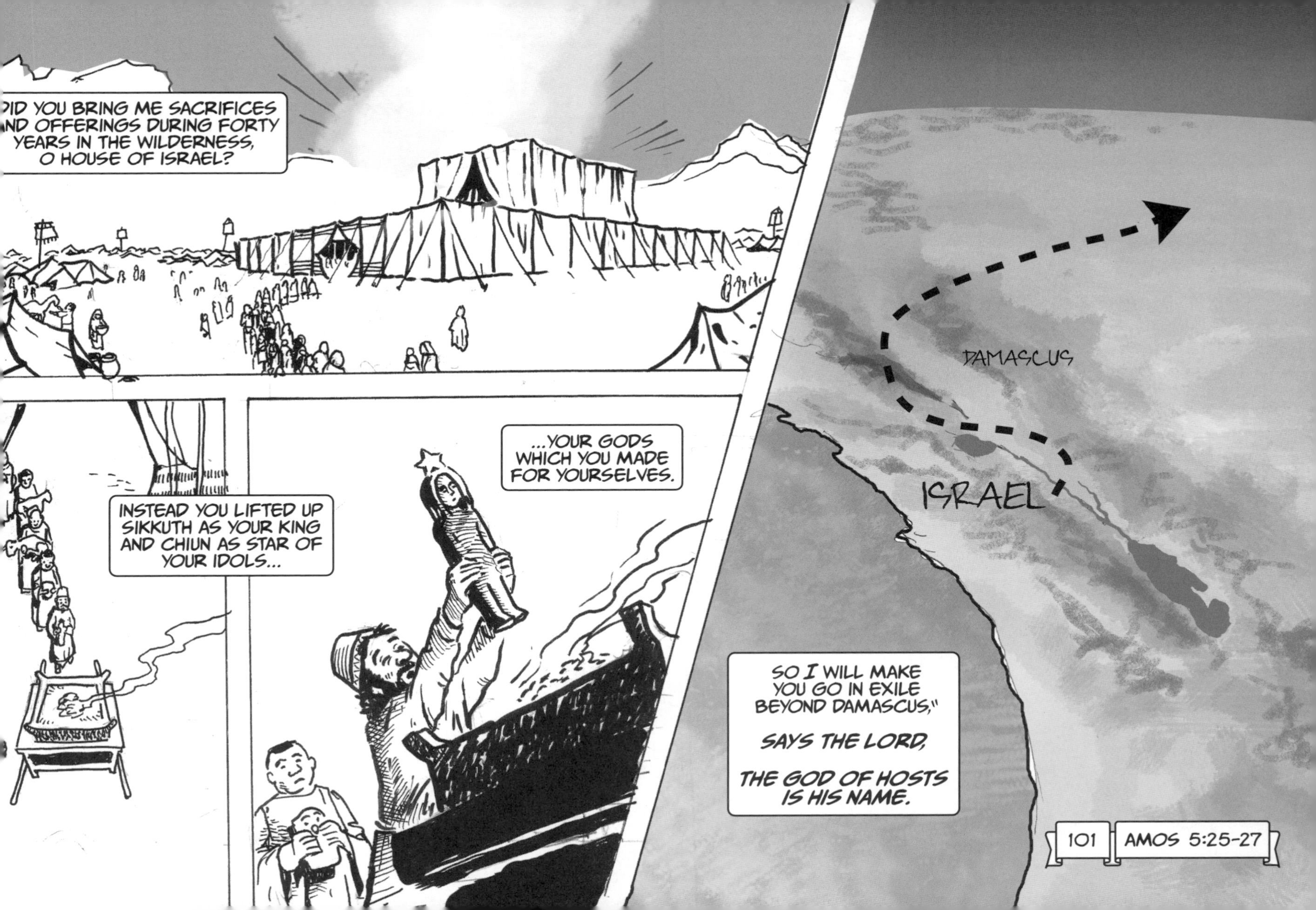
DID YOU BRING ME SACRIFICES AND OFFERINGS DURING FORTY YEARS IN THE WILDERNESS, O HOUSE OF ISRAEL?
INSTEAD YOU LIFTED UP SIKKUTH AS YOUR KING AND CHIUN AS STAR OF YOUR IDOLS...
...YOUR GODS WHICH YOU MADE FOR YOURSELVES.
DAMASCUS
ISRAEL
SO I WILL MAKE YOU GO IN EXILE BEYOND DAMASCUS,"
SAYS THE LORD,
THE GOD OF HOSTS IS HIS NAME.
101
AMOS 5:25-27

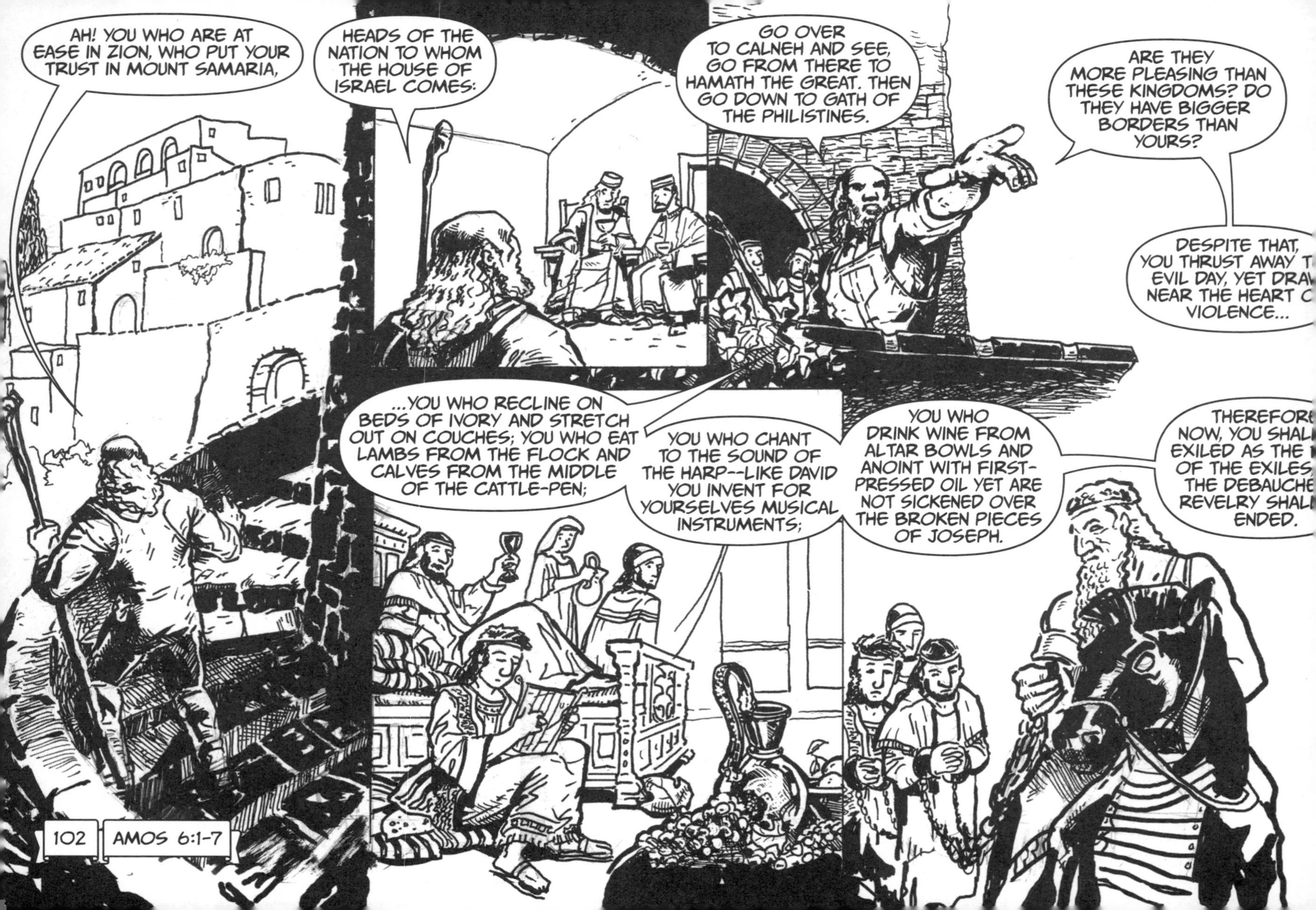
AH! YOU WHO ARE AT EASE IN ZION, WHO PUT YOUR TRUST IN MOUNT SAMARIA,
HEADS OF THE NATION TO WHOM THE HOUSE OF ISRAEL COMES:
GO OVER TO CALNEH AND SEE, GO FROM THERE TO HAMATH THE GREAT. THEN GO DOWN TO GATH OF THE PHILISTINES.
ARE THEY MORE PLEASING THAN THESE KINGDOMS? DO THEY HAVE BIGGER BORDERS THAN YOURS?
DESPITE THAT, YOU THRUST AWAY T EVIL DAY, YET DRAW NEAR THE HEART O VIOLENCE...
...YOU WHO RECLINE ON BEDS OF IVORY AND STRETCH OUT ON COUCHES; YOU WHO EAT LAMBS FROM THE FLOCK AND CALVES FROM THE MIDDLE OF THE CATTLE-PEN;
YOU WHO CHANT TO THE SOUND OF THE HARP--LIKE DAVID YOU INVENT FOR YOURSELVES MUSICAL INSTRUMENTS;
YOU WHO DRINK WINE FROM ALTAR BOWLS AND ANOINT WITH FIRST-PRESSED OIL YET ARE NOT SICKENED OVER THE BROKEN PIECES OF JOSEPH.
THEREFORE NOW, YOU SHALL EXILED AS THE OF THE EXILES THE DEBAUCHE REVELRY SHALL ENDED.

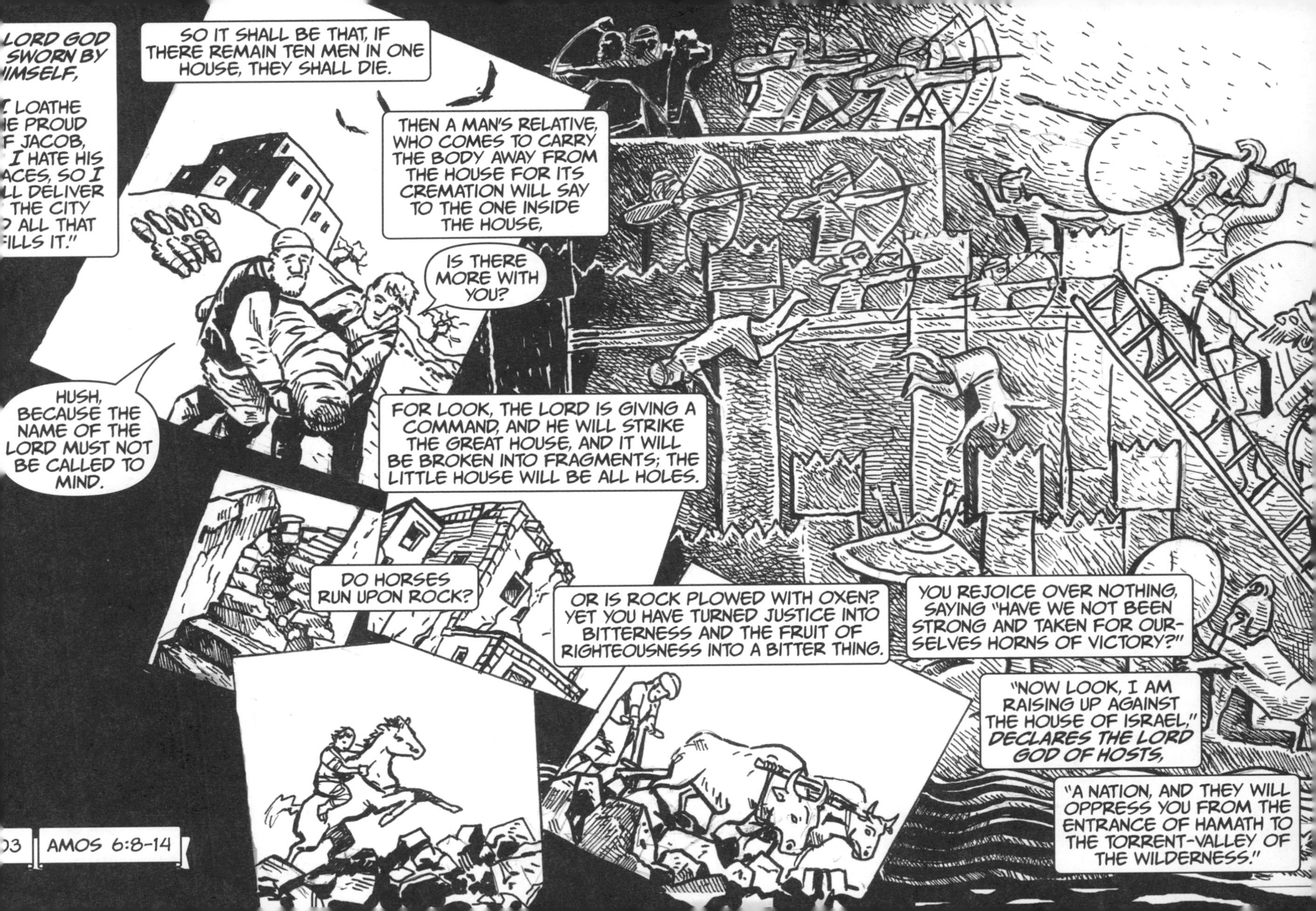
LORD GOD SWORN BY IMSELF,
T LOATHE IE PROUD F JACOB, I HATE HIS ACES, SO I LL DELIVER THE CITY D ALL THAT FILLS IT."
SO IT SHALL BE THAT, IF THERE REMAIN TEN MEN IN ONE HOUSE, THEY SHALL DIE.
THEN A MAN'S RELATIVE, WHO COMES TO CARRY THE BODY AWAY FROM THE HOUSE FOR ITS CREMATION WILL SAY TO THE ONE INSIDE THE HOUSE,
IS THERE MORE WITH YOU?
HUSH, BECAUSE THE NAME OF THE LORD MUST NOT BE CALLED TO MIND.
FOR LOOK, THE LORD IS GIVING A COMMAND, AND HE WILL STRIKE THE GREAT HOUSE, AND IT WILL BE BROKEN INTO FRAGMENTS; THE LITTLE HOUSE WILL BE ALL HOLES.
DO HORSES RUN UPON ROCK?
OR IS ROCK PLOWED WITH OXEN? YET YOU HAVE TURNED JUSTICE INTO BITTERNESS AND THE FRUIT OF RIGHTEOUSNESS INTO A BITTER THING.
YOU REJOICE OVER NOTHING, SAYING "HAVE WE NOT BEEN STRONG AND TAKEN FOR OURSELVES HORNS OF VICTORY?"
"NOW LOOK, I AM RAISING UP AGAINST THE HOUSE OF ISRAEL," DECLARES THE LORD GOD OF HOSTS,
"A NATION, AND THEY WILL OPPRESS YOU FROM THE ENTRANCE OF HAMATH TO THE TORRENT-VALLEY OF THE WILDERNESS."

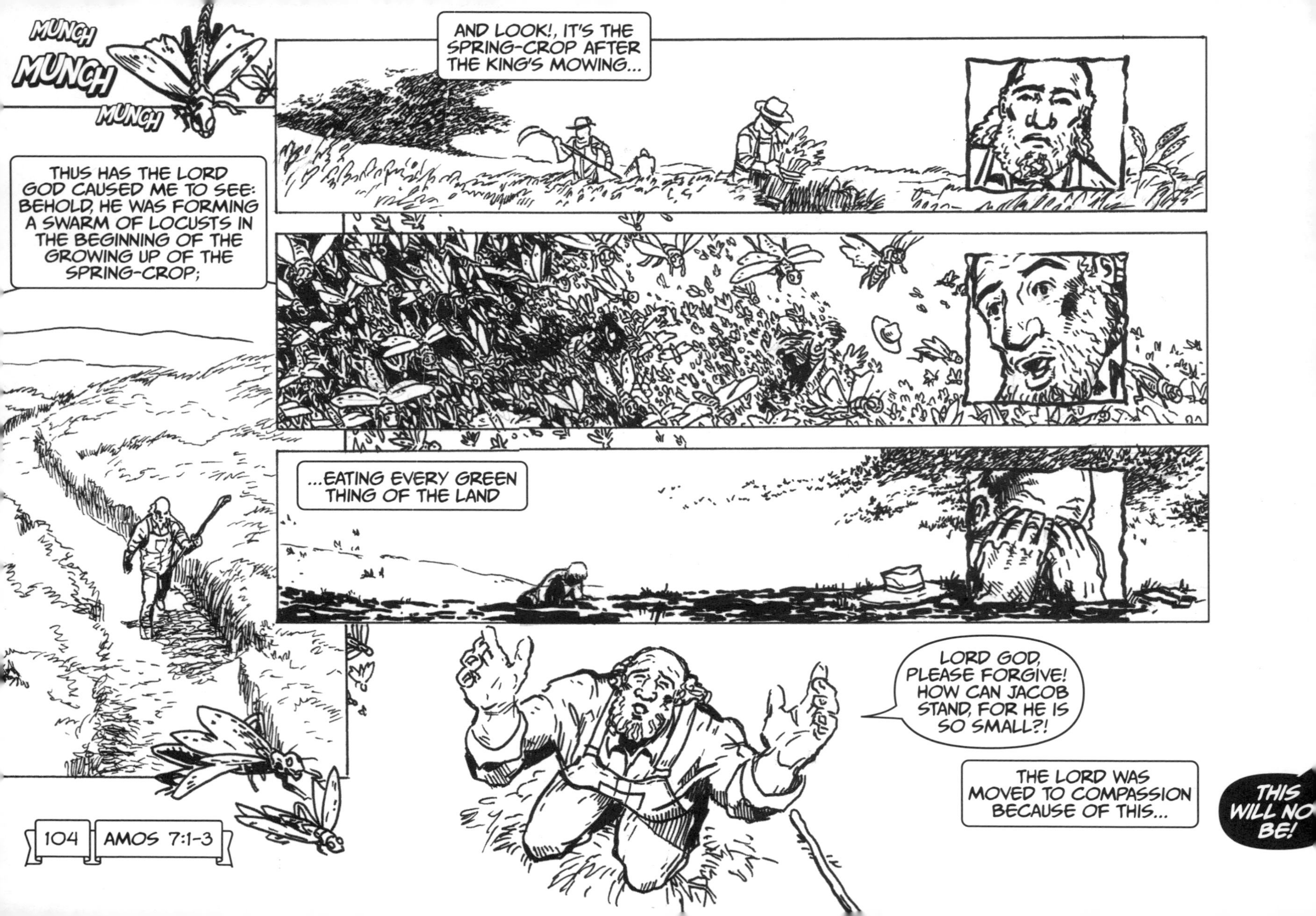

MUNCH
MUNCH
MUNCH
THUS HAS THE LORD GOD CAUSED ME TO SEE: BEHOLD, HE WAS FORMING A SWARM OF LOCUSTS IN THE BEGINNING OF THE GROWING UP OF THE SPRING-CROP;
AND LOOK!, IT'S THE SPRING-CROP AFTER THE KING'S MOWING...
...EATING EVERY GREEN THING OF THE LAND
LORD GOD, PLEASE FORGIVE! HOW CAN JACOB STAND, FOR HE IS SO SMALL?!
THE LORD WAS MOVED TO COMPASSION BECAUSE OF THIS...
THIS WILL NO BE!

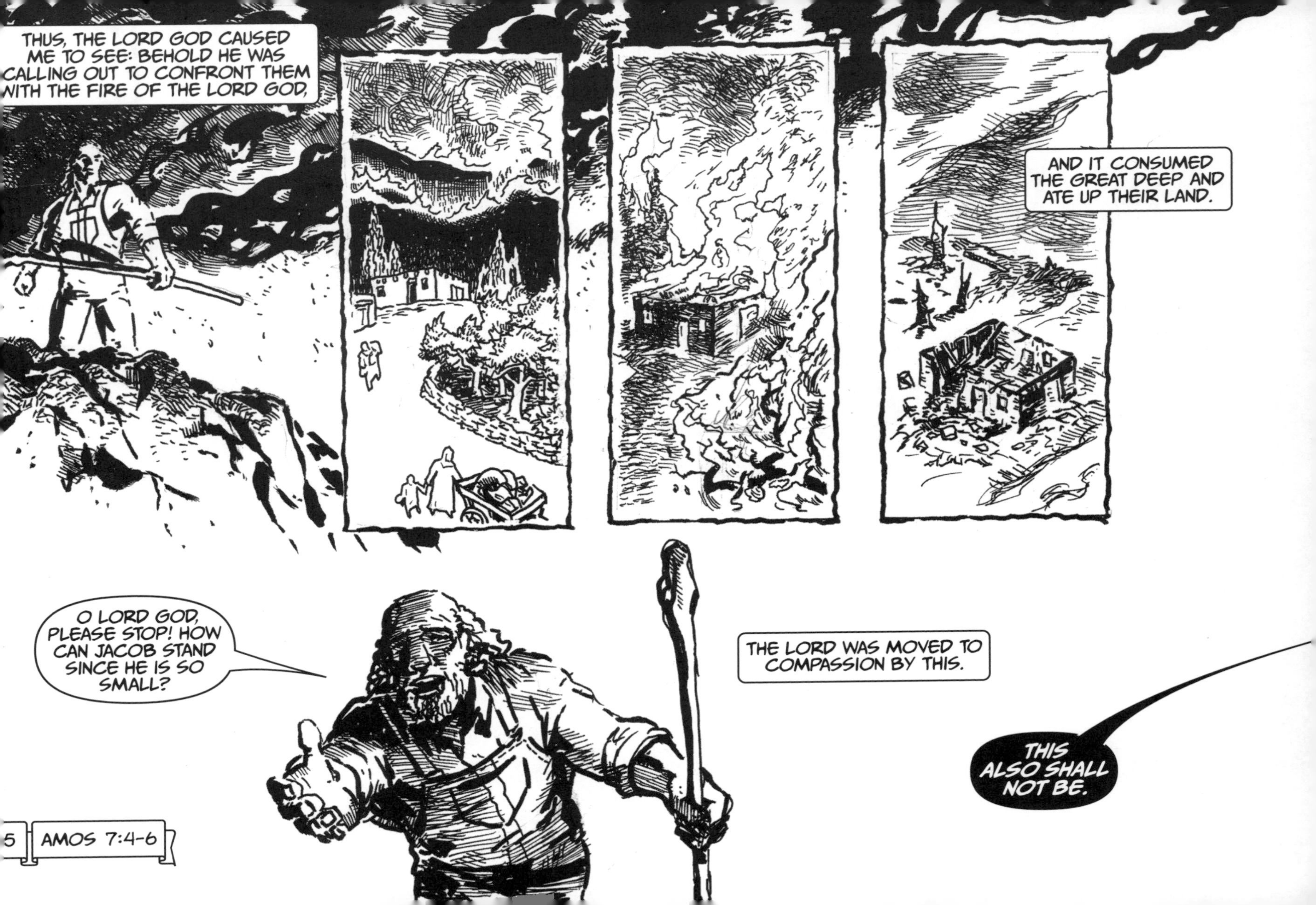
THUS, THE LORD GOD CAUSED ME TO SEE: BEHOLD HE WAS CALLING OUT TO CONFRONT THEM WITH THE FIRE OF THE LORD GOD,
AND IT CONSUMED THE GREAT DEEP AND ATE UP THEIR LAND.
O LORD GOD, PLEASE STOP! HOW CAN JACOB STAND SINCE HE IS SO SMALL?
THE LORD WAS MOVED TO COMPASSION BY THIS.
THIS ALSO SHALL NOT BE.
AMOS 7:4-6

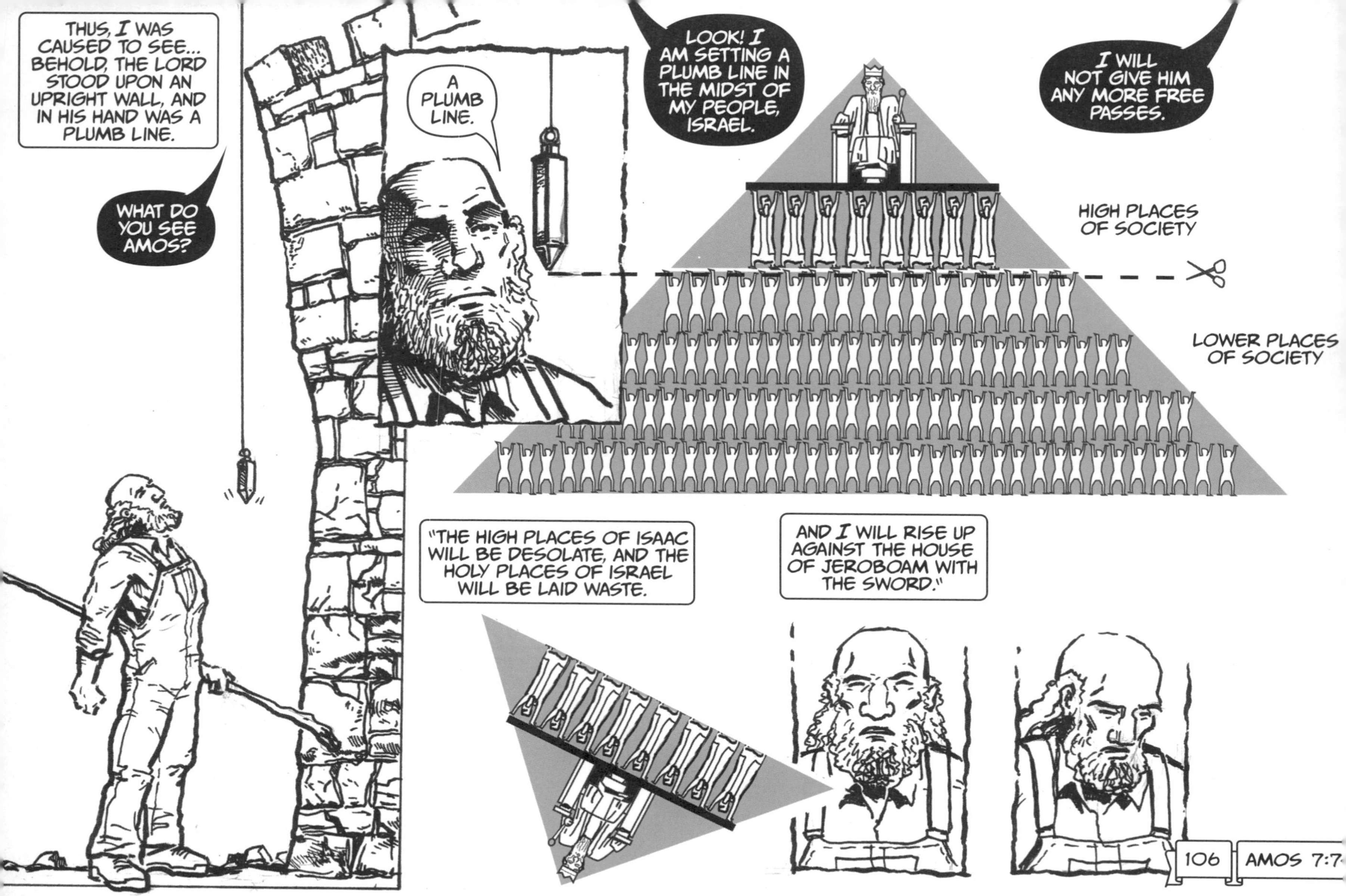
THUS, I WAS CAUSED TO SEE... BEHOLD, THE LORD STOOD UPON AN UPRIGHT WALL, AND IN HIS HAND WAS A PLUMB LINE.
WHAT DO YOU SEE AMOS?
A PLUMB LINE.
LOOK! I AM SETTING A PLUMB LINE IN THE MIDST OF MY PEOPLE, ISRAEL.
I WILL NOT GIVE HIM ANY MORE FREE PASSES.
HIGH PLACES OF SOCIETY
LOWER PLACES OF SOCIETY
"THE HIGH PLACES OF ISAAC WILL BE DESOLATE, AND THE HOLY PLACES OF ISRAEL WILL BE LAID WASTE.
AND I WILL RISE UP AGAINST THE HOUSE OF JEROBOAM WITH THE SWORD."

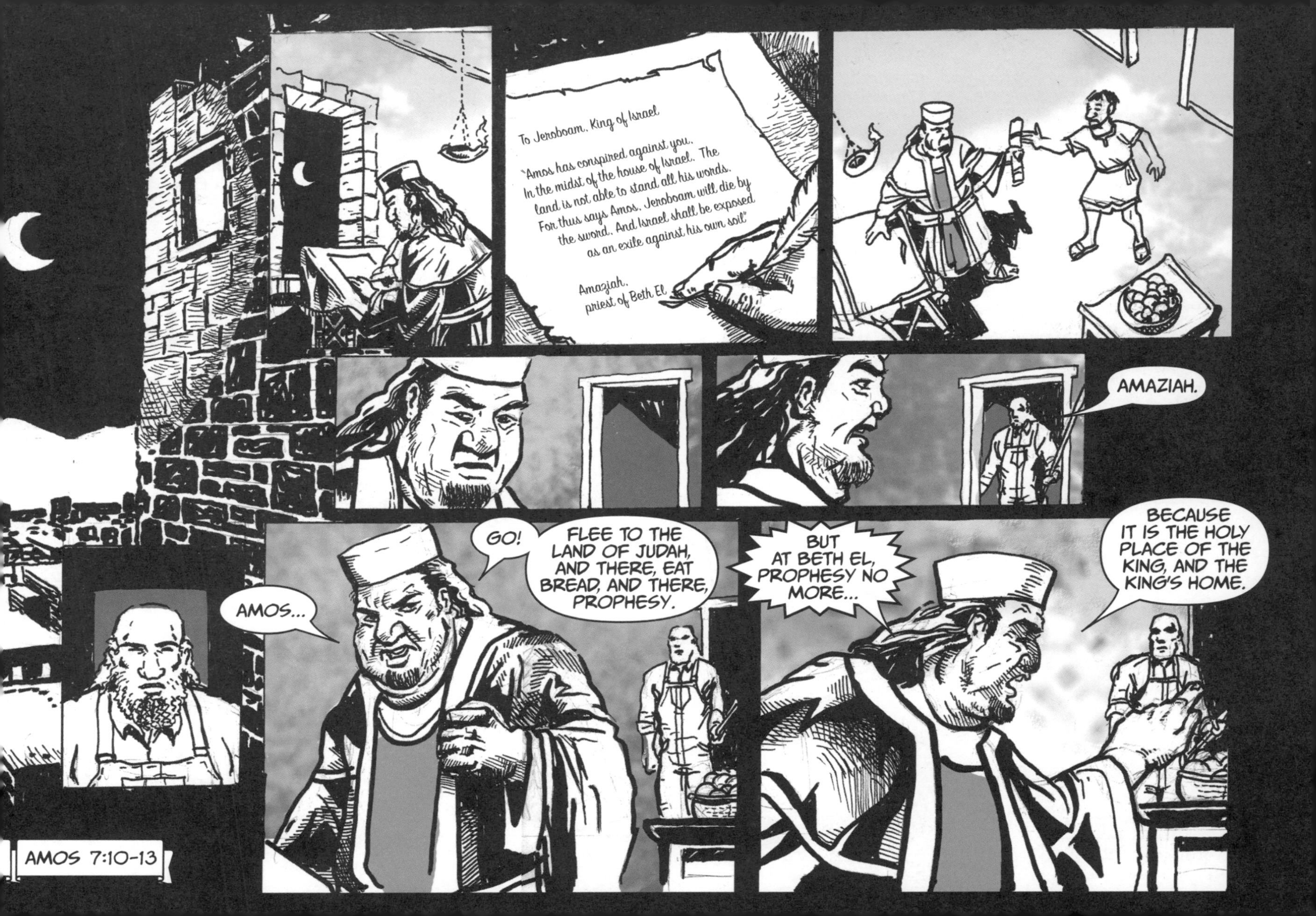

To Jeroboam, King of Israel
"Amos has conspired against you. In the midst of the house of Israel. The land is not able to stand all his words. For thus says Amos, Jeroboam will die by the sword, And Israel shall be exposed as an exile against his own soil"
Amaziah, priest of Beth El
AMAZIAH.
AMOS...
GO!
FLEE TO THE LAND OF JUDAH, AND THERE, EAT BREAD, AND THERE, PROPHESY.
BUT AT BETH EL, PROPHESY NO MORE...
BECAUSE IT IS THE HOLY PLACE OF THE KING, AND THE KING'S HOME.
AMOS 7:10-13

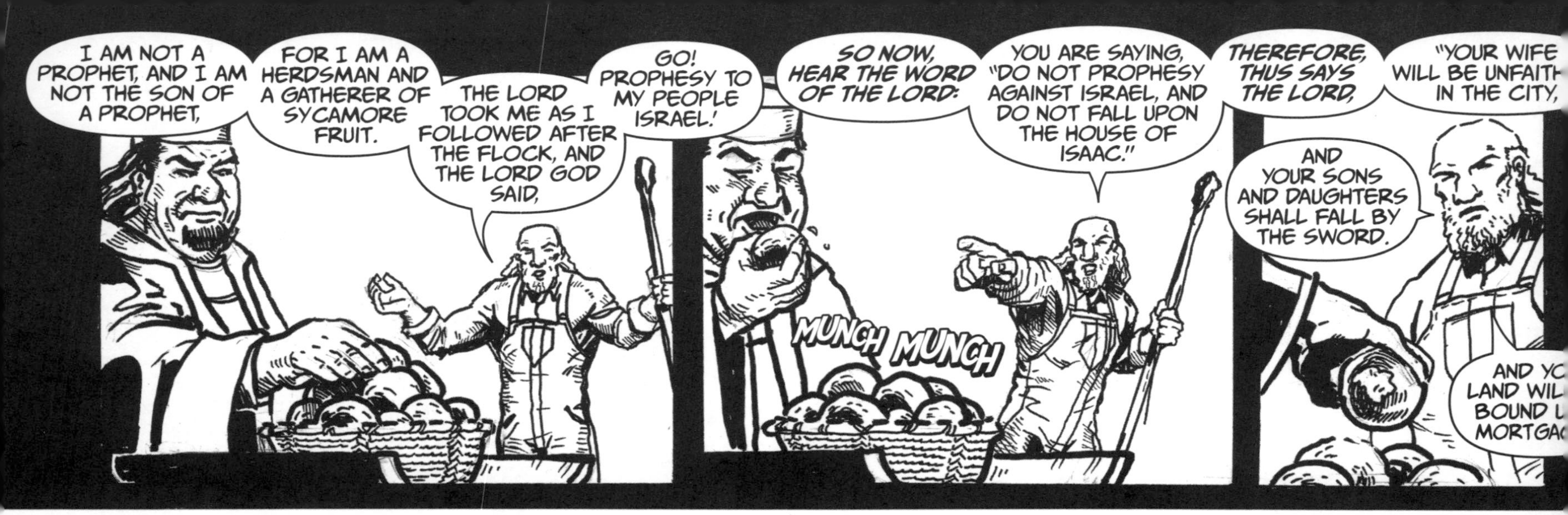
I AM NOT A PROPHET, AND I AM NOT THE SON OF A PROPHET,
FOR I AM A HERDSMAN AND A GATHERER OF SYCAMORE FRUIT.
THE LORD TOOK ME AS I FOLLOWED AFTER THE FLOCK, AND THE LORD GOD SAID,
GO! PROPHESY TO MY PEOPLE ISRAEL.'
SO NOW, HEAR THE WORD OF THE LORD:
YOU ARE SAYING, "DO NOT PROPHESY AGAINST ISRAEL, AND DO NOT FALL UPON THE HOUSE OF ISAAC."
MUNCH MUNCH
THEREFORE, THUS SAYS THE LORD,
"YOUR WIFE WILL BE UNFAITH IN THE CITY,
AND YOUR SONS AND DAUGHTERS SHALL FALL BY THE SWORD.
AND YO LAND WIL BOUND U MORTGA

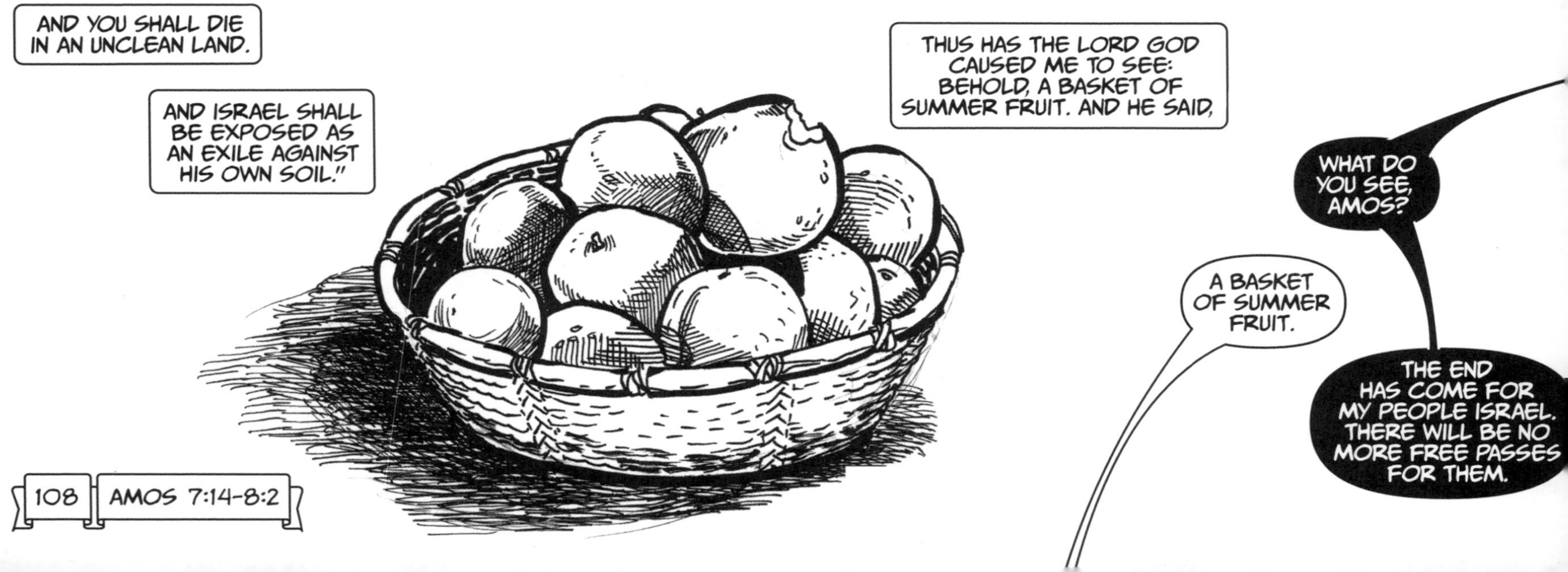
AND YOU SHALL DIE IN AN UNCLEAN LAND.
AND ISRAEL SHALL BE EXPOSED AS AN EXILE AGAINST HIS OWN SOIL."
THUS HAS THE LORD GOD CAUSED ME TO SEE: BEHOLD, A BASKET OF SUMMER FRUIT. AND HE SAID,
WHAT DO YOU SEE, AMOS?
A BASKET OF SUMMER FRUIT.
THE END HAS COME FOR MY PEOPLE ISRAEL. THERE WILL BE NO MORE FREE PASSES FOR THEM.

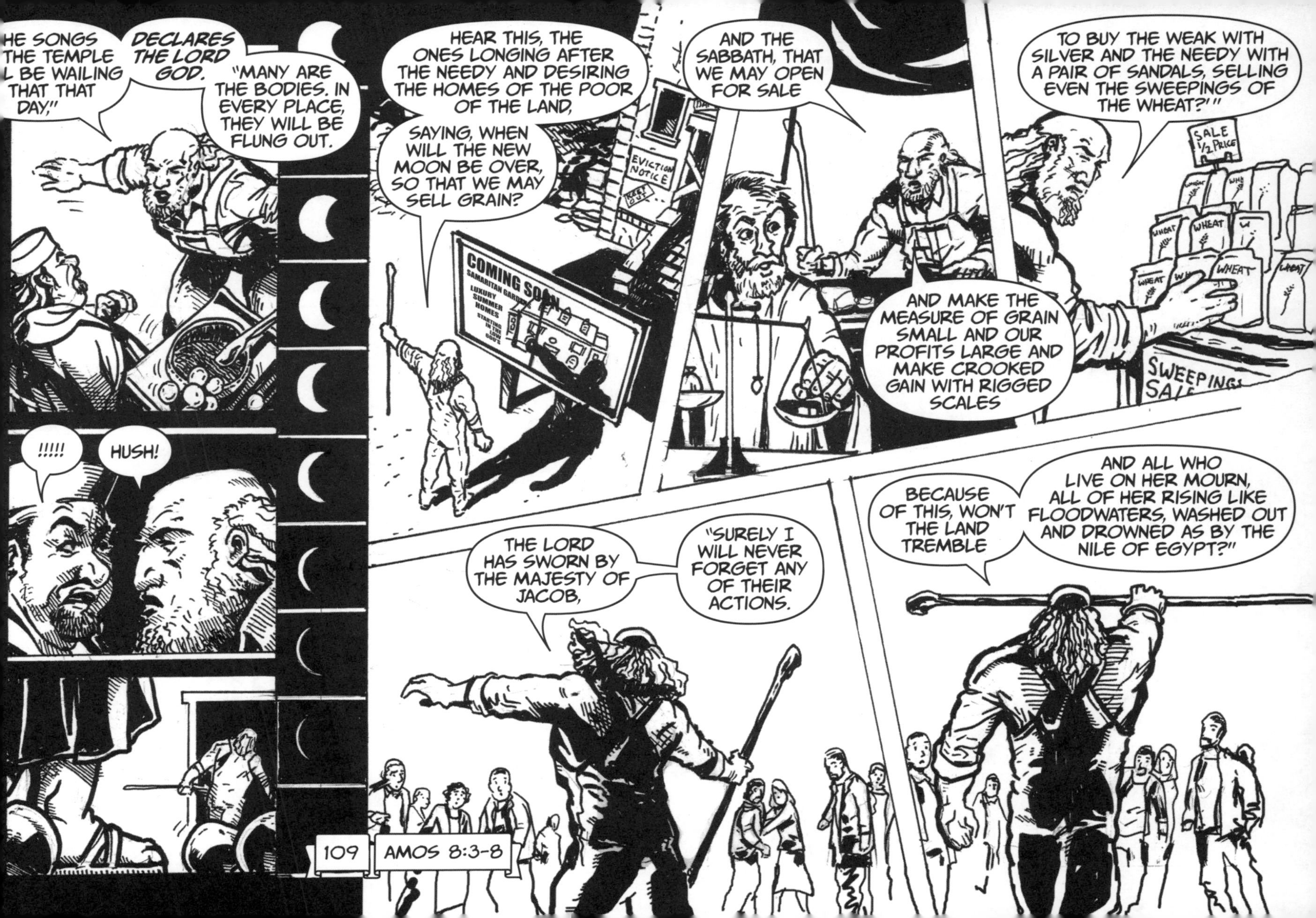
HE SONGS THE TEMPLE L BE WAILING THAT THAT DAY,"
DECLARES THE LORD GOD.
"MANY ARE THE BODIES. IN EVERY PLACE, THEY WILL BE FLUNG OUT.
!!!!!
HUSH!
HEAR THIS, THE ONES LONGING AFTER THE NEEDY AND DESIRING THE HOMES OF THE POOR OF THE LAND,
SAYING, WHEN WILL THE NEW MOON BE OVER, SO THAT WE MAY SELL GRAIN?
COMING SOON
SAMARITAN GARDEN
LUXURY SUMMER HOMES
STARTING IN THE LOW 600'S
EVICTION NOTICE
KEEP OUT
AND THE SABBATH, THAT WE MAY OPEN FOR SALE
AND MAKE THE MEASURE OF GRAIN SMALL AND OUR PROFITS LARGE AND MAKE CROOKED GAIN WITH RIGGED SCALES
TO BUY THE WEAK WITH SILVER AND THE NEEDY WITH A PAIR OF SANDALS, SELLING EVEN THE SWEEPINGS OF THE WHEAT?'"
SALE 1/2 PRICE
WHEAT
SWEEPINGS SALE
THE LORD HAS SWORN BY THE MAJESTY OF JACOB,
"SURELY I WILL NEVER FORGET ANY OF THEIR ACTIONS.
BECAUSE OF THIS, WON'T THE LAND TREMBLE
AND ALL WHO LIVE ON HER MOURN, ALL OF HER RISING LIKE FLOODWATERS, WASHED OUT AND DROWNED AS BY THE NILE OF EGYPT?"

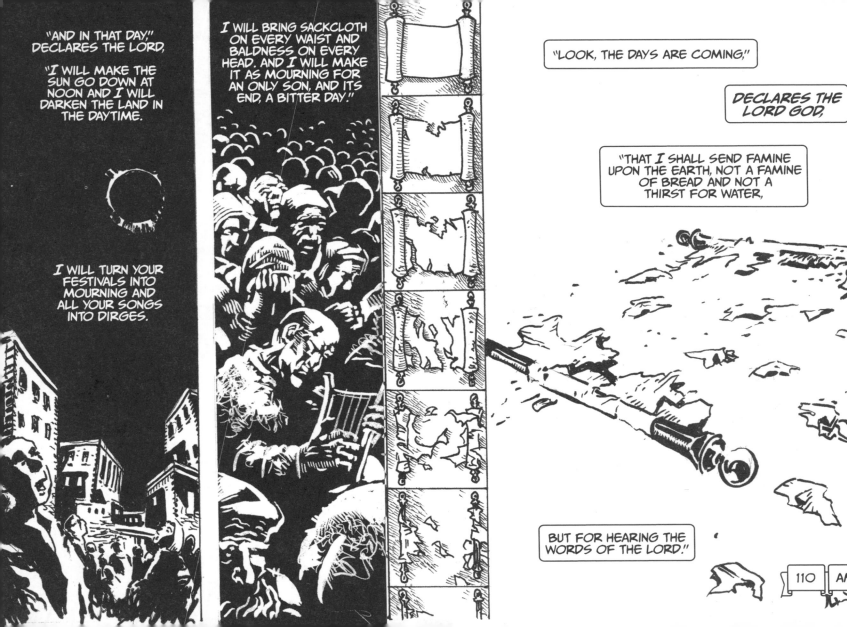

"AND IN THAT DAY," DECLARES THE LORD,

"I WILL MAKE THE SUN GO DOWN AT NOON AND I WILL DARKEN THE LAND IN THE DAYTIME.

I WILL TURN YOUR FESTIVALS INTO MOURNING AND ALL YOUR SONGS INTO DIRGES.

I WILL BRING SACKCLOTH ON EVERY WAIST AND BALDNESS ON EVERY HEAD. AND I WILL MAKE IT AS MOURNING FOR AN ONLY SON, AND ITS END, A BITTER DAY."

"LOOK, THE DAYS ARE COMING,"

DECLARES THE LORD GOD,

"THAT I SHALL SEND FAMINE UPON THE EARTH, NOT A FAMINE OF BREAD AND NOT A THIRST FOR WATER,

BUT FOR HEARING THE WORDS OF THE LORD."

110   AMOS 8:

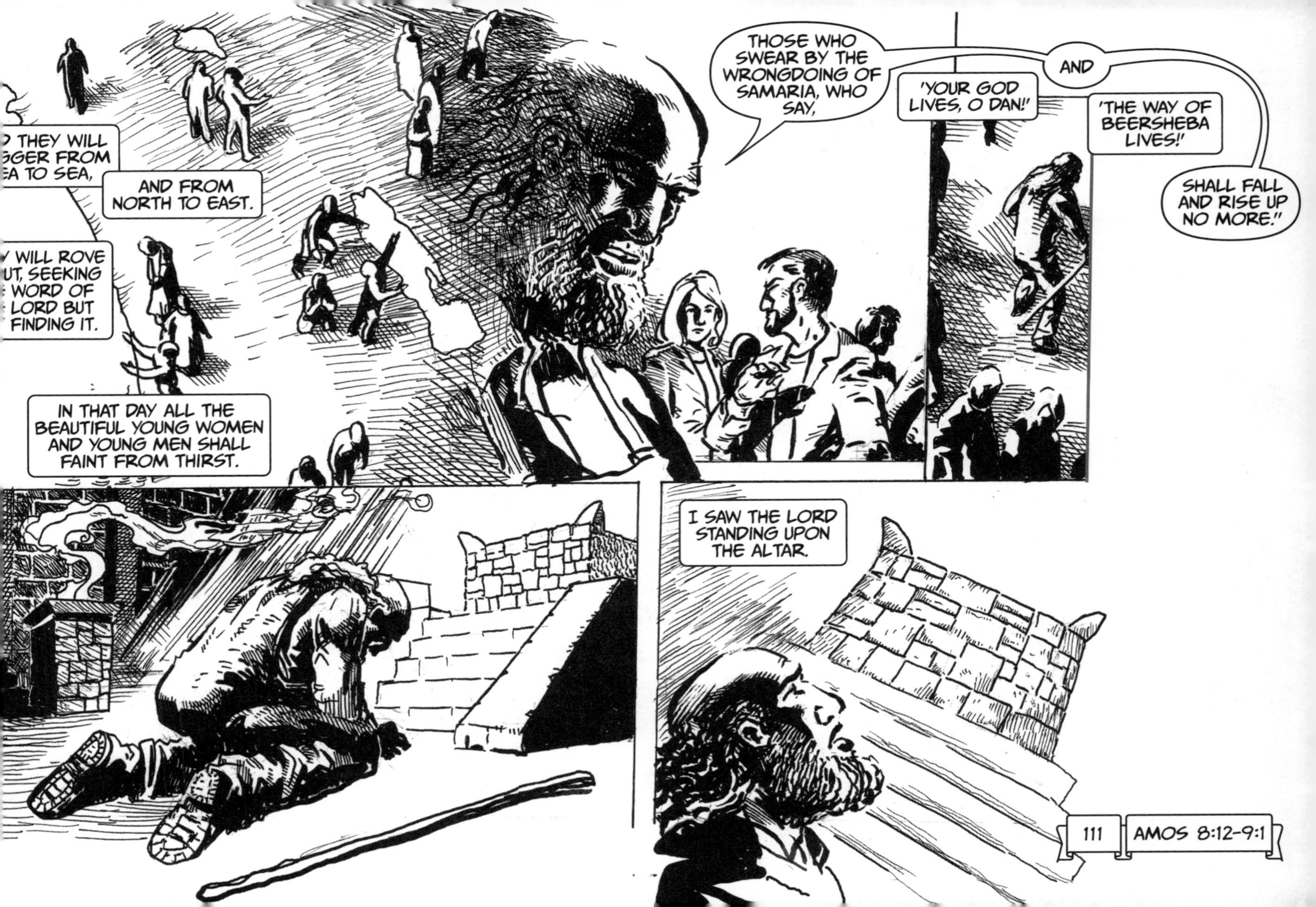
D THEY WILL
GGER FROM
EA TO SEA,
AND FROM NORTH TO EAST.
Y WILL ROVE
UT, SEEKING
WORD OF
LORD BUT
FINDING IT.
IN THAT DAY ALL THE BEAUTIFUL YOUNG WOMEN AND YOUNG MEN SHALL FAINT FROM THIRST.
THOSE WHO SWEAR BY THE WRONGDOING OF SAMARIA, WHO SAY,
'YOUR GOD LIVES, O DAN!'
AND
'THE WAY OF BEERSHEBA LIVES!'
SHALL FALL AND RISE UP NO MORE."
I SAW THE LORD STANDING UPON THE ALTAR.

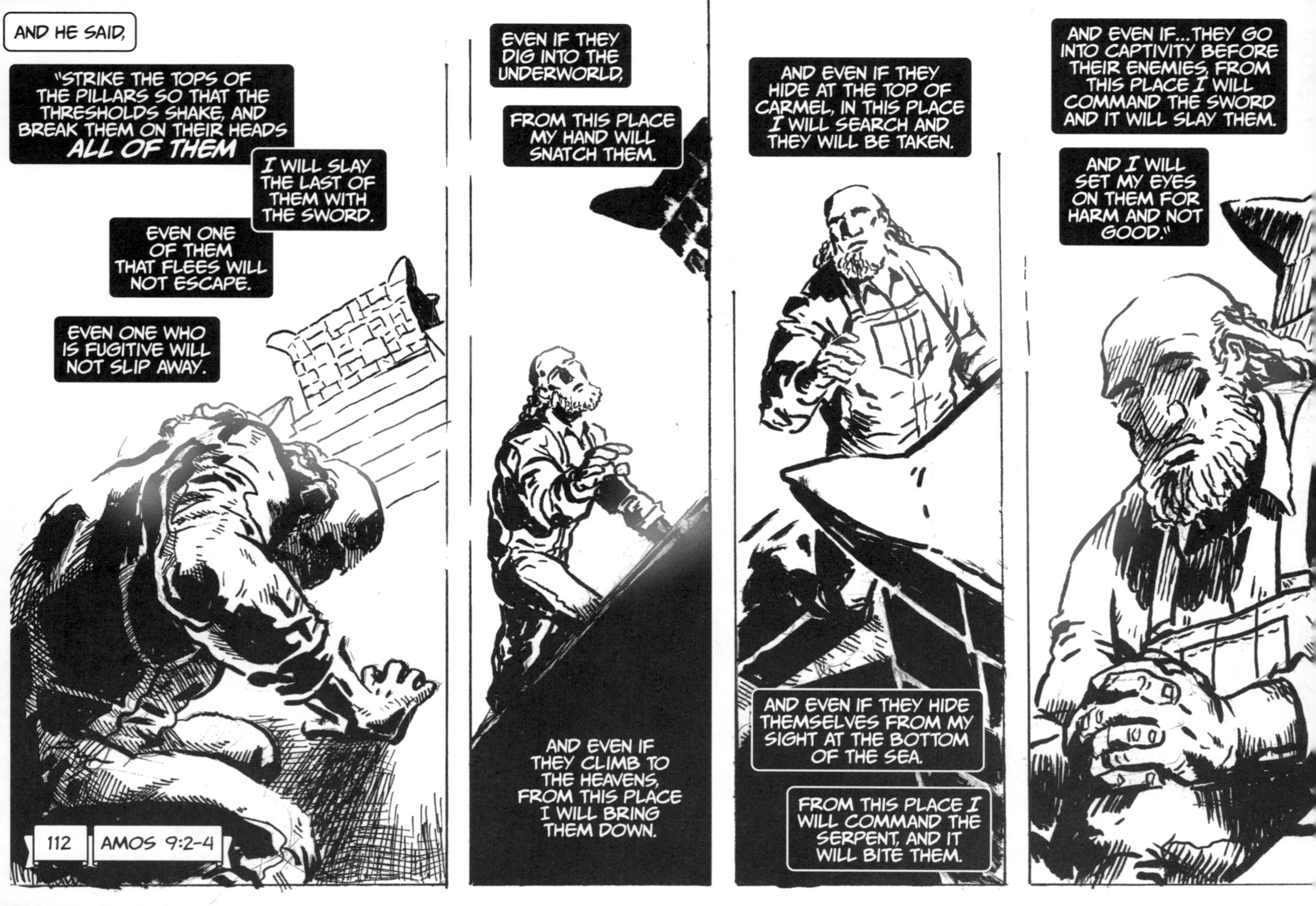
AND HE SAID,
"STRIKE THE TOPS OF THE PILLARS SO THAT THE THRESHOLDS SHAKE, AND BREAK THEM ON THEIR HEADS ALL OF THEM
I WILL SLAY THE LAST OF THEM WITH THE SWORD.
EVEN ONE OF THEM THAT FLEES WILL NOT ESCAPE.
EVEN ONE WHO IS FUGITIVE WILL NOT SLIP AWAY.
EVEN IF THEY DIG INTO THE UNDERWORLD,
FROM THIS PLACE MY HAND WILL SNATCH THEM.
AND EVEN IF THEY CLIMB TO THE HEAVENS, FROM THIS PLACE I WILL BRING THEM DOWN.
AND EVEN IF THEY HIDE AT THE TOP OF CARMEL, IN THIS PLACE I WILL SEARCH AND THEY WILL BE TAKEN.
AND EVEN IF THEY HIDE THEMSELVES FROM MY SIGHT AT THE BOTTOM OF THE SEA.
FROM THIS PLACE I WILL COMMAND THE SERPENT, AND IT WILL BITE THEM.
AND EVEN IF...THEY GO INTO CAPTIVITY BEFORE THEIR ENEMIES, FROM THIS PLACE I WILL COMMAND THE SWORD AND IT WILL SLAY THEM.
AND I WILL SET MY EYES ON THEM FOR HARM AND NOT GOOD."

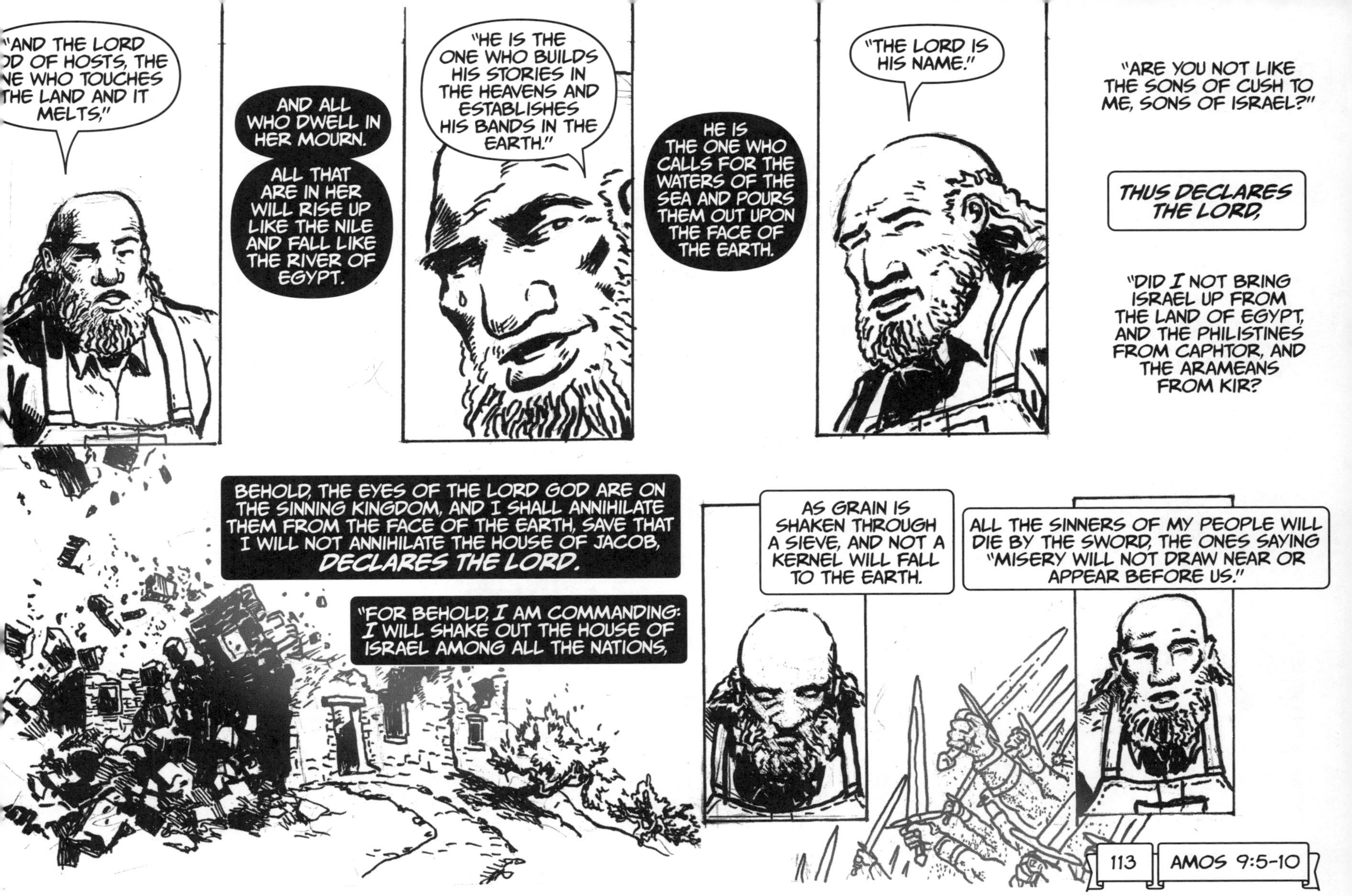
"AND THE LORD
OD OF HOSTS, THE
NE WHO TOUCHES
THE LAND AND IT
MELTS,"
AND ALL WHO DWELL IN HER MOURN.
ALL THAT ARE IN HER WILL RISE UP LIKE THE NILE AND FALL LIKE THE RIVER OF EGYPT.
"HE IS THE ONE WHO BUILDS HIS STORIES IN THE HEAVENS AND ESTABLISHES HIS BANDS IN THE EARTH."
HE IS THE ONE WHO CALLS FOR THE WATERS OF THE SEA AND POURS THEM OUT UPON THE FACE OF THE EARTH.
"THE LORD IS HIS NAME."
"ARE YOU NOT LIKE THE SONS OF CUSH TO ME, SONS OF ISRAEL?"
THUS DECLARES THE LORD,
"DID I NOT BRING ISRAEL UP FROM THE LAND OF EGYPT, AND THE PHILISTINES FROM CAPHTOR, AND THE ARAMEANS FROM KIR?
BEHOLD, THE EYES OF THE LORD GOD ARE ON THE SINNING KINGDOM, AND I SHALL ANNIHILATE THEM FROM THE FACE OF THE EARTH, SAVE THAT I WILL NOT ANNIHILATE THE HOUSE OF JACOB, DECLARES THE LORD.
"FOR BEHOLD, I AM COMMANDING: I WILL SHAKE OUT THE HOUSE OF ISRAEL AMONG ALL THE NATIONS,
AS GRAIN IS SHAKEN THROUGH A SIEVE, AND NOT A KERNEL WILL FALL TO THE EARTH.
ALL THE SINNERS OF MY PEOPLE WILL DIE BY THE SWORD, THE ONES SAYING "MISERY WILL NOT DRAW NEAR OR APPEAR BEFORE US."

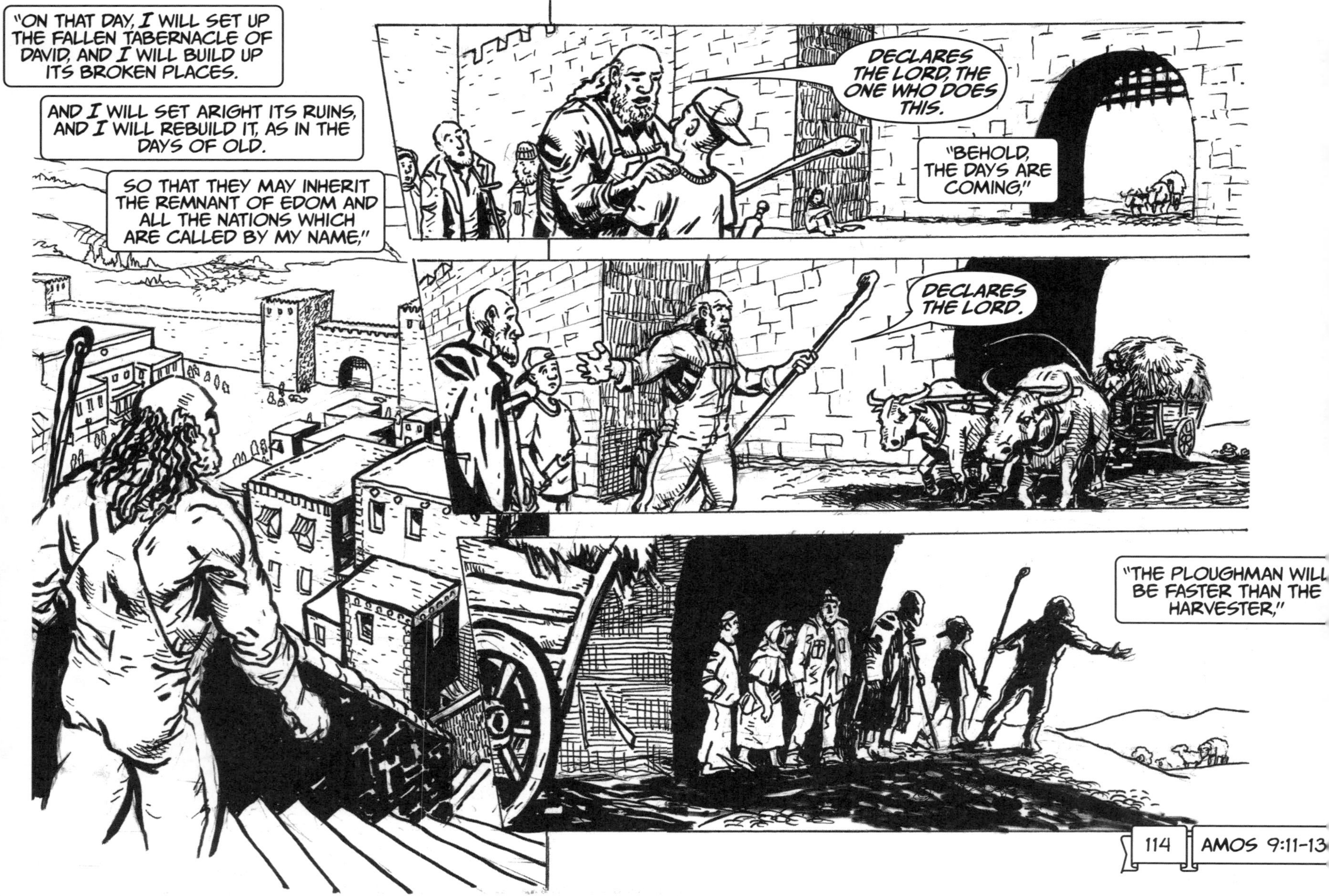
"ON THAT DAY, I WILL SET UP THE FALLEN TABERNACLE OF DAVID, AND I WILL BUILD UP ITS BROKEN PLACES.
AND I WILL SET ARIGHT ITS RUINS, AND I WILL REBUILD IT, AS IN THE DAYS OF OLD.
SO THAT THEY MAY INHERIT THE REMNANT OF EDOM AND ALL THE NATIONS WHICH ARE CALLED BY MY NAME,"
DECLARES THE LORD, THE ONE WHO DOES THIS.
"BEHOLD, THE DAYS ARE COMING,"
DECLARES THE LORD.
"THE PLOUGHMAN WILL BE FASTER THAN THE HARVESTER,"

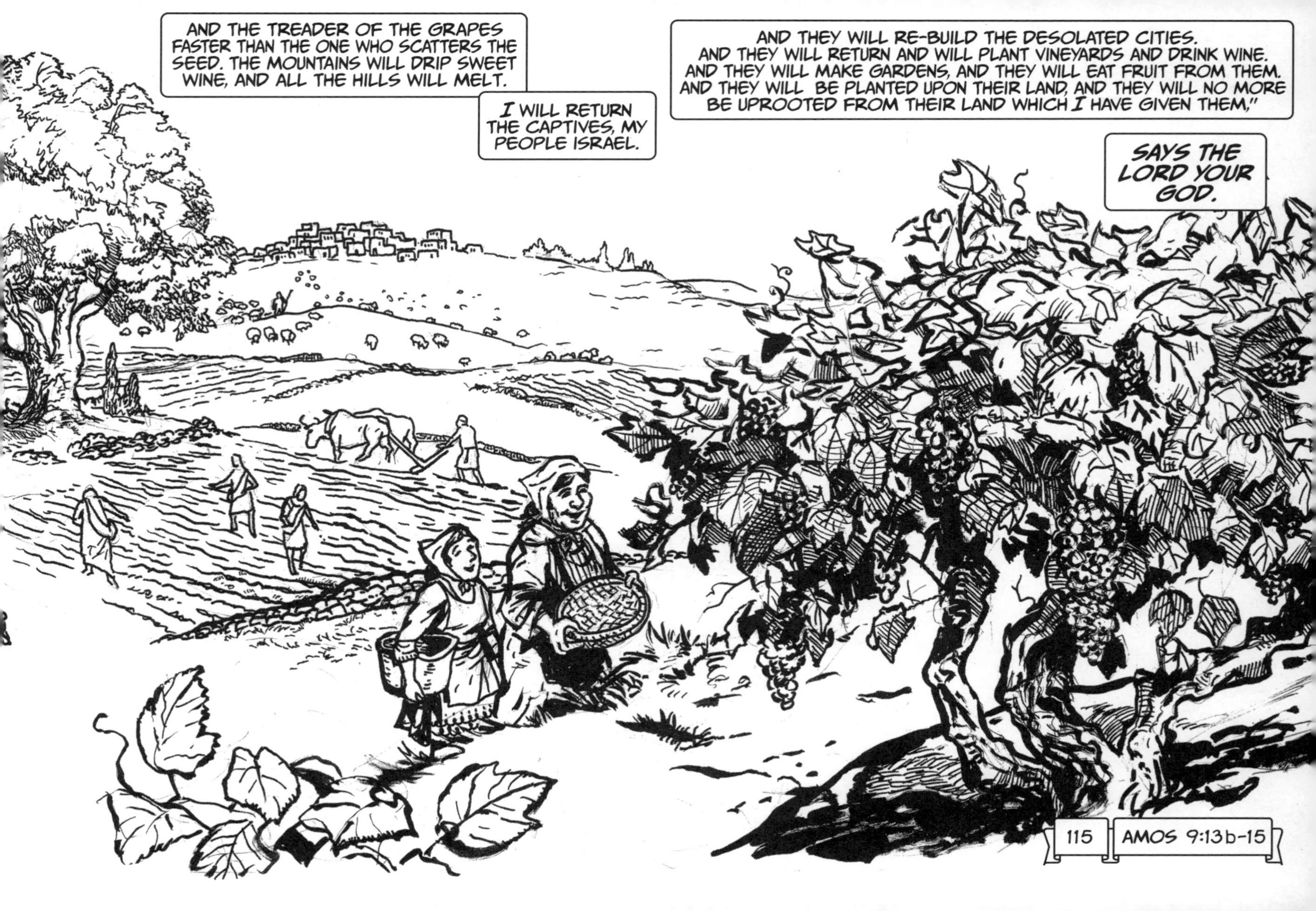
AND THE TREADER OF THE GRAPES FASTER THAN THE ONE WHO SCATTERS THE SEED. THE MOUNTAINS WILL DRIP SWEET WINE, AND ALL THE HILLS WILL MELT.
I WILL RETURN THE CAPTIVES, MY PEOPLE ISRAEL.
AND THEY WILL RE-BUILD THE DESOLATED CITIES. AND THEY WILL RETURN AND WILL PLANT VINEYARDS AND DRINK WINE. AND THEY WILL MAKE GARDENS, AND THEY WILL EAT FRUIT FROM THEM. AND THEY WILL BE PLANTED UPON THEIR LAND, AND THEY WILL NO MORE BE UPROOTED FROM THEIR LAND WHICH I HAVE GIVEN THEM,"
SAYS THE LORD YOUR GOD.

g Deeper into the Stories:

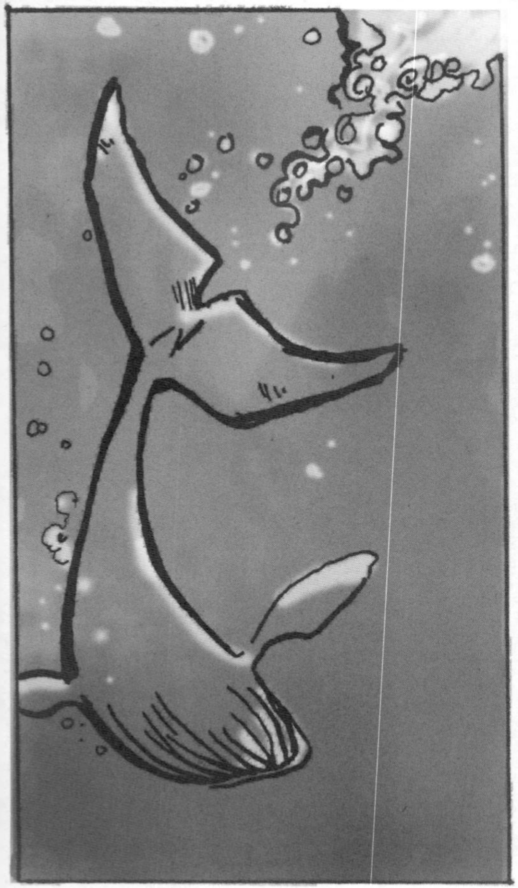

A guide for thought, study and discussion

Part I: Jonah

Page 2

"And the word of the Lord was ..." In Hebrew (the original language in which the of Jonah was written,) the phrase translated as "the word of the Lord" also can the "thing of the Lord" or the "event of the Lord." In the Old Testament, ofte "word" feels like an event.

Perhaps God always has an event ready for us and is just waiting for us to "go fi ing", or to plop our fishing hook in the water. What "event" (ordinary or extraor nary) recently happened to you which might have been a "word of the Lord" mom coming to you?

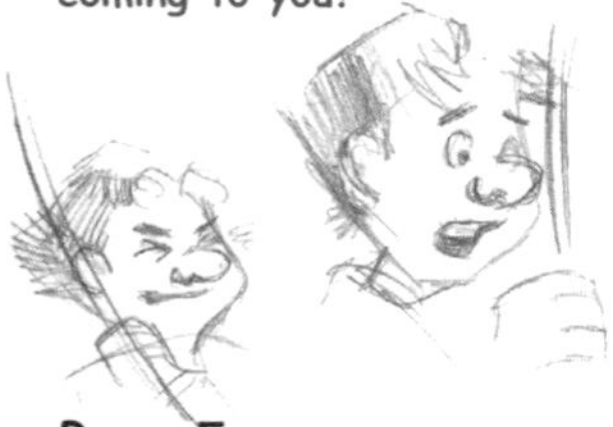

Page 3-4

Look at the reactions that Jonah has to the fish at the other end of his line. Which one most looks like how you feel?

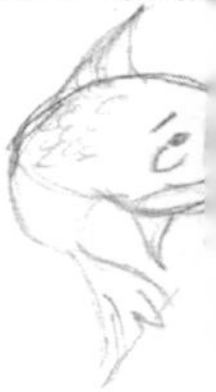

Page 5

We know from the Hebrew's history that they suffered under Assyrian soldiers. The Assyrian soldier who is dragging away the Hebrews to put them in prison looks threatening, fierce and unsympathetic. In the Bible we often see life circumstances in which there is a powerful force that feels threatening or fierce.

Is there a force in your life, neighborhood or school that feels threatening or fierce?

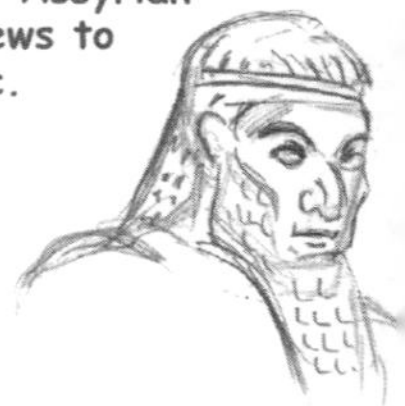

Page 6

Jonah hears God calling him to action. However this call to action seemingly come out of nowhere and doesn't make sense to him. Maybe Jonah didn't understand h the bad things happening in Nineveh had anything to do with him. But God chose recruit Jonah to play a part in Nineveh's turnaround.

What kind of hurt do you see going on in your world that God might want to turn around?

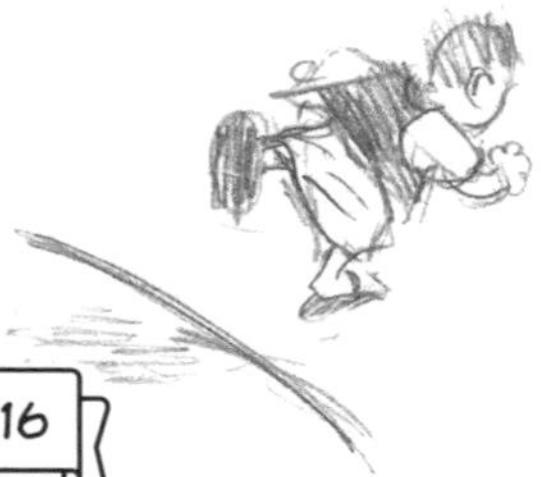

Page 7

We usually think of people as being drawn to God, but when Jonah has a close encounter with God, he runs "away from the face of the Lord."

Why do you think Jonah ran away from God?
Have you ever felt like running away? What did you d

9
even finds running away difficult. First he has to decide where to run to.
God called him to go to Nineveh, Jonah wants to go the furthest he can away
Nineveh - which is Tarshish.

does this tell you about Jonah and what he is like? (Hint: Few Bible characters
perfect as we may think they should be.)

your answer to the previous question, how do you think God might use Jonah's
cter (what he is like) for good?

11
er 1, verse 5 says that the sailors each cried out to their own God. In the
t world, as now, different people had different names for God and different
standings of who God is and the power God has. What does it mean to you that
ilors turned to their own gods for help?

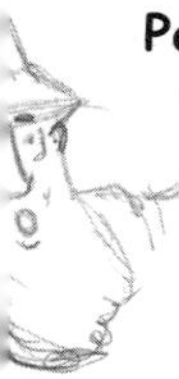

Page 12
The Master and Commander (or captain of the ship) hopes that God will "spare us a thought" and save the people on the ship. Sometimes we think of God as being so big that we think God is concerned only with the big things of life. Yet the stories of the Bible remind us that God is interested in us (as some of the small things of life) and that God considers us to be deserving of God's care. When have you felt too small for God to pay attention to?

13
ing dice or casting lots is an ancient practice that our
w and Christian ancestors picked up from ancient cultures.
ractice appears in many books of the Bible including Leviticus,
a, Nehemiah, Jonah, Esther and the Book of Acts.

does it mean to you that throwing dice - an act associated
luck and gambling - has been used in discerning what is true
hat is the will of God?

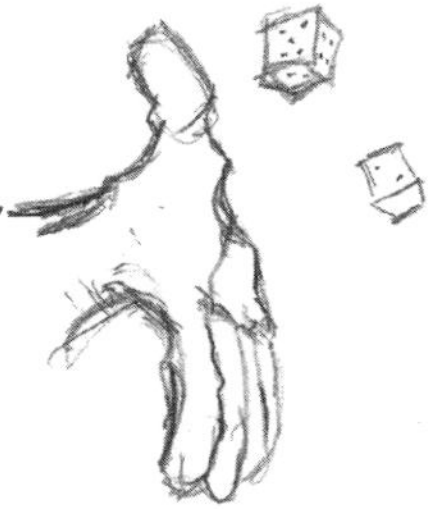

14
times nature seems to reflect how well (or not well) things are with people.
of how the Lord sends an east wind that brings in the swarms of locusts in
(Exodus 10:12-20). Jonah recognizes the storm as somehow reflecting the
iness of his own situation (running away from God and the bad things happening
eveh).

example can you think of that shows nature reflecting how well (or not well)
are going in human life?

Page 14
In chapter 1, verse 9, Jonah says he is a Hebrew foreigner because he is traveling in a part of the world where the Hebrews do not live. The Hebrew people we associate with the names Israel and Judah lived near people of other cultures. Often they wondered how to live alongside others who were different from them. Often the Hebrews competed with other peoples for basic resources like food, water and land.

The Hebrews understood themselves to be people specially appointed by God to live according to the Covenant, but not necessarily chosen over other people. So the Hebrews wondered how they should behave toward their non-Hebrew neighbors.

How do you see Jonah struggling with this question? Does Jonah like the people of Nineveh? Who likes the people of Nineveh more, Jonah or God? Why?

Page 15
Clearly the sailors think that, by throwing Jonah into the sea, they are murdering him. They ask God not to hold their crime against them. ("Do not charge us with innocent blood.")

What does this tell you about how important the sailors think human life is? Who do the sailors feel accountable to?

Page 19
Can you think of a time when you spent three days away from home in a place that was so far away that you would not have been able to get yourself home? What did that feel like? What did you do?

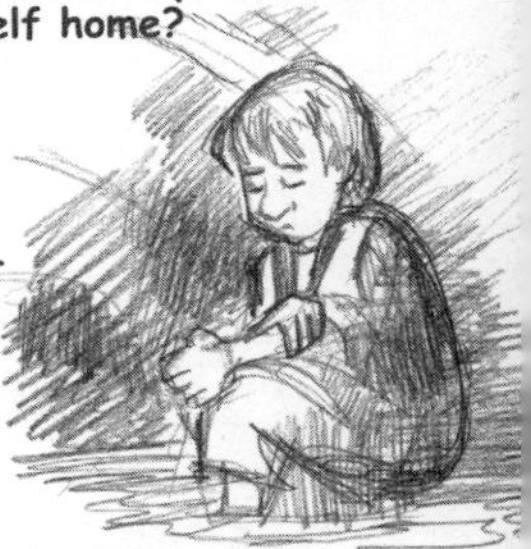

Page 20
When Jonah is lost in the belly of the fish, he remembers the psalm that describes the experience he is going through now.

Have you ever heard a story that is so true to your own experience that it could have been your story? Did knowing the story help you? How?

Page 22
In our culture, going down is often associated with a bad time and coming up is associated with things getting better. We see this down-up idea here when Jonah feels as if he has sunk to the bottom of the world (to the bottom of the mountains, down to the earth, I went down, and her bars passed over me forever). But even as bad as things were for Jonah when he was in the belly of the fish, he remembered that God could raise his life up "from the pit."

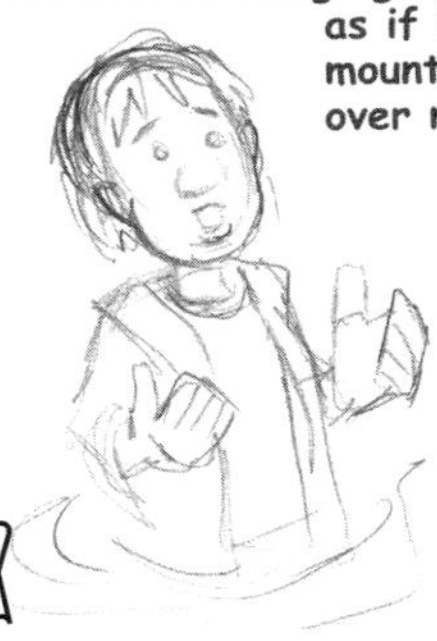

When things are bad for you, how do you remind yourself that God can raise you up?

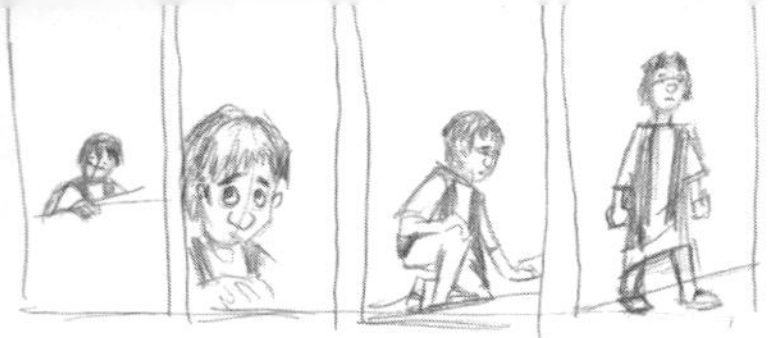

Page 25
In chapter 3, verse 1, God gives Jonah the same message after the fish-event that God did before: "Rise up! Go to Nineveh the great city...." Why do you think God tried again?

Page 26
God tells Jonah to "rise up" or stand up. In Hebrew (the original language in which Jonah was written) the word for "rise up" occurs frequently, especially when someone is about to do something important. "Rise up" could mean "get to your feet." What else could "rise up" mean if someone is about to do something important?

Page 27-29
What kinds of people do you see in the pictures of the city of Nineveh?
What kinds of jobs do you think the people do?
What ages of people do you see?

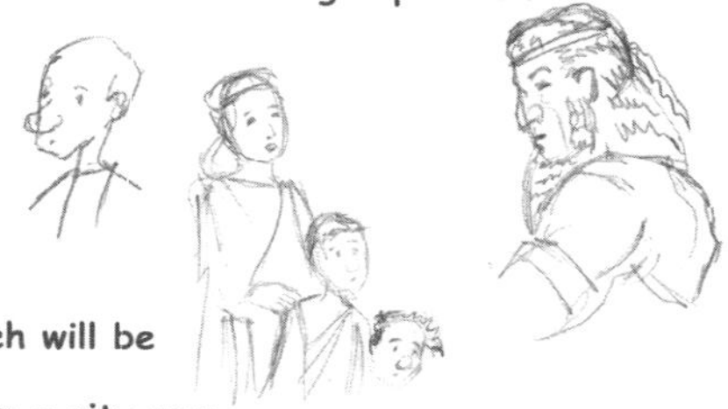

Page 29
What do you think Jonah means by saying Nineveh will be "turned upside down"?
Can you think of examples from the Bible of when a city was "turned upside down"? In those cases, why do you think this happened?

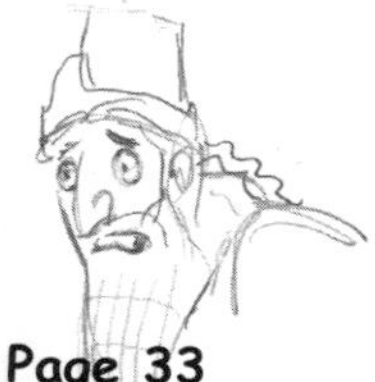

Page 31-32
The surprise for Jonah is that the people of Nineveh trust in God and do what God desires (p. 29) even though they are not Hebrews.

Which picture on pages 30 or 31 tells you Jonah is surprised that they are doing what God desires?

Page 33
The Bible is full of examples of God asking people to turn away from doing evil. Page 32 shows examples of what it might look like to not do evil.
What actions of "not evil" do you see drawn here?

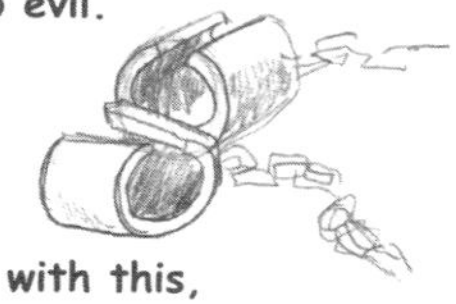

Page 34
The people of Nineveh turn away from evil. God is pleased with this, but Jonah gets angry.

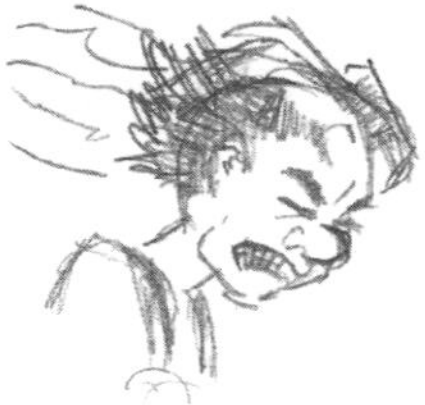

Why do you suppose Jonah is angry?
Have you ever felt so angry that it seemed like you were "burning" inside?
What did you do?

Page 35
Look at what Jonah says to God on page 34.
What does Jonah know about God that he reveals here?
Jonah says that one of the things he knows about God is that God "repents of ev
What do you think this means?

Jonah seems to be saying that God is capable of evil.
What might evil done by God look like?

Page 36
The Book of Jonah doesn't tell us Jonah's answer to God's question, "Is it good f this anger to burn in you?"

What do you think Jonah's answer was?
Would you answer the same way or differently?

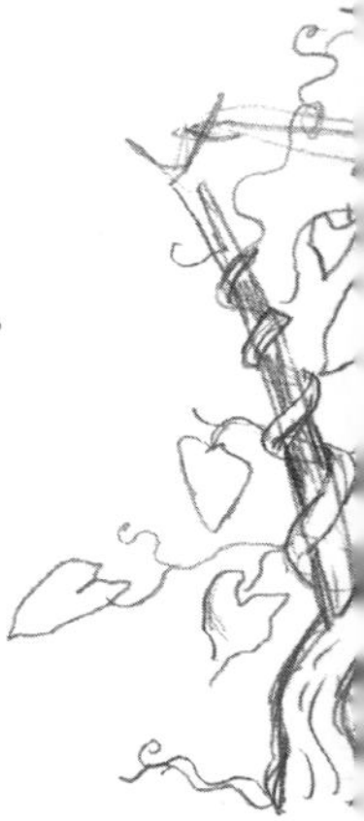

Page 37
Jonah works hard to save his own life by building a shelter to protect him from the blazing sun.
What happens to the shelter and his effort to protect himself?

Page 38
Look at how the vine grows into full leaves and grapes and how well it protects Jonah from the sun.
What did Jonah do to make the vine grow?

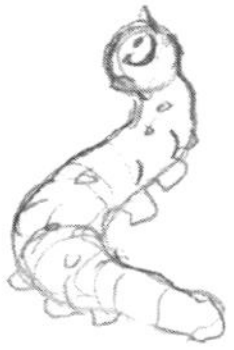

Page 39
What did the "vine weevil" do to the vine?
Who sent the "vine weevil"?

Page 40
How does Jonah feel about his vine-shelter being destroyed?
How does that compare to his feeling about the prospect of Nineveh being destroyed?

Just like God has sent Jonah the same message twice, God has asked the same q tion twice: "Is it good for this anger to burn in you ...?" What does this repeate question tell you about God?

Page 41
God compares Jonah's caring for the vine with God's own caring for the people and creatures of Nineveh.
Just as Jonah wanted the vine to live, so God wants the people of Nineveh to live. This surprises Jonah.

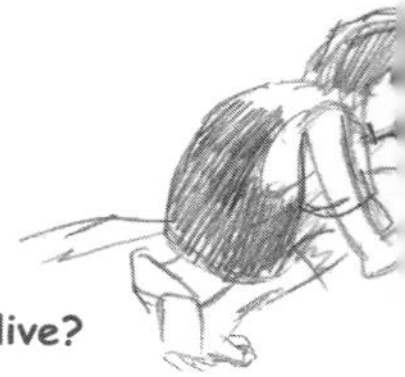

Does it surprise you that God wants the people of Nineveh to live?
Why, or why not?

t II: Esther

g's name in the original Hebrew text is written as The King Ahasuerus. Even
this could be translated as King Ahasuerus, the more literal phrase "The King
rus" gives us an idea of how important he and others think his power is. Later
story, Ahasuerus gives his power to others.
, is he The King or the king?

ing in Shushan (the capital of Persia) is done in a big way. The text says The
rinking party lasted for 180 days.
What does this tell you about The King?

g gives his big-chiefs options – whether to drink wine at the party or not.
t in this small matter, The King is not a tyrant who insists that everyone must
he does.

story progresses, see whether The King sticks to this policy or whether he
.

een (and her beautiful appearance) give The King status and make him look good
of others.
igns of status are present in your daily life?

g's anger burned within him. Do you remember when Jonah's anger burned in
low does The King act when he is angry, as compared with Jonah?

Hint: The King respects the law and follows it. This
(the law and how it is used and changed) is a
theme throughout the Book of Esther.

The King's attendant Memucan argues that, because
Vashti has disobeyed The King, all of the
women throughout the kingdom will also disobey their
husbands. Do you think this is likely?

g's attendant refers to Vashti's status of queen as being her "ambition."
n, or plans that a person develops for himself/herself, is another theme in the
Esther.
oes ambition mean to you?

King Ahasuerus' kingdom was actually a collection of geographical areas that had been
combined under the power of the Persian army. Each of these areas named on page
forty six would have had their own culture and language, which would have been
different from the others. So, each area would have traditions of its local area in
addition to the ones that The King Ahasuerus' law imposed on them.

How important do you think the law was to The King's ability to rule over a large
kingdom?

Page 47
After King Ahasuerus got over his anger, he realized he no longer had a queen (oops!).
His advisers recommend hosting a beauty contest in all the geographic areas (provinces) to find the most beautiful women from the kingdom. Then a winner would be
selected from this group of finalists.

From what you've learned about The King, why do you think he liked this plan?

Page 48
We meet Esther first through her uncle Mordecai.
We learn that their family had experienced many hardships:
they were refugees from Jerusalem and had been brought
forcibly to Shushan by a different king, the King of Babylon.
While some of the Jews in the Babylonian captivity returned to
Jerusalem when the Persian Empire took over the region,
many Jews, like Esther's family, remained in Persia.
What countries of the world today can you think of that have
suffered military defeat and/or have seen its people become
refugees?

How do you think Esther's situation is similar to or
different from today's world?

Page 49
"Exalted in favor" is a phrase that appears again and again in the Bible. Its signifi-
cance comes from the practice of lifting up or exalting prized objects or persons.
Thus, kings would sit on a high throne because they were exalted.

As the story progresses, take note of why Esther is "exalted."

Have you wondered why the women who were finalists for the "most beautiful woman
in Persia" contest would need to have a year worth of beauty treatments?

Page 50

We are told that, at first, The King doesn't know Esther's "people or ancestry." This is a different way of saying it than we'd use today. Today we'd ask someone's family name and ethnicity or race. Esther's people were Jews, and her family lineage (same as Mordecai's) was her ancestry.

Do you think this was the only time in the Bible that someone hid their identity as a Jew and hid their family connections?
What other examples can you think of?

In cities especially, people from lots of different nations and ethnicities live in the same areas. What different people groups do you see in your school or work environment? At the grocery store? In fast food restaurants?

Concubinage is the practice of women being kept by powerful men for the purpose of satisfying the men's sexual pleasure without giving the women freedom or equal rights. Some might say that King Ahasuerus' model of concubinage was generous in that the women could keep whatever they wanted after their night with The King.
What did the women lose by being concubines to The King?

Page 51

Esther is "exalted in grace in the eyes of all who saw her."

Is Esther exalted because of going up to The King, or for her virtue in not asking for a lot of things to take with her, or because The King loved her "more than all the women"?

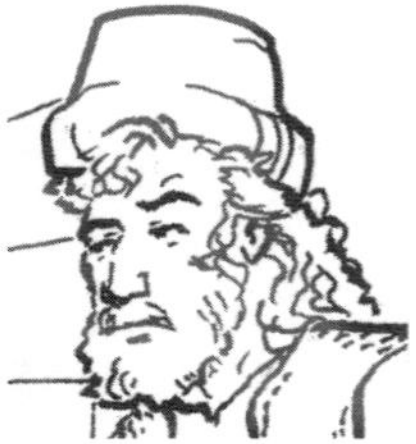

Page 52-53

Mordecai overhears two eunuchs plotting to harm The King. Then Mordecai reports the crime to Esther. Then Esther reports it to The King. Finally the two eunuchs are killed for their crime of seeking to harm The King.

What does this tell you about the law in the kingdom of Persia under Ahasuerus?

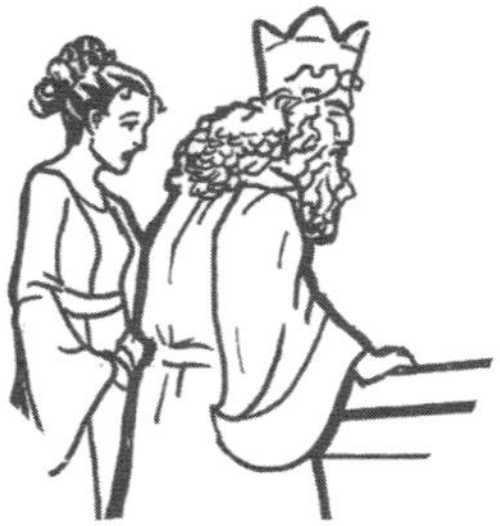

Page 54

Chapter three introduces us to a new character: Haman. Haman acts like The King's "right hand man" because The King has given his authority and power to Haman.

Does Mordecai respect Haman's authority?

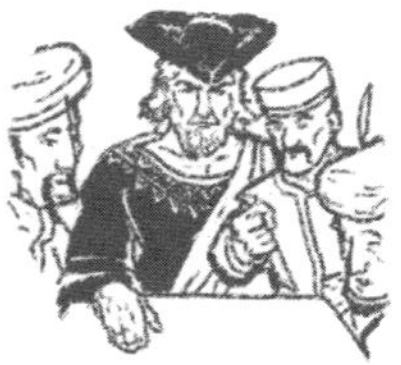

Page 55

Haman is now the third character we've met who suf
burning anger. The first character is Jonah, and th
second is The King Ahasuerus.
What does Haman do with his anger?
How many people will suffer as a result of Haman's

Haman wants to annihilate the Jews because he resents Mordecai (although he is only one man). Yet the reason Haman presents to The King for wanting to destroy the Jews is different from his real reason.
What reason does Haman give The King?

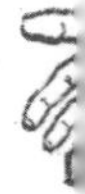

Genocide is a word developed in the 20th Century in the United Nations to desc
what happened to the Jews of Europe under the Nazis from 1933 to 1945, whe
over six million Jews were systematically killed simply because of their identity
Jewish). In our own day, the United States has named the violence against pec
Darfur, Sudan as genocide.

Do you think God is opposed to genocide? Why?
How is genocide different from killing a single person?

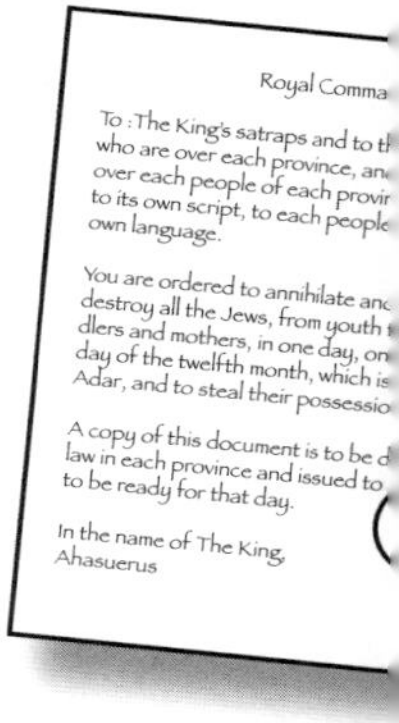

Royal Comma

To : The King's satraps and to th
who are over each province, an
over each people of each provir
to its own script, to each people
own language.

You are ordered to annihilate anc
destroy all the Jews, from youth
dlers and mothers, in one day, on
day of the twelfth month, which is
Adar, and to steal their possessio

A copy of this document is to be d
law in each province and issued to
to be ready for that day.

In the name of The King,
Ahasuerus

Page 56

"The Royal Command" is a copy of the genocide order issued by Haman under The King's authority.

What shocks you about this command?
Do you think The King should have this authority?
Are there any limits on The King's authority?
Is there another law that trumps The King's law?

Page 57

What is Mordecai's reaction to the Royal Command?
What do you see Mordecai doing?

Page 58

Why does Queen Esther want Mordecai to put his ordinary clothes on?

Mordecai asks Esther to beg The King to reverse his order and so "ask for her people."

What's the first problem she will face?
Do you think Esther remembers that she is a Jew?
Do you think The King knows she is a Jew?

Page 59

Through the intermediary Hathach, Mordecai reminds Esther that she needs to be "delivered" or rescued from this death sentence, just like all the other Jews.

Why do you think Mordecai is confident that, if Esther doesn't act to rescue the Jews, someone else will?

[O]f the most famous words of the Bible are these: [] who knows, if for a time such as this you were brought to the kingdom?" [Mordec]ai believes that specific persons have a specific role to play in a specific time in

[What] do you think about this?
[What] help does Esther request from the Jewish people? Why?

[Page] 61

[] The King extends the golden scepter to Esther, [] safe to come near him.

[Why doesn't] she immediately ask The King to save [Je]ws from death, instead of waiting to [make her] request?

[Page] 62

[Th]e second time, The King promises to give Esther "up to half of the kingdom." [Remem]ber now how easily The King gave up his authority to Haman.
[Is the]re anything wrong with the way The King so easily gives up his authority? If [so, wh]at?

[Page] 63

[Haman] considers himself "exalted" in the eyes of Queen Esther and King Ahasuerus. [What] evidence does Haman have of this?

[Page] 64

[In the] original language of the Book of Esther, the words literally say "sleep ran away [from T]he King."

[Why d]o you think we [are tol]d this about [the Ki]ng?

Page 65

There is a case of mistaken identity going on here.
Who does The King have in mind for being rewarded?
Who does Haman think The King is planning to reward?

Haman's answer about what the reward should be is influenced by who he thinks is going to get the reward. In other words, Haman's policy of what should be done is based on who Haman thinks the policy will apply to.

When you have a decision to make, is your decision different when you think of its effect on one person as opposed to another person?

Page 66

Why does Mordecai do what The King has commanded?

What does this say about the importance of the law (and The King's decrees) in Persian society?

Page 67

The King unwittingly speaks of Haman as "so full of himself in his heart" that he would plan genocide.

What does it mean to be full of yourself?
Does someone always get hurt when a person is full of himself/herself?

Why does Queen Esther call Haman evil?
How is Haman different from King Ahasuerus, if he is?

Page 69

Haman dies under punishment the same way that the two eunuchs did who had been planning to harm The King.

Is Haman guilty of the same crime as the two eunuchs?
What is Haman actually guilty of?

Page 70

The King no longer is concerned about the Jews causing harm and not being fit residents of his kingdom.

Do you think originally he was truly worried about this threat?

The King gives his authority (symbolized by his signet-ring) to Mordecai in just the same way that he had given his authority over to Haman.

Is this act of giving over his power any better now than it was with Haman?
What power or responsibilities do you have?
Do you sometimes give up your responsibilities too easily? How?

Page 71

The execution of Haman does not end the threat to the Jews or reverse the genocide order. What does Esther have to do in order to be rescued herself?

Why does she do this?

The King says that an order written in his name cannot be changed, even by him. If that is true, then The King can't just cancel the genocide order against the Jews but must tell the Jews to defend themselves against those who are attacking them.

What would have to happen in order to prevent the violence entirely?

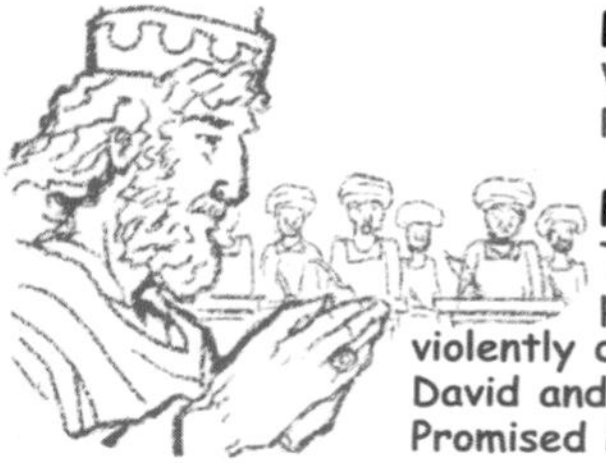

Page 72

Who is really responsible for writing this second Royal Command?

Page 73

This is one of several cases in the Bible in which the people of historic Israel seem empowered by God to violently defeat those who are their enemies (reference David and the Philistines and the Hebrew slaves moving into the Promised Land). Yet God created all human life, and all people are precious to God.

How do you reconcile the violence of an army with God's high regard for human life?

Both of the Royal Commands authorize the attackers to steal the possessions of those they kill, which is an ancient practice called plundering. However the Jews do not take the possessions of those they kill. Why is this important? (Compare with 1 Samuel 15:10-23)

Page 75

Queen Esther asks The King for the permission to have more Persians killed. Why might she want this power?

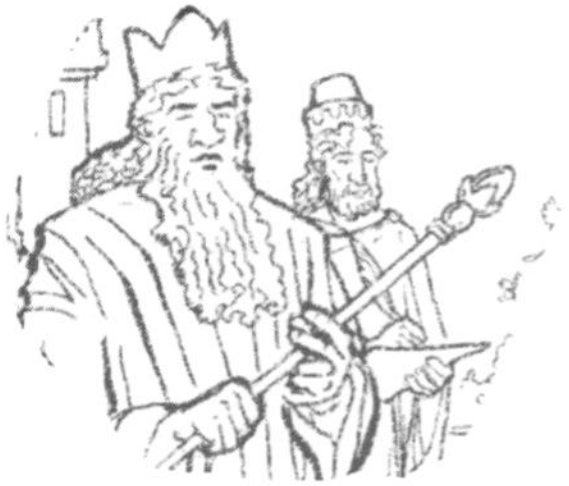

This book of the Bible is called Esther, but the book ends with Mordecai being the hero of the story. The King shows his high regard for Mordecai by taxing people (setting up a tribute) to provide income to support Mordecai's status in the kingdom.

There are other stories in the Bible in which a Jew becomes second in command to a king. Where are those stories?

Part III: Amos

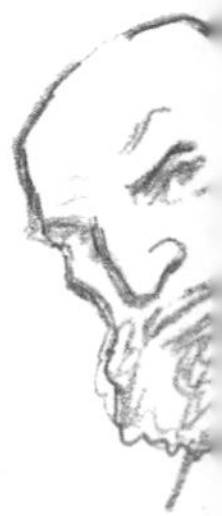

Page 79

When we read the Bible, we are reading words. In some cases those words describe a vision (or picture) that a person has had. Words and pictures both can express God's revelation of God's self to us.

As you read this graphic translation of Amos, does what you see and read make more sense to you as a vision or as a story?

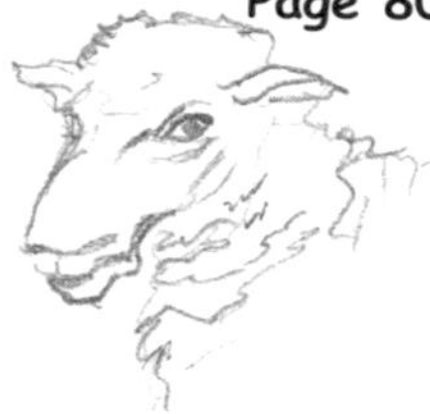

Page 80

At the beginning of the story, we see Amos being a shepherd. What are shepherds supposed to do? If you don't know, how could you find out?

In the beginning of the story of Amos, Amos says "the Lord r from Zion," and the artist chose to picture a lion appearing in midst of the sheep.

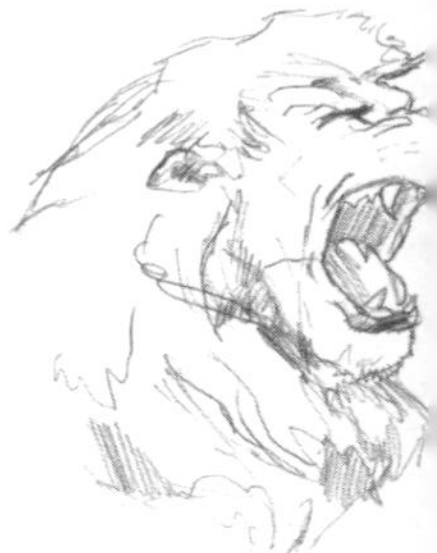

What might the presence of the lion mean for the sheep?

If the lion represents God, why might God be roaring?

Page 81

Many translations say that from Jerusalem God utters or thunders. In this translation, God "gives up his voice." The original Hebrew literally says "he gives his voice." Giving voice could mean raising God's voice like a yell, or God giving up or handing over his voice.

Which of these two interpretations helps you make sense of what happens: that all the plants and vegetation dry up?

Note: Remember that, in the Book of Jonah, what was happening in nature re ed what was happening in the lives of the people.

Page 82

The time and place that Amos lived in was very different from our time and plac we need to learn what it was like then. The artist has included some pictures t us learn.

Who and what do you see here?
What looks similar to your world?
What looks different?

83

following five pages, God makes God's case against specific groups of people
ve hurt others. The bottom line (or indictment) against them is always the
but the ways they have hurt others are different.
:harges (or indictments) do you see God making against the various groups?

king a list of the names of the people-groups and the charges God makes
them. (Doing this will help you understand the story.)

is an important pattern in the beginning of Amos: God charges people with a
and then God announces what the punishment will be for their crime.
do you think of the idea of God punishing people?
seem unfair or wrong?
good, if any, can you see the punishment doing?
urpose do you think punishment might serve?

ost every case, the crime God describes each people-group committing creates
harm after the original crime. As chapter 1, verse 11 says, "His anger has
rpetually, so his transgression keeps continuing."
his happen in your life? Can you think of times when one bad thing done leads
r harms?

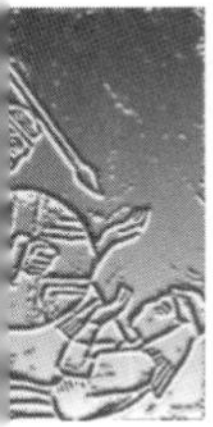

Page 84

In the ancient world, it was common, after a war, for the people who lost the war to be taken into captivity. Sometimes that captivity was slavery; sometimes it was a gentler form of exile, as we see of the Jews in Persia in the story of Esther. Here, God accuses Gaza of delivering (as if in a package) a whole people-group to Edom, their historic enemy and the ones who will treat them the worst.How is this act of delivering a whole people-group to their enemy an act that lacks compassion?

85

n of the charges against the people, God accuses them of breaking covenants.
n't know exactly what the covenants were in these cases, but we do know that
nt is a very important concept throughout the whole Bible (the Old Testament
e New Testament.)
do you think covenant means?
ets involved in a covenant?
specifically might you learn more about the covenants
od makes with God's people?

to why these awful crimes are done appears
original Hebrew. On this page, what does it
s happened to compassion?
s compassion?
night it mean for compassion to be corrupted?
passion essential to human life?
passion important to God?
u guess why?

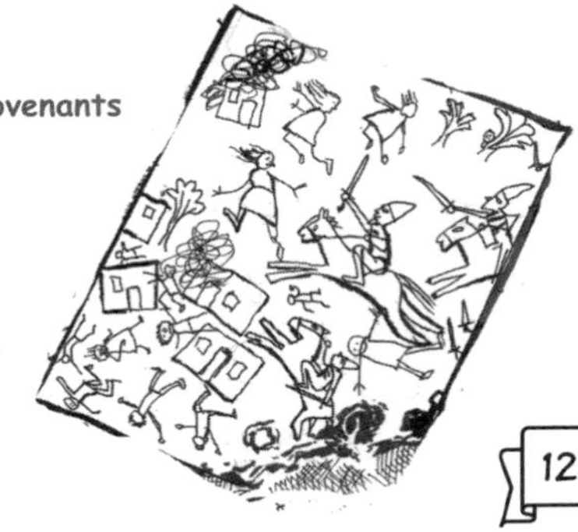

Page 86

Judah's crime is not hurting another people-group but hurting God, of "rejecting the instruction of the Lord." Instruction here could mean the word of the Lord or the commands of the Lord.

Why would God be upset that people had rejected his instructions?

Page 87

On this page, several crimes are pictured.
What are the crimes?
What do these crimes have in common?

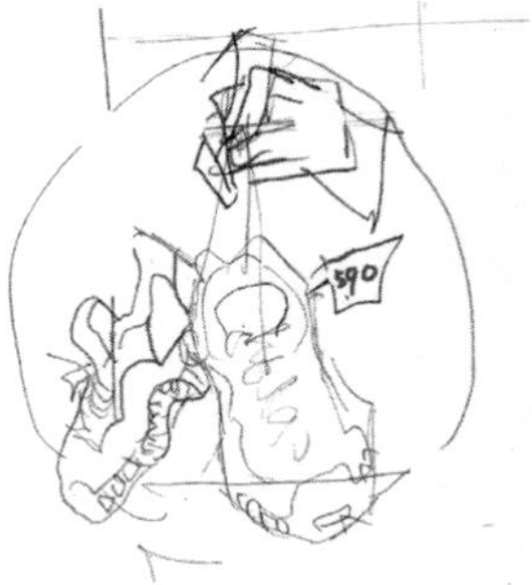

Page 88

God describes some of the things God has done to protect the people in the past.

What has God done for them? Make a list.
Why do you think God gives this contrast of what God has done to help them?

Page 89

God begins to describe the punishment God has in mind for the people. But one of the descriptions of punishment doesn't seem to fit; it doesn't seem like a bad thing. How might it be bad to be like an oxen cart that is loaded too full with grain (or food)?

Can you think of another example from the Bible of when the people are so well fed that they suffer (or they get sick) as a result?

Page 90

Most of the people don't like Amos' revelation, and they turn away to leave. The artist imagines one person remaining.
What do you see in this picture?
Why do you think it is important to the story?

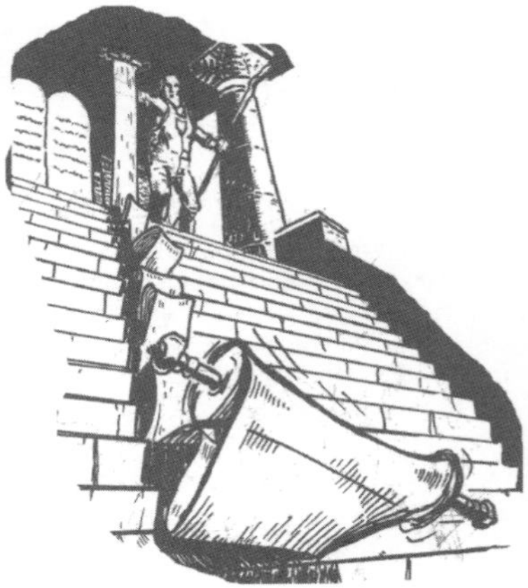

This page shows Amos rolling a scroll down the steps of the Temple. In ancient times and up through the time of Jesus, the Bible was written by hand on scrolls, which were stored in the Temple or in places of study.

Why might Amos be throwing the scroll down the steps of the Temple?

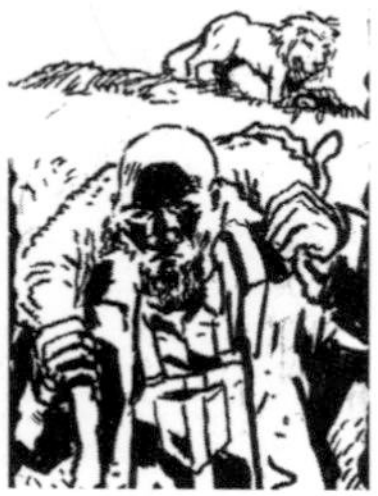

Page 91

On this page, the lion comes back. All the examples make the point that, if an event happens, there must be a reason. So, if the lion roars, and people are afraid because of the lion, there must be a reason for their fear.
What is the reason for their fear?
Is fear always bad?
Can fear lead to good or helpful things? If so, what?

Page 92

The Lord describes the people as not knowing how to do what is right.
Have you ever been in the situation of not knowing what to do?
What were your options for figuring out what to do?
What would you do if you realized you needed a set of instructions after you had already thrown them away?

Page 93

The Lord talks both about saving people from danger (from the mouth of the lion) and about destroying places of importance to the people.

How could these two different things fit together?
How do you make sense of this?

Page 94

God emphasizes that the people have so lost their moral compass that they now are happy to be doing what is the very worst thing to do. They no longer recognize God, and this moral decay is reflected in nature.
What natural disasters do you see drawn here?

Page 95

Because the people no longer recognize God, God describes God's self to them:
"For look, the one who forms the mountains, he who creates the wind and reveals to man what his thought is, who makes darkness black and treads on the high places of the earth, the Lord, the God of hosts is his name."
How would you draw this description of God?

Page 96

God knows that the people have forgotten the instructions, so God gives a single instruction as a simple replacement.
What is this one simple instruction?
Where else in the Bible do you find this same instruction?
(Hint: check the Internet for websites that will let you search the Bible by typing in a word or phrase.)

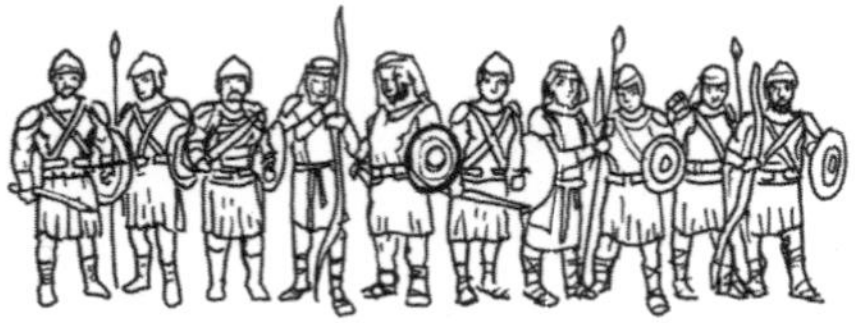

Page 97

In the Bible, justice and righteousness are the best things, right next to the st
fast loving-kindness of God. Also, justice and righteousness are attributes of G
So if the people have turned justice into a bitter thing, and if they have killed
teousness, what have they done toward God?

Page 98

Make a list of the crimes you see on this page.
What is the remedy or cure that God offers through the words of Amos?

Page 99

In both the Old Testament and the New Testament, "the day of the Lord" is a future date when God will come on earth to re-establish justice and order. As a result, "the day of the Lord" is a good thing but is also a fearsome thing: things that are not just will be destroyed. "The day of the Lord" is good news for people who are seeking justice, but the process of getting to that justice will involve some destruction. Some things will get torn down before they are built up.

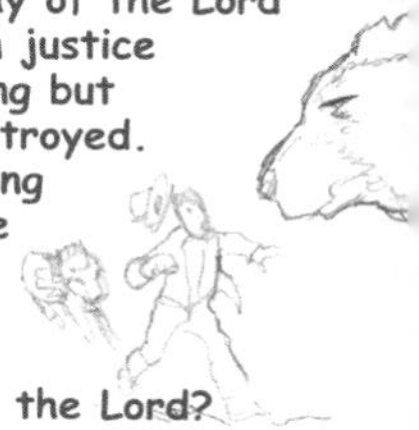

What words and images do you see that describe the day of the Lord?

Page 100

In ancient Israel, animals would be sacrificed in the Jerusalem Temple as one of
ways of exalting God. But, through the words of Amos, God criticizes the peopl
exalting God with sacrifices at the same time they are abusing people.

Which would God prefer to happen, sacrifices made at the Temple or justice don
the people?

One of the most treasured verses of the Bible is here: "but let justice run down
waters, and righteousness like a perpetual torrent-valley."
But being in the middle of a flashflood of water could be harmful.
How is this description good news?

Page 101

God accuses the people of worshipping gods they have made.
Which of the Ten Commandments prohibits this behavior?
Why do you think God cares whether or not people worship idols?

Page 102

God accuses the people of being excessive in their luxury.
What were they doing?
Why do you think those things would not be consistent with justice and righteous
Why does doing these things bring them "near the heart of violence"?

Page 103

The people's bitter actions lead to the bitterness God will send through the natio
that will punish (oppress) them.
What nations occupied and oppressed Israel after the time of Amos' prophecy?
Where might you look to find this historical information?

104
steadily tells the people about the punishments
ill come as a result of their own bad deeds,
en Amos isn't tough enough to hold up under
last words of punishment.

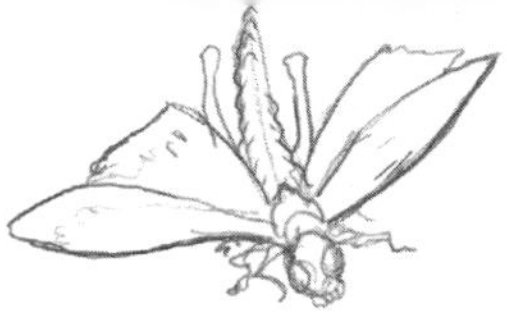

finally causes Amos to beg God to have compassion on the people?
other story in the Bible does this remind you of?

105
knows the people's actions deserve punishment, but he feels sorry for them
eless. Justice calls for punishment (or a remedy), but the flip side of the coin
of justice is mercy (or compassion).

How does God show that God is willing to change his mind and withhold
the punishment?

Page 106
A plumb line is used as a measure to determine what is crooked and
needs to be straightened. God is determined to make the house
straight, to make the people well.
How does this page show this straightening happening?

107
gh Amos, God accuses the king and the religious leaders of being "crooked."
o they respond to this message?
response of the king and religious leaders similar to how people responded to
, in the case of Nineveh?

108
says he is not a prophet (and he certainly does not look like one!). Yet he also
hat God told him to prophesy.
do you think God chose someone as unlikely as Amos for the job?

ells Amos that the people will receive no more "free passes."
s context what might a free pass be?
nber the story of the first Passover in Exodus 12:27. What happened then
God passed over the Hebrew children?

109
when warned, the people keep being greedy.
examples of greed do you see on this page?
eed different than earning a fair wage? How?

110
s another place where the natural world becomes a mirror image of human life
apart.

are the "unnatural" images of nature that you see here?

Page 110-111
Usually a famine means a lack of food. During famines
people go hungry and even die for lack of food.
What might a famine "for hearing the words
of the Lord" be like?

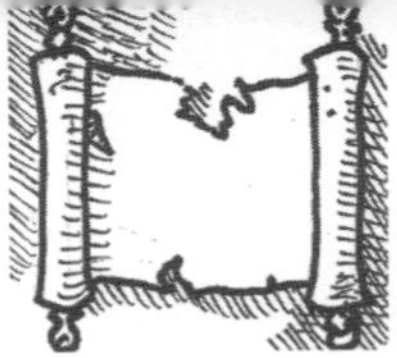

Page 112
The message of hope has been this: "Seek the Lord and live." But now the message
has changed; not being in the presence of the Lord (having the Lord
"set eyes on them") brings harm.
What accounts for the difference?

Page 113
Through the words of Amos, God says God will "shake out the House of Israel … as
grain is shaken through a sieve."
Is this good news?

According to Amos' message, the people who have sinned will die.
What could prevent this outcome?
Is such punishment an example of God's harshness or God's goodness, or both?

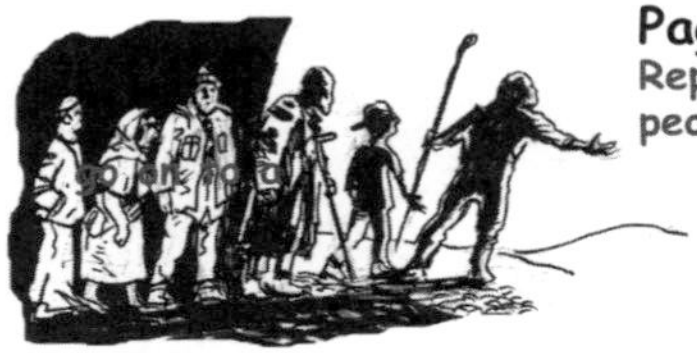

Page 114
Repeatedly in the Old Testament, a disaster happens to a
people-group and then a remnant of the people survives to
a new future.

What does God plan to do with the "remnant" of
people who are not destroyed?

Page 115
The Book of Amos ends with the good news of the remnant people, who will enjoy an
abundance of food, plentiful land and will enjoy peace to live in that land.
This is the classic image of justice in the Old Testament: each person
having enough food, shelter and peace to live. This image of justice is
found in the prophecies of Isaiah, Micah and Amos as well in the
teachings of Jesus.

What is your favorite part
of this good news?
Why?

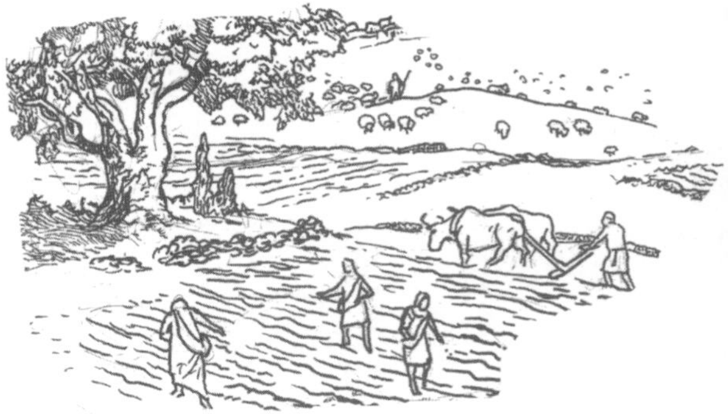